"*Exodus Old and New* is a fascinating, w
a masterful job of demonstrating that th
throughout both the Old and New Testaments—indeed, it lies at the very heart of biblical theology. This is a fresh and insightful study of a very important theme. This book makes a very important contribution to the field of biblical theology and is a must-read for all who preach, teach, or write in this field."

J. Daniel Hays, professor of biblical studies, Ouachita Baptist University

"A key to understanding the coherent nature of scriptural revelation is to have a firm grasp on the biblical theological themes that stretch from Genesis to Revelation. Michael Morales has given us an impressive study of one of the most pervasive and interesting themes found in the Bible—the exodus. *Exodus Old and New* is based on solid scholarship, and the writing is extremely clear and accessible. I recommend this book for all serious readers of Scripture."

Tremper Longman III, distinguished scholar and professor emeritus of biblical studies, Westmont College

"With academic expertise Michael Morales offers an insightful overview of the Bible centered on the themes of exile and exodus. He helpfully demonstrates how the Exodus account of God's dramatic deliverance of the enslaved Israelites from Egypt provides a paradigm for a greater exodus centered on Jesus Christ, the perfect Passover sacrifice. His thought-provoking analysis of the broad sweep of Scripture from Genesis to Revelation is compelling, even when one might differ on minor details. *Exodus Old and New* highlights admirably how the concept of exodus is highly significant, leading to life with God by reversing the tragic consequences of humanity's exile from God's presence."

T. Desmond Alexander, senior lecturer in biblical studies and director of postgraduate studies at Union Theological College, Belfast

"The exodus is just as important as Michael Morales says it is, and this book (and the series) will rejoice the hearts of all who, having been saved through the judgment that fell on the Lamb, now pass through the wilderness sustained by the bread of life on the way to the new and better Jerusalem. *Exodus Old and New* will send its readers back to the Bible with fresh eyes and new questions. As with all books on biblical theology, readers should test everything by the Scriptures themselves, and Morales's vigorous prose and provocative ideas provide great exercise for those seeking to stretch their biblical-theological limbs and lungs. Enjoy!"

James M. Hamilton Jr., professor of biblical theology at Southern Baptist Theological Seminary

"Morales's book is well worth reading. Advanced students will relish the opportunity to put their Bibles back together after years of studying its parts. Morales harnesses elegant prose to convey biblical insights with theological depth. His book is a gift to the church."

Carmen Joy Imes, associate professor of Old Testament at Prairie College, author of *Bearing God's Name: Why Sinai Still Matters*

EXODUS OLD AND NEW

A Biblical Theology of Redemption

L. MICHAEL MORALES

IVP Academic
An imprint of InterVarsity Press
Downers Grove, Illinois

InterVarsity Press
P.O. Box 1400, Downers Grove, IL 60515-1426
ivpress.com
email@ivpress.com

InterVarsity Press® is the book-publishing division of InterVarsity Christian Fellowship/USA®, a movement of students and faculty active on campus at hundreds of universities, colleges, and schools of nursing in the United States of America, and a member movement of the International Fellowship of Evangelical Students. For information about local and regional activities, visit intervarsity.org.

All Scripture quotations, unless otherwise indicated, are the author's own translation.

All interior figures, except where noted, are by Eric Chimenti and are used by permission
Figure 0.1: Gustave Doré, The Vessel, *engraved by Hélidore-Joseph Pisan / Wikiart.org*
Figure 4.1: Gustave Doré, The Destruction of Leviathan, Doré's English Bible / *Wikimedia Commons*

Cover design and image composite: David Fassett
Interior design: Daniel van Loon
Images: vector mesh pattern: © By Eve Livesey / Moment Collection / Getty Images

ISBN 978-0-8308-5539-1 (print)
ISBN 978-0-8308-5540-7 (digital)

Printed in the United States of America ♾

InterVarsity Press is committed to ecological stewardship and to the conservation of natural resources in all our operations. This book was printed using sustainably sourced paper.

Library of Congress Cataloging-in-Publication Data
A catalog record for this book is available from the Library of Congress.

P 22 21 20 19 18 17 16 15 14 13 12 11 10 9 8 7
Y 39 38 37 36 35 34 33 32 31 30 29 28 27 26 25 24 23 22

For:

Luis and Ana Morales

And for the risen generation:

Armando, Augustine, Alejandro, and Andres

Alyssa, Stephen, Matthew, Amelia, and Josephine

Kayla, Aliana, and Carlos

Aidan and Isabel

Elise and Elizabeth

And:

Für Elise

Psalm 71:17-20

CONTENTS

SERIES PREFACE

BENJAMIN L. GLADD

THE ESSENTIAL STUDIES IN BIBLICAL THEOLOGY is patterned after the highly esteemed series New Studies in Biblical Theology, edited by D. A. Carson. Like the NSBT, this series is devoted to unpacking the various strands of biblical theology. The field of biblical theology has grown exponentially in recent years, showing no sign of abating. At the heart of biblical theology is the unfolding nature of God's plan of redemption as set forth in the Bible.

With an influx of so many books on biblical theology, why generate yet another series? A few reasons. The ESBT is dedicated to the fundamental or "essential" broad themes of the grand story line of the Bible. Stated succinctly, the goal of the ESBT series is to explore the *central* biblical-theological themes of the Bible. Several existing series on biblical theology are generally open-ended, whereas the ESBT will be limited to ten or so volumes. By restricting the entire series, the scope of the project is established from the beginning. The ESBT project functions as a whole in that each theme is intentional, and each volume does not stand solely on its own merits. The individual volumes interlock with one another and, taken together, form a complete and cohesive unit.

Another unique dimension of the series is a robust emphasis on biblical theology, spanning the entire sweep of the history of redemption. Each volume traces a particular theme throughout the Bible, from Genesis 1–3 to Revelation

21–22, and is organically connected to the person of Christ and the church in the New Testament. To avoid a "flat" biblical theology, these projects are mindful of how the New Testament develops their topic in fresh or unexpected ways. For example, the New Testament sheds new light on the nature of the "kingdom" and "messiah." Though these twin themes are rooted and explored in the Old Testament, both flow through the person of Christ in unique ways. Biblical theology should include how Old Testament themes are held in continuity and discontinuity with the New Testament.

The audience of the series includes beginning students of theology, church leaders, and laypeople. The ESBT is intended to be an accessible introduction to core biblical-theological themes of the Bible. This series is not designed to overturn every biblical-theological rock and investigate the finer details of biblical passages. Each volume is intentionally brief, serving as a primer of sorts that introduces the reader to a particular theme. These works also attempt to apply their respective biblical-theological themes to Christian living, ministry, and worldview. Good biblical theology warms the heart and motivates us to grow in our knowledge and adoration of the triune God.

AUTHOR'S PREFACE

L. MICHAEL MORALES

"MIDWAY UPON THE JOURNEY OF OUR LIFE I found myself in a dark wilderness, for I had wandered from the straight and true."[1] Many years ago now, these famous opening lines of Dante's *Inferno* pierced my heart, resonating deeply with me—just as their author, with his use of "our life," had intended. Although a son of the church since early childhood, slowly and subtly I had been drifting away, not necessarily into scandalous or public sin but nevertheless away from fellowship with God, from seeking his face and kingdom—from the goal of Creation. As I continued reading through the whole of the *Divine Comedy*, the canticles led me through a sort of exodus, out of my complacency and back to God, back to the meaning of life. More on Dante in my introduction, but suffice it to say here that his poem, followed by my dissertation work under Gordon J. Wenham on Genesis and Exodus, opened for me the splendors of the exodus motif in Scripture, along with its profound implications for biblical theology. Being assigned the exodus theme for this series, therefore, has been a wonderful burden, a weight of joy. My hope and prayer is that this book may in some small way lead readers through their own "sort of exodus," closer to God.

[1]Dante Alighieri, *The Inferno*, trans. Anthony Esolen (New York: Modern Library, 2002), 3.

How does one possibly do justice to the exodus theme, especially so in keeping with the accessible, introductory nature of the ESBT series? One may, for example, trace allusions to the exodus from Genesis through Revelation, for the exodus as a literary motif may be discerned in narratives like the books of Ruth and Esther. Even in Psalms, the influence of the exodus is found well beyond any references to the historical exodus out of Egypt; rather, the recurring pattern of suffering and glory—of dying and rising, of being drawn out of the waters of Sheol—found in the psalms, is an exodus pattern. For this book, however, I have not traced such allusions, with the exception of the second chapter, on the life of Abraham. In that chapter I hope you will taste the deep significance of the exodus motif in the patriarch's life and perhaps in your own as well. My more modest approach in this volume has been to cover the three major exodus movements in Scripture: (1) the historical exodus out of Egypt, (2) the prophesied second exodus, and (3) the new exodus accomplished by Jesus Christ. In the first part, I cover major themes of the historical exodus like God's signs and wonders, Passover, and the mediation of Moses, since in various ways these will feed into the second two parts.

Chapters twelve and thirteen explore the new exodus, looking only at the Gospel of John. There are now hundreds upon hundreds of studies—articles, dissertations, monographs—on the exodus motif in the New Testament as a whole and within particular books like Matthew, Romans, or Revelation; it would have taken another book altogether to cover that topic more widely. In any case, every biblical theology is incomplete, a drawn-up bucket out of an endless well, and the Gospel of John is able to serve as something of a summary of New Testament theology for us—at least on the exodus theme. A bit more applicatory in nature, chapter fourteen closes our journey with a reflection on the centrality of the Messiah's resurrection in the life and writings of the apostle Paul. I should also note here that all Scripture quotations are my own translation and follow English versification (which occasionally differs from the Hebrew text), with italics sometimes added for emphasis.

I am thankful for my wife, Elise, and boys—young men now—Armando, Augustine, Alejandro, and Andres, who bring much joy to life. Words cannot fully express my gratitude also for Eric Chimenti, whose fine and helpful tables and charts adorn this book—thank you, friend. I am thankful too for Ben Gladd, not only for the invitation to participate in this series but also for his valuable feedback as editor. Appreciation is also due Anna Gissing at InterVarsity Press for her labors on this project. Finally, my love and life to the One who in taking my judgment on himself has redeemed my soul from destruction and now leads his sheep into the dawning glory of a new creation, to the Son who served me, the risen Lord Jesus Christ—to you, together with the Father and the Spirit, be all glory and praise.

INTRODUCTION

> Who was your guide or who your lantern
> to lead you forth from that deep night
> which steeps the vale of hell in darkness?[1]

Penning a letter to his benefactor, Dante Alighieri explained the significance of the exodus in Scripture and for the Christian life.[2] In doing so, he was offering the key for understanding his *Divine Comedy*, one of the greatest poems ever written. Referring to the opening line of Psalm 114, "When Israel went out of Egypt," Dante wrote that while historically the verse refers to the children of Israel's exit out of Egypt under Moses, this exodus prefigured the redemption accomplished by Jesus Christ. The exodus, he continued, also describes the soul's conversion out of the estate of sin and misery and into the grace of salvation. Finally, the exodus even points us to the church's consummate deliverance out of the enslavement of this corrupt old creation as God's people are brought into the glories of the new Jerusalem in the new creation. The medieval church's use of the fourfold interpretation of Scripture

---

[1]Dante Alighieri, *Purgatorio*, trans. Jean Hollander and Robert Hollander (New York: Doubleday, 2003), 7.

[2]For a defense of the letter's authenticity, see Robert Hollander, *Dante's Epistle to Cangrande* (Ann Arbor: University of Michigan Press, 1993).

(the so-called *Quadriga*) has been criticized with good reason, open as it is to unbounded misuse. It is, nevertheless, a token of Dante's genius that he narrowed in on one instance, the exodus out of Egypt, that Scripture itself uses as a multifaceted theological symbol, not only for Christ's departure out of the grave in the "new exodus" but also for the soul's deliverance out of the domain of darkness by spiritual rebirth.

In a brilliant passage of his poem (canto II of *Purgatorio*), Dante unveils his biblical theology with multiple layers of exodus symbolism streaming together onto a single scene.[3] Having emerged from the pit of Sheol onto the shores of the afterlife, his face washed of death's grime, Dante the pilgrim watches as a divinely navigated ship draws ashore, bearing the souls of the redeemed who have recently died (see Gustave Doré's illustration in figure 0.1 at the end of this introduction). The souls are singing Psalm 114 in Latin (Psalm 113 in the Vulgate): *In exitu Israël de Aegypto*, a song that, as we learn from Dante's letter, bears testimony to the historical exodus of Israel out of Egypt even as these singers are themselves undergoing an exodus, their deliverance out of corrupt creation into glory. Meanwhile Dante the pilgrim is himself experiencing spiritual conversion, symbolized by his emergence out of Sheol while still a living mortal. This scene, moreover, takes place at the dawn of Easter, celebrating the resurrection out of the grave of Jesus Christ, in whose footsteps the pilgrim follows. Resolving the ultimate exile, Dante's exodus leads to his reentry of Eden on the summit of God's mountain (*Purgatorio* XXVII-XXXIII), and his spiritual conversion is described as his being granted to come from Egypt to behold Jerusalem (*Paradiso* XXV.55-57).

Even the threefold structure of the poem follows the pattern of the exodus story: *Inferno* relates to Israel's exodus out of Egypt, symbolic of Sheol; *Purgatorio*, centering on a great mountain and dealing with themes of sanctification and perseverance, relates to Israel's wilderness experience with Mount Sinai as its focus (note the Moses-like figure of Cato encountered here); and *Paradiso* relates to Israel's dwelling in the land with God, a foretaste of paradise. Dante's theological journey—his spiritual conversion—

[3]See Marguerite M. Chiarenza, *The Divine Comedy: Tracing God's Art* (Boston: Twayne, 1989), 56-59.

traces the route both of Israel's historical exodus out of Egypt *and* Jesus Christ's path of death, burial, and resurrection—even his ascension into heaven. The end of redemption is not to live a bodiless, ethereal existence in the afterlife of heaven but rather to be raised up in glory with a real, new-creation body for a life of unending joy with God the Father, Son, and Holy Spirit. All of God's people from every nation will be ushered into a renovated heavens and earth—the final exodus, which is only (but surely) anticipated in Dante's poem.

Throughout the *Divine Comedy*, the drama of Christ's "harrowing of hell," performed in mystery plays of the Middle Ages, functions as a conceptual backdrop. Following the pattern of the historical exodus, such harrowing-of-hell dramas portrayed Jesus at his death literally and spatially descending into hell in order to deliver the awaiting Old Testament saints, having redeemed them by his blood, and as a new Moses leading them triumphantly into paradise in a grand and wondrous exodus out of hell. These dramas attempted to portray a doctrine confessed in one of the early creeds of the church, the Apostles' Creed, namely that Jesus "descended into hell" as our Savior (echoing Ephesians 4:9). John Calvin understood this line as referring to Jesus' suffering the pangs of hell—God's just wrath for the sins of his people—on the cross, and the later council of theologians known as the Westminster Assembly interpreted "he descended into hell" as referring to Jesus' descent into the grave.[4]

These understandings of Jesus' descent are profound, indicating a reality that in large measure remains for us an enigma, that the man of sorrows, smitten and forsaken, drank the bitter wine of the cup of God's unrelenting wrath—this in place of sinners to redeem them from their own just condemnation. The medieval harrowing-of-hell drama was an attempt to portray visually and physically something of the reality of what Jesus Christ has accomplished for his people through his death and resurrection. In a sense, we may think of Israel's historical exodus out of Egypt as God's own harrowing-of-hell drama, a historical deliverance he ordained ultimately to teach us

[4]On this topic, see Mark Jones, "John Calvin's Reception at the Westminster Assembly (1643–1649)," *Church History and Religious Culture* 91, no. 1-2 (2011): 215-27.

about the manifold glories of Jesus' redemption. Thus, while Jesus did not physically enter a hellish cavern under the earth as found in the *Inferno*, one should nevertheless be careful neither to dismiss nor neglect the awe-inspiring reality of his experience and accomplishment through the crucifixion, burial, and resurrection. Ultimately, the redemption of God's people is indeed an exodus out of a justly deserved hell and a conveyance into the paradise of God. The harrowing-of-hell drama, like the spatially structured story of the *Divine Comedy* itself, presents a picture of what is a profound spiritual reality—one based on God's leading Israel out of Egypt by the hand of Moses. The historical exodus, then, became the archetypal expression of Israel's future hope, a *mythos*, explained by Michael Fishbane as a paradigmatic story and life teaching through which an objective past recurrently gave way to a subjective event of the present.[5]

Suffice it to say, then, that if Dante were asked what has today become a controversial question in academic circles—namely whether there is a center of biblical theology, and, if so, what it is—he would answer: "Yes, the central theme and story of the Bible, and of history itself, is the exodus." Put differently, literary critic Northrop Frye once remarked that the exodus "is the only thing that ever happens" in the Bible, with the New Testament revolving around Christ's resurrection, the antitype of the exodus.[6] Understood in their widest sense, exodus traditions include not only the exodus out of Egypt but also the wilderness journeys and the inheritance of life in the good land. God's aim, in both creation and redemption, is to dwell with his people in the house of his creation, the cosmos. With this goal in mind, then, the exodus surely is the literary seed that unfolds into the deepest theological roots of Scripture, sprouts upward to form its sturdy trunk and overshadowing branches, and blossoms forth to bear its life-yielding fruit. More particularly, the *new* exodus of Jesus' resurrection—with *resurrection* as shorthand for the death, burial, resurrection, and ascension of the Lord Jesus Christ—is what the Bible is all about, inasmuch

[5]Michael A. Fishbane, "The 'Exodus' Motif/The Paradigm of Historical Renewal," in *Biblical Text and Texture: A Literary Reading of Selected Texts* (Oxford, UK: Oneworld, 1998), 121-22.
[6]Northrop Frye, *The Great Code: The Bible and Literature* (New York: Harcourt, 1981), 171-72.

as the new exodus will lead the redeemed of God into the joys of eternal life in the new heavens and earth of glory. "Biblical theology," wrote Floyd Filson, "finds its clearest starting point and interpreting clue in the resurrection of Jesus Christ," the new exodus.[7]

So with Israel's exodus out of Egypt through Moses, God had established a paradigm, the pattern, for understanding the salvation of all his people, including Israel and the nations, through Jesus the Messiah. It would be a grand mistake, therefore, to presume that the New Testament is but spiritualizing the exodus out of Egypt, for Jesus' emergence out of death is no less historical than Israel's emergence out of the sea, and his resurrection, again, will lead to the bodily resurrection of all his people when he returns to put an end to history. Rather, by God's own design, the exodus out of Egypt enables us to grasp the manifold realities accomplished by Jesus' resurrection. For example, the redemption of Israel's firstborn sons by means of the blood of a Passover lamb helps us to grasp something of the significance of Jesus' death as substitutionary atonement, that by his blood the cross has become the doorpost of salvation, redeeming God's people from death and judgment. Similarly, the bitter bondage of Egypt enables us to appreciate more deeply the tyranny of sin, how it shackles the will in and through our own deep-seated desires, and so on—realities that the New Testament authors draw out in a rich manner.

The accomplishments of Jesus the Messiah, in sum, may be comprehended more fully by the study of the Old Testament Scriptures even as he reciprocally opens them up under the light of his own suffering and glory. Once what God is up to has been unveiled definitively through Jesus Christ, then steadily, on a backward glance at the previous history of redemption, the unity of God's purpose and the marvelous logic of his ways begin to inundate the mind and, hopefully, the heart:

> Oh, the depth of the riches both of the wisdom and knowledge of God! How unsearchable are his judgments and his ways past finding out! (Romans 11:33)

---

[7]Floyd V. Filson, *Jesus Christ the Risen Lord: A Biblical Theology Based on the Resurrection* (Nashville: Pierce & Washabaugh, 1941), 25; see also F. X. Durrwell, *The Resurrection: A Biblical Study* (New York: Sheed and Ward, 1960).

O come, O come, Immanuel, and ransom captive Israel
That mourns in lonely exile here until the Son of God appear.
O come, O Branch of Jesse's stem, unto your own and rescue them!
From depths of hell your people save, and give them victory
o'er the grave.
Rejoice! Rejoice!
Immanuel shall come to you, O Israel.[8]

Figure 0.1. Gustave Doré, *The Vessel*, c. 1868

[8]"O Come, O Come, Immanuel," trans. composite, originally by J. M. Neale (1851).

Chapter One

EXILE BEFORE EXODUS

THE OPENING ELEVEN CHAPTERS of Genesis unfold a theological history of humanity that serves as the backdrop for the rest of the Bible's story of redemption, including the role of Israel within that story. This backdrop, as we will see, narrates humanity's exile from God's presence and life-yielding fellowship. Separated from Yahweh God, the fountain of life and being, humanity's condition is one of death. As such, the return to God—the exodus—can only be life from the dead, deliverance from death.

CREATED TO LIVE WITH GOD ON EARTH

The story of the Bible begins with a creation account that sets forth humanity's fellowship with God on earth as the goal of creation. Created in the image and likeness of God, humanity's highest purpose—the meaning of life and existence—was to be found in the awe-inspiring prospect of engagement with the uncreated Being who transcends all creation. Genesis 1 portrays God as a workman who builds the cosmos as a three-storied house (heaven, earth, and seas) and then takes up Sabbath rest and refreshment on the seventh day. More than this, he sanctifies the Sabbath day as time set apart to enjoy fellowship and communion with humanity. This divine relationship was set within the context of the earth as *home*, a place of security and joy. While being made in God's image both qualified and commissioned Adam to rule caringly over the house of creation on God's behalf, yet the chief delight and privilege of such likeness to God was in humanity's unique ability to gaze heavenward, to lift our faces to God and relate to him—no other creature could enjoy such friendship with the Eternal.

Genesis 2 elaborates further on the intimate nature of God's relationship with his first human creatures within the land of Eden. Yahweh God personally formed Adam's body, breathed into him the breath of life, brought him into paradise, a well-watered garden filled with life-giving fruit. Finally, God created a woman for Adam so that together the couple would know human companionship, the embrace of love, the yielding of new life in children, and the daily fellowship of mutual help in their God-given labors. Adam would shepherd his family, and all creation, in the knowledge and praise of Yahweh's name.

HUMANITY'S ALIENATION FROM GOD

The idyllic life in the Garden of Eden did not last long. Deceived by the serpent who would later be identified as the fallen angel Satan (Revelation 12:9; 20:2), the woman took fruit from the only tree God had forbidden and then gave some to her husband Adam, who also took and ate. Rather than using God's single command as an opportunity to demonstrate loyalty—loving obedience—to their Maker, to show fealty through grateful submission to his authority, humanity rebelled against God, grasping at the serpent's lie that by doing so they could become as gods themselves. Adam's sin changed the nature of humanity, corrupting it with the principle of rebellion, the power of sin. As a consequence, the human couple was spiritually severed from God, whose purity and holiness were now a threat, and they fell under his just sentence of death—for "the wages of sin is death" (Romans 6:23). Adam and the woman were cast out of the Garden of Eden, and God stationed cherubim (fierce, composite creatures) and a flaming sword to guard the Garden's entrance, barring humanity from the tree of life. Crucial for understanding the theology of the Bible, the expulsion from the Garden of Eden means that the restoration of humanity must be in the form of an exodus back to God, a deliverance out of exile.

In being driven out of the Garden of Eden, humanity did not merely lose life defined as paradisal existence. Rather, people lost the fountain of life and source of all peace, joy, and fulfillment—that is, they lost their relationship with God himself. What's more, exiled from God they lost something of their own selves as well. Created for life with God, to find their highest satisfaction and rest in him, banished humanity lost its defining purpose and basis for significance. Possessing the divine gift of a rational soul with its wondrous and fearful capacity to relate to God, set apart from all other creatures in being created in his divine image and likeness, human beings, whose natures are now deeply bent by the principle of sin, reject the purpose of God's gift and live instead for things like bodily pleasures alone. Seeking happiness in carnal ambitions, people live with aims no higher than the mongrel skulking in the streets—a denial and utter waste of the image and likeness of God. In this way, humans squander the divine gift of life, of the soul's noble openness to the Infinite. As Shakespeare put it: "What is a man, / If his chief good and market of his time / Be but to sleep and feed? A beast, no more."[1]

Soberingly, divine justice may give human beings over to becoming as the beasts in whose image and likeness they have lived and then finally, apart from God's mercy, to lose forever the possibility of fellowship with the Creator, along with the fruits of peace, joy, life, and contentment that only communion with God yields. The path of exile through Eden's gates was, therefore, a path from life to death, from light to darkness, from harmony to dysfunction and strife, from health to sickness, from security to violence, from compassion to inhumanity, from wholeness to brokenness, from peace with God to enmity—from a life of friendship with God to alienation. This is the anthropology of our fallen world, an integral aspect of what it now means for us to be human. This fallen condition is also the genuine cause of our fears, anxieties, depression, and restlessness—we are exiles, alienated fugitives, within a cosmos that was created to be our home with God. And yet there is nothing within creation itself that can fulfill our soul's capacity and longing to have fellowship with the One who transcends the night sky and all the works of his hands.

---

[1]William Shakespeare, *Hamlet*, in *Shakespeare the Complete Works*, ed. G. B. Harrison (New York: Harcourt Brace Jovanovich, Inc., 1968), IV.iv.33-35; 919.

THE EXILE INTENSIFIES

In addition to disrupting humanity's relationship with God, the plummet into sin affected every other possible relationship—between husband and wife, between brothers, with animals, with the earth's soil, with one's vocation and labor, and with childbearing. The shadow of divine judgment, the curse of God, was cast over all of life. Nature, life, reality—all writhe too in the pollution of death unleashed by humanity's sin. The bitter reality becomes manifest in the next story as Cain murders his brother Abel and ends up banished farther east of Eden (Genesis 4). In response, Cain builds a city. Within its literary and theological context, this city can only be understood as an effort to replace Eden's framework for humanity's life together with God. As such, Cain's city building marks corrupt humanity's transition to a new goal of fulfillment, a fabricated purpose, the quest for self-realization apart from God's own agenda for creation and human history. Cain has set in motion the city-of-man project. The narrative betrays his city building as founded on three motivations: the desire for glory, protection, and permanence.

First, Cain built a city and named it after his son—this marks the quest for glory and immortality. In the ancient Near East as elsewhere, one's name lived on through building projects, battle glory, or childbearing. In the ancient Sumerian poem *The Epic of Gilgamesh*, the oldest recorded story in the world, when Gilgamesh's quest for immortality from the gods fails, he resolves to build up his royal city of Uruk—indeed, the story's prologue guides the reader to gaze with wonder at Uruk's walls, temple, and foundations as a tribute to the hero's lasting glory. Similarly, in Homer's *Iliad* the warrior Achilles faces the choice of gaining immortality, a name, either through death in battle glory or by returning home to a quiet, if obscure, life wherein his children would live on in his stead. He chose the former. Cain both bears a son and builds a city, uniting them by naming the city after his son.

Second, his city also marked an attempt to claim safety and protection. Separated from the refuge of God, he had said that "whoever finds me will kill me" (Genesis 4:14), and then, slighting God's protective mark, he built his city. The impulse rings true from a sociological perspective, as ancient cities, encircled by walls, developed from a posture of defense.

Third, and more deeply, in exiling Cain, God had cursed him to be a "fugitive and wanderer on the earth" (Genesis 4:12-14). Estranged further from God, Cain's place on earth is no home, but a vast, no-man's land bare of comfort. In Hebrew the word for "wandering" is *nod*, so there is no small irony when the narrative goes on to recount how Cain departed from the face of Yahweh and dwelled in the land of Nod—that is, he made his home in the land of wandering, located east of Eden. The farther one is removed from God, the greater one's disorientation becomes. Such rebellion, welling up out of a heart polluted by sin, is all the more tragic as the Maker of heaven and earth reveals himself to be abounding in mercy and steadfast love.

Alongside the city builders of human history, there are also the sojourners, those who by divine grace understand that God is both willing and able to return his original gift of paradise and who now wait on him in humble submission. While Cain's family builds a city, the family of his brother Seth would become known as those who "call upon the name of Yahweh" (Genesis 4:25-26), an act that portrays a life of dependence on and loyalty to God, expressed liturgically by invoking Yahweh's name in worship. Such sojourners understand that before Yahweh will descend out of heaven to reestablish paradise on earth, the unleashed evil residing within the human heart must be dealt with, and humanity's sins and consequent death sentence must be resolved by God himself. These two gestures, city building and worship, are paradigmatic: Abraham will later build an altar and call on the name of Yahweh (Genesis 12:8), and when Pharaoh enslaves the Israelites to build Egyptian cities, he is conscripting them for the city-of-man project, that is, for rebellion against God's purposes for human history (Exodus 1:10-14).

The narrative history of Genesis 1–11 continues with other tragic stories of exile, tracing the ever-deepening path of humanity's separation from God. And this growing alienation is matched by an intensification of sin and rebellion as human civilization is increasingly marked by injustice and violence. Genesis 6 describes a great transgression, a boundary crossing, understood traditionally either as the intermingling of heavenly beings with humans or of Yahweh worshipers ("sons of God") with the line of Cain. As a result, the way of Yahweh was corrupted, that is, the knowledge of how to have a restored relationship with God was forsaken and almost completely lost. The earth was filled with the tyranny of "men of renown" (literally "men of name [*shem*]"), people set on self-glorification to godlike proportions, rather than on the praise of the living God. We are told God saw "that the wickedness of man was great upon the earth, and that every intention of the thoughts of his heart was only evil all the day" (Genesis 6:5). Grieved in his heart, God destroyed most of humanity, putting a temporary halt on the advance of wickedness. Yet, even after cleansing the earth of an utterly corrupt generation, saving only Noah and his household through the deluge, God's verdict on humanity is no less dismal: "the imagination of the human heart is evil from youth" (Genesis 8:21), a divine assessment that would soon prove fully justified.

THE NATIONS SCATTERED FURTHER INTO EXILE

Turning to the last story of the primeval era (Genesis 11:1-9), the Tower of Babel portrays humanity in ways remarkably like the earlier depiction of Cain. "Come," the people say, "let us build ourselves a city and a tower with its summit in the heavens; let us make a name for ourselves, lest we be scattered over the face of the whole earth" (Genesis 11:4). As with Cain, there is here the reciprocal interplay between fear and colossal pride, betrayed in similar desires for the immortality of vain glory, self-preservation, and permanence as an end to wandering.

First, the city builders desire to make a "name" for themselves, *name* again being an expression of human glory, a grasping effort at immortality. The people unite to build, brick by brick, a name for themselves, a ziggurat city to display human achievement. Somewhat mockingly, the story ends without our ever discovering the names of these builders. Their clutching after immortality through prideful love of self proves to be a grasping after the wind.

Second, the temple-ziggurat, with its summit reaching into heaven, also stands as a monument to human enterprise and perverse religion, the attempt to access heaven and its divine power for self-preservation. Out of fear, the people endeavor to create a channel to heaven, to access heavenly power by human device—occult power tapped for protection. (The actual name of the city is "Babylon," which in Akkadian means "gate of god," reflecting their understanding of the ziggurat as a gateway to heaven, but the title is punned in the Hebrew as *Babel*, as in "nonsense" or "confusion," reflecting God's judgment.)

Third, the builders, as with Cain, desire permanence, rootedness—"lest we be scattered over the face of the whole earth." And yet once more the result is only the bitter reverse of their aim. Unmistakably, the point is twice repeated within this very short story: "Yahweh scattered them over the face of all the earth" (Genesis 11:8, 9). While the root for "wandering" was given threefold punctuation in the story of Cain, here the root for "scattered" surfaces three times. "Wandering" and "scattered" well capture humanity's plight outside the gates of Eden's garden. "Our heart is restless," St. Augustine wrote in his *Confessions*, "until it rests in you."[2]

Separated from the One who is himself the only true source of life and peace, human beings are fugitives and wanderers on earth. Still, humanity ever endeavors to reclaim the benefits of life with God—immortality, protection, rootedness—apart from God himself. Having been expelled from his heavenly presence in Eden, humanity's natural bent is to deny the exile and to reclaim the good life through science, technology, and art, a pursuit as hapless as it is endless, destined to failure. Such pursuits in themselves are the good gifts of God, but they were used to circumvent God rather than for his glory. City building is thus portrayed as a humanistic attempt to defy God, a sadly arrogant energy of self-will and self-assertion that shakes a fist in the face of God to one's own utter and inevitable demise, ever grasping for the deceitfully just-out-of-reach allurements of the city-of-man project. The scattered nations, each now within its own ethnic context, return to their building endeavors so that rather than praising the Maker's name, they, steeped in their dark plight of exile, continue the anthem, "Let us make a name for ourselves" (Genesis 11:4), living to exalt their own reputation, power, and glory. The whole drama of human history and God's redemption of the nations turns on this subject of the glory of Yahweh's name.

In retrospect, we can see that the material of Genesis 1–11 has been shaped so as to present two layers of deepening alienation from God (see figure 1.1). While creation and re-creation initiate exodus movements toward life with

[2]Saint Augustine, *Confessions*, trans. Henry Chadwick (New York: Oxford University Press, 1991), I.1; 3.

God, these are followed by continual exile movements away from life with God. Broadly, the history of humanity is presented as an eastward descent from the summit of Eden, the holy mountain of God, outward to the scattering of the nations in an ever-deepening exile of separation from God. The last episode of human history in Genesis 1–11 is, therefore, the story of an already bitter exile pressed more deeply out into darkness. God responded to the city builders with devastating judgment, scattering them over the face of the earth.

Table 1.1. Two layers of deepening alienation

Genesis 1–7	**Genesis 8–11**
Creation, Adam (Genesis 1)	Re-creation, Noah (Genesis 8)
Fall, Cain's curse (Genesis 3–4)	"Fall," Canaan's curse (Genesis 9)
Men of "name" (Genesis 6)	City builders seeking a "name" (Genesis 11)
Deluge destruction (Genesis 7)	Scattering of nations (Genesis 11:8-9)

Worse still, the people are separated into nations, divided by languages. While at first glance the judgment on the city builders may seem less harsh than the flood of destruction brought on humanity in Noah's generation (Genesis 6–7), yet it is more than likely that throughout history the tally of death from wars and battles between the nations, played out on the streets of every major city and ever bolstered by cultural and ethnic pride, has surpassed the population of the ancient world destroyed in the flood—not to mention how the atrocities of inhumane acts during war far exceed the grim nature of death through a deluge—and this with no near hope of political peace in sight. Humanity's sinful nature, with its deeply ingrained love of self, spawns into violence and divisiveness not only within households but among nations as well, enough to ensure that there cannot and will not be any humanly devised peace on earth. Cain viciously murders his brother; the city builders bearing his image and likeness do the same, now on a worldwide scale. Separated from God, the peoples of the earth are also separated from one another. All told, Genesis 1-11 employs a fivefold use of the term "curse" (see Genesis 3:14, 17; 4:11; 5:29; 9:25), an apt if dismal assessment of the human condition in sin.

CONCLUSION

Millennia of humanity's highest endeavors in philosophy, political thought, education, science, and even conquest have done nothing to reduce the ancient curse—arguably the situation has gotten much worse. In his famed song "Imagine," John Lennon dared to hope for a life of peace by inspiring his listeners to imagine a world without countries.[3] Such a perceptive longing for harmony based on a unity not unlike that set forth in Plato's *Republic* rests ultimately on a misguided view of human nature, one that may be traced to the city builders of Babel, who had been united by language and ideal yet opposed to God—they had indeed been a fraternity of man living as one. Yet, in imagining no countries, Lennon was tracing the source of war to its budding flower, not its root. God's solution, as this book will endeavor to show, is to bring the nations out of exile to himself in a great exodus of deliverance. Rather than obliterating the differences among the peoples, he will create a beautiful selfless harmony among them, reconciling them to himself and to each other, creating a new humanity. This new reality will be possible because God will deal with the core problem of sin, the principle of self-love that poisons every human thought, act, and relationship, and he will deal decisively with death, opening the gates of Eden into a new heavens and earth. While the structural parallel between the flood and the scattering of the nations portrays the reality of their exile as a kind of death, the difference is nevertheless to be appreciated. Having spared their existence, mitigating the progress of evil inclination somewhat by disuniting the people, God will begin to reverse their exile by calling Abram out from among them.

In summary, Genesis 1–11 describes humanity's progressively deepened exile from God, an alienation mirrored naturally by a corresponding intensification of human sin and depravity. Separated from God, humanity dwells in the land of wandering and lives in the realm of death. The quest for eternal significance through accomplishment, for security derived from power, for lasting reality by rootedness in a place; the search for meaning and the ache for hope; the undermining of every happy occasion through the profound awareness of its fleeting nature; in short, the longing to find a home so as

[3]John Lennon and Yoko Ono, "Imagine," *Imagine*, Ascot Sound Studios, 1971.

finally to come home—these are all the inescapable burdens of life in exile from God, of the human soul turned in on itself. Apart from life with the Creator, creation itself groans in futility, stripped of meaning, emptied of significance, void of purpose. Severed from the fountain of life, humanity's inner longings and deepest desires find no ultimate objective, no *telos*—neither goal nor guide. And then long before we have tasted it, life runs out—and to dust we return. The New Testament describes people under the power of sin as helpless, ungodly, sinners, and the enemies of God (Romans 5:6-10). The plight of the nations in exile is further described as their being strangers, having no hope and without God in the world (Ephesians 2:12), a dark and desperate dilemma.

Crucial for understanding the message of the Bible, the exile of the nations is the backdrop for the story of Israel. The nations are the target of God's redemptive acts in history, and Israel was brought forth as God's means to that redemption. God had called out Abram and created Israel to undo the curse, to bring blessing to all the families of the earth. He promised that one day the scattering from Babel's ruins would be reversed and all the nations would be regathered together, streaming to God's holy Mount Zion, the new Eden, and to the house built for Yahweh's name—for his reputation, his fame, and his glory (Isaiah 2:1-4). The nations will magnify the glory of Yahweh and sing praise to his name.

Within this context, Israel's calling as the servant of Yahweh is to bring blessing to the nations, to reclaim the nations for Yahweh. Israel will be created to shine the light of the knowledge of God and his glory into the darkness of the nations' plight. Israel was to be a living catechism for the nations—that was their public, international calling. By observing Israel, the lost nations were to understand that, as the Westminster Shorter Catechism puts it, humanity's chief end is "to glorify God and enjoy him forever."[4] Ultimately, a restoration of the nations to God will require an exodus, for the exodus pattern is nothing less than the reversal of exile, nothing less than resurrection from the dead.

[4]*Westminster Shorter Catechism* 1.

PART 1

THE HISTORICAL EXODUS OUT OF EGYPT

Chapter Two

THE EXODUS PREFIGURED

"LEKH! LEKH!" Abram swung his staff vigorously, yelling, "*Lekh! Lekh!*—Go! Go!" The vultures bounded back several yards, hopping with outspread wings. He turned back to the *cutting* Yahweh had bidden him to perform. There before him lay the bloody path between the split carcasses of a heifer, a female goat, a ram, and two birds. He had cut the animals in half, laying each side opposite the other, creating a pathway through death. Under the sweltering sun, much of the blood and offal had begun to congeal and the odor had already drawn a horde of flies, not so easily driven off as the vultures (though the vultures patiently lurched closer as soon as he turned his back). The sun was now beginning to set, and Abram, the sweat of his brow having dried in rivulets of salt around his lids and down his cheeks, knew that soon both the dark and the cold would overtake him. He sat on a large stone, waving his staff rhythmically as a warning signal to the preying scavengers. He was drifting in and out of slumber when, suddenly, a deep sleep fell on him and he was plunged into thick darkness, black as pitch, submerging him in horrific dread—he was full of fear and terror.

Out of the primordial dark, Abram heard the voice of Yahweh: "You must know that your descendants will be strangers in a land not their own. They will slave for the inhabitants and be afflicted by them for four hundred years. But know also that I will judge the nation enslaving them, and afterward your descendants will come out with great possessions." Then a fire appeared, pushing back the shroud of darkness. Abram watched intently, straining his eyes as the wonder unfolded: A pot with a billowing pillar of smoke and a torch whose flame ascended in a column of blazing fire stood before the *cutting*, spreading an auburn haze over the slaughter. Steadily, the pillars of smoke and fire began to pass between the carcasses, moving slowly through the path of death.

Silent and motionless, Abram exhaled. The cold sweat drenching his body jerked him into movement. Discarding sandals and staff, he sank onto his knees and bowed low until his forehead rested on the ground. Dust and the musky scent of shrubs entered his nostrils as he stretched out his arms before him.

The vision of Yahweh, as recorded in Genesis 15, had confirmed that one day Abram's seed would be delivered through death and brought in to possess the land of God as an inheritance.

GENESIS 12–22: THE EXODUS OF ABRAHAM

God's character and attributes are changeless. Even before delivering the Israelites out of Egypt, he was the God of the exodus. In this chapter, we will look at the major events in the life of Abraham and find that they were divinely stamped with an exodus impress.

Genesis 12:1-9: Abraham's exodus out of Ur. Thankfully, Genesis 11 does not end with humanity's exile from God and the scattering of nations from the ruined city of Babel. The Tower of Babel story (Genesis 11:1-9) and the call of Abram, whom we will come to know as "Abraham" (Genesis 12:1-3), are linked inseparably by the family line of Shem (Genesis 11:10-32). In Hebrew, Shem means "name," connecting him not only to the primary motivation of the city builders, who wanted to make a name for themselves, but also to Shem's descendant Abram, to whom God promises, "I will make your name [*shem*] great" (Genesis 12:2)—a hint that every human longing finds its end in God himself. Indeed, by his grace God offers Abram restoration in terms of everything humanity had sought through defiant self-assertion: his descendants would experience abundant life and security with God in the land.

For our purposes here, it is critical to understand that God called out Abram precisely in order to reverse the exile of the nations. Abraham's narrative life begins with God's promise that "in you all the families of the earth shall be blessed" (Genesis 12:3) and ends with his confirming oath that "in your seed all the nations of the earth shall be blessed" (Genesis 22:18). Abram's call out of Ur, moreover, employs a fivefold use of the Hebrew root for "bless," likely intended to signal that through Abram's calling the fivefold "curse" found throughout Genesis 1–11 would finally be undone. As Abraham's seed, Israel's vocation will be to bring the light of salvation to the nations, the storyline of Israel culminating with the Messiah's gathering of a new humanity, of both Jewish people and Gentiles, to dwell in fellowship with God in a new creation. This dawning hope of glory begins with God's call of Abram to "Go get yourself out of your land, and from your kinfolk, and from your father's house" (Genesis 12:1), that is, *leave* all that you know behind, forsaking every defining element of your life—sacrifice your past, your *self*.

In calling Abram out of Ur of the Chaldees, God was delivering an ancient Mesopotamian man, along with his wife Sarai, out of exile and initiating a relationship that would serve as the kernel for all humanity's new life with God. The divine call to leave Ur was also a deliverance out of Ur, out of the plight of the nations' exile. As the first human being to experience a reversal of the spiritual exile narrated in Genesis 11, Abraham himself stands as the firstfruits of an international deliverance—the call out of Ur was, in other words, an exodus. And the goal of Abram's exodus, the land that Yahweh would show him, was the land of Canaan. Centuries later, Abram's exodus out of Ur and entry into Canaan would be followed by Israel's exodus out of Egypt and entry into Canaan. In Genesis 15 God will proclaim to Abram, "I am Yahweh who brought you out of Ur of the Chaldeans to give you this land to inherit" (Genesis 15:7), a divine declaration—an "exodus formula"—that will be echoed in the proclamation to Israel: "I am Yahweh your God who brought you out of the land of Egypt, out of the house of bondage" (Exodus 20:2; Deuteronomy 5:6). In both instances, God defines himself as his people's deliverer. To his people Yahweh is, and can only be known as, the God of the exodus.

Genesis 12:10-20: Abraham's exodus out of Egypt. After his departure from Ur, Abram underwent a deliverance out of Egypt whose outline would later be traced by the Israelites in their own exodus experience. Genesis 12:10-20 narrates Abram's descent into Egypt due to a severe famine in the land. Fearing the Egyptians would kill him to obtain his wife, Abram bid Sarai to say she was merely his sister. As it turned out, her beauty was reported to the Pharaoh himself, who took her into his harem, giving Abram many sheep, oxen, donkeys, male and female servants, and camels—an enormous hoard of wealth in the ancient Near East. Yahweh intervened, however; he "plagued Pharaoh and his household with great plagues" (Genesis 12:17) so that Pharaoh sent Abram and his wife away, along with the many possessions Abram had amassed in Egypt. Genesis 13:1 reads: "And Abram ascended out of Egypt, he and his wife and all that he had." In whatever manner Abram's behavior may have been understood within the thought-world of the ancient Near East, in the alchemy of divine providence his experience served as a foretaste of Israel's deliverance out of Egypt.

A severe famine would also lead Jacob and his twelve sons to descend into Egypt (Genesis 41–50), and even as Abram feared he would be killed while his wife would be allowed to live, so the Egyptians would later plot to kill Israelite sons while keeping the daughters alive (Exodus 1:22), presumably to integrate them into Egyptian life by marriage. Just as Yahweh had plagued the Pharaoh who had taken Abram's wife, causing him to send them away, so too the Pharaoh of the exodus would be plagued until finally he sent the Israelites out (Exodus 7–12). Even the verb used for Pharaoh's sending Abram and Sarai away (*shalach*, Genesis 12:20) echoes throughout the exodus narrative (Exodus 3–11), as does his command for them to "take and go" (Genesis 12:19; Exodus 12:31-32). Moreover, Abram's departure out of Egypt with great possessions foreshadowed the plundering of the Egyptians by Israel (Exodus 12:31-36). Many of these parallels are anchored by unique words common to both accounts. For example, Genesis 12:17 and Exodus 11:1 are the first two occurrences of the word "plague" in the Pentateuch, and the "severe famine," which led Abram to "descend" into Egypt, uses the same vocabulary that describes the "severe famine" that led to Israel's own "descent" into Egypt (Genesis 12:10; 43:15; 47:4). These and other parallels were brought out by ancient interpreters, underscoring the principle that everything written about Abraham's children was also written about Abraham himself.[1]

Later on, Abraham and Sarah will be delivered out of Gerar (Genesis 20) in a manner that corresponds closely to their previous sojourn in Egypt. In the literary structure of the Abraham narrative, these two episodes complement one another and stand in parallel. Both stories include Abraham's claim that Sarah is only his sister, the king's taking Sarah for himself, a divine threat to the foreign king, the rescue of Abraham and Sarah, and Abraham's amassing of plunder. Profoundly, the story of Abram's rescue out of Egypt, and then again out of Gerar, demonstrates that the life-shaping and identity-establishing event of Israel, the exodus, was by degree true also of Israel's patriarchs—and *is* true for all of God's people still.

Genesis 15: Abraham's vision of Israel's exodus out of Egypt. In Genesis 15, Abram has two wondrous exchanges with God (Genesis 15:1-6, 7-21). Both accounts include visions and are similarly structured: they begin with a declaration by Yahweh, followed by a question from Abram, which is then answered by Yahweh with a sign confirming his original word. In the first scene, God promised that Abram, although still childless, would have descendants as numerous as the stars in the heavens. Such a reality led naturally to another concern: where would they live? The land of Canaan was as yet filled with ten threatening groups of disturbingly violent and idolatrous inhabitants.

The second scene thus begins with a word of assurance to Abram, grounded in God's own being and character—the exodus formula: "I am Yahweh who brought you out of Ur of the Chaldeans, to give you this land to inherit" (Genesis 15:7). The designation *Yahweh* brings us within the realm of the exodus, for beyond notions of what the name means literally (for example, "I am who I am"), Yahweh is defined fundamentally as "the God of the exodus." With these words, Yahweh points Abram back to his own deliverance out of Ur, from the hopeless life of the nations exiled from the Creator, and he points him forward to the next stage of his calling, for God to establish his

---

[1]See *Genesis Rabbah* 40:6.

descendants as a redeemed nation in the land of Canaan. This opening declaration by Yahweh, as already observed, will be echoed by later divine proclamations to Israel: "I am Yahweh your God who brought you out of the land of Egypt, out of the house of bondage" (Exodus 20:2; Deuteronomy 5:6). Yahweh is the God who brings his people out of exile—home, to himself. Such parallel expressions create an analogy between Abram's departure out of Ur and that of Israel out of Egypt—the deliverance of the descendants was foreshadowed by that of their patriarch.

In response to Abram's request for a guarantee, God directs him to perform the cutting ritual. Abram cuts various sacrificial animals in half (although the birds are not cut), creating a bloody pathway. After warding off buzzards from the slaughter, he eventually falls into a deep sleep and is plunged into a night of horrific darkness. Then on the bloody pathway he sees a column of smoke created by a kiln and a column of fire created by a torch. It is difficult to understand precisely every element of the scene, although the smoking oven and flaming torch, using imagery found in other theophanies, clearly refer to Yahweh's presence. Some scholars believe that Yahweh's walking between the pieces stands as a self-maledictory oath. This understanding derives from the words of Jeremiah 34:18, which speak of Judeans who have transgressed the words of the covenant that they had made with God "when they cut the calf in two and passed between the pieces." By the system of clean and unclean animals later revealed (Leviticus 11), it may be that Israel is represented by the sacrificial animals of the ritual while the encroaching buzzards represent the threat of the nations, so that Abram's fending them off reflects his concern over his posterity's wellbeing. What is more certain, by comparing God's words (Genesis 15:13-16) with the vision (Genesis 15:17), the scene that unfolds before Abram forms a symbolic enactment of the exodus of Israel, led by Yahweh's pillars of cloud and fire (Exodus 13:21-22).

As retold in song afterward, Israel's path through the sea is described as a journey between walls of death (Exodus 15:1-10), mirrored in the second half of the song by Israel's journey into the land through the death threat of the nations who are stayed by God's hand like so many hostile waters (Exodus 15:14-17; see also Psalm 78:50-54). Psalm 136:13 renders praise to God "who divided the Sea of Reeds into *parts*," using the same Hebrew term as Genesis 15:17's description of the smoking kiln and flaming torch passing "between the *parts*," a connection that led ancient rabbis to interpret Genesis 15 as Yahweh's showing Abram a vision of the parting of the sea.[2] Plunged into and delivered out of this night of darkness and deathly terror, Abram had experienced a foretaste of Israel's exodus. Through this vision, Yahweh assured Abram that he would indeed deliver his children out of foreign oppression—and more, he showed him *how* that deliverance would be accomplished: through the blood of sacrifice, the seed of Abram would pass through walls of death.

Yahweh's passing through the pieces in Genesis 15:17 is described in the next verse as his making a covenant with Abram. By its association with this ceremony, Israel's Passover meal obtains a covenantal character, and celebrates first of all God's faithfulness to the nation's patriarch.

Genesis 18–19: Lot's exodus out of Sodom. The exodus of Lot out of Sodom is imbedded within the story of Abraham and laced with Passover terminology and themes.[3] In the Sodom and Gomorrah story Abraham and Lot serve their divine guests "cakes" and "unleavened bread," respectively (Genesis 18:6; 19:3)—both of which not only have strong associations with Passover and its feast of Unleavened Bread (almost exclusively so) but are also not found again until the Passover story (Exodus 12:8, 15, 17, 18, 20, 39; 13:6, 7). By this unmistakable association between unleavened bread and Passover, Rashi, the medieval French rabbi and popular biblical commentator (AD 1040–1105), glosses the story of Lot's departure from Sodom in Genesis 19 with a famously simple statement: "It was Passover."[4] Recalling that the Israelites "baked the dough which they had brought out of Egypt, unleavened cakes" (Exodus 12:39), the original audience of Genesis likewise could hardly have missed the connection to Passover in

---

[2]*Genesis Rabbah* 44:21.

[3]Several of the following points are found in Jeffrey C. Geoghegan, "The Abrahamic Passover," in *Le-David Maskil: A Birthday Tribute for David Noel Freedman*, ed. David Noel Freedman, Richard Elliott Friedman, and William Henry Propp (Winona Lake, IN: Eisenbrauns, 2004), 47-62.

[4]Rashi, *The Torah: With Rashi's Commentary: Bereishis/Genesis*, trans. Yisrael Herczeg, Sapirstein edition (New York: Mesorah Publications, 1995), 194; cf. Jeffrey C. Geoghegan, "The Abrahamic Passover," 43.

the story of Lot, especially given the presence of other verbal links between the two narratives. In only these two stories, for example, does the Bible relate that Yahweh heard "the cry" and responded by "descending" to "see" and "know" the matter (Genesis 18:20-21; Exodus 3:7-9). Moreover, the meals with Abraham and Lot and the birth of Isaac one year later appear to have taken place in the spring, interpreted widely as during the feast of Passover. Noted three times in Genesis, the birth of Abraham's son Isaac takes place "at the appointed time" (Genesis 17:21; 18:14; 21:2), a phrase otherwise reserved for Passover, being used three times for the feast of Unleavened Bread (Exodus 13:10; 23:15; 34:18).

Other terms and phrases shared between Lot's exodus out of Sodom and Israel's exodus out of Egypt include Yahweh's "passing" (*'avar*) by or through, the divine act of "destroying," the need for God's people "to hurry," and the command to "rise up and go" (see Genesis 18:3, 5; 19:14; Exodus 12:23, 31). Both stories also highlight the safety found behind a door (Genesis 19:6-11; Exodus 12:7-14). The rescues from Sodom and Egypt both focus on being closed within a house and then the need to depart that house without delay.

Interestingly, the Passover liturgy celebrated in Judaism today (in the Ashkenazic tradition) includes a poem by Rabbi Eleazar Kallir (c. AD 570–640) that draws on many of the associations we have considered here:

> You revealed Your great power on Passover.
> You placed above all festivals Passover.
> You revealed Yourself to Abraham at midnight on Passover.
> This is the festival of Passover.
> In the heat of the day, You knocked on Abraham's door on Passover.
> He fed the angels cakes of unleavened bread on Passover.
> And he ran to the herd to offer a calf on Passover.
> This is the festival of Passover.
> The men and women of Sodom provoked God and were consumed by fire on Passover.
> Lot was saved and he baked unleavened bread on Passover.
> Egypt was swept away when You passed through it on Passover.
> This is the festival of Passover.

You killed the firstborn on the night of Passover.
You spared Israel's firstborn on Passover.
The destroyer was not allowed to enter Israel's doors on Passover.
This is the festival of Passover.[5]

The deliverance out of Egypt will be described as an exodus from "the house of bondage" (Exodus 13:3, 14) and Israel will be commanded not to go back to Egypt (Deuteronomy 17:16) for the bonds to life in exile must be severed. Abram's exodus out of Ur had also involved the forsaking of a house: "Go, get yourself out . . . from your father's house" (Genesis 12:1). Precisely here one detects the hesitancy of Lot's household in forsaking the life of exile; we read that Lot "lingered" in his house, a gesture more fully exposed when his wife, contrary to explicit command, "looked back behind him" to Sodom and turned into a pillar of salt (Genesis 19:16, 26). The outward departure must be formed and informed by an inward, spiritual break with the past—separation unto God requires separation from the world. In his original choice to dwell near Sodom, Lot had seen that the plain of the Jordan was as "the garden of Yahweh, like the land of Egypt" (Genesis 13:10), unveiling his yearning to find paradise within the cities of exile—and creating a correspondence between Sodom and Egypt as well. Lot's exodus, unlike Abram's, will not lead to the summit of God's holy mountain but into a dark cave. On their pilgrimage, the first generation of Israelites out of Egypt too would continually stumble by a backward gaze, with a longing for a return to their former house of Egypt (see Numbers 11:4-6; 14:1-4).

Lot's story reminds one that an exodus involves much more than crossing a threshold in departure. Indeed, the primal exile itself was more than a mere departure out of Eden's gates but involved an ever-deepening alienation from God throughout the long eastward trek of human history, a separation that steadily darkened humanity's understanding of God's character and purposes even while fostering the clenching fists of rebellion, sinking the whole race into graver depths of depravity. Even so, the reversal of exile, the exodus, is a journey more profound than any geographical departure out of Ur, Sodom, or Egypt; it involves a lifelong *leaving*, a process of sanctification, whereby

[5]Elie Wiesel, *A Passover Haggadah* (New York: Simon & Schuster, 2004), 126.

one steadily dies to the life, religion, and world of exile, and steadily learns to live the new life of restoration to God. The path out of Ur is the path to Mount Moriah—every episode of Abraham's life adumbrates Israel's exodus journey out of Egypt to Mount Zion.

Genesis 22: Abraham's Passover journey. Biblical exegetes have noted a variety of other allusions to the exodus in Genesis. The Cain and Abel story (Genesis 4), for example, with its themes of the firstborn son, sheep and sacrifice, and shed blood, has traditionally been related to Passover.[6] The two departures of Hagar mirror the exodus ironically, as she is an Egyptian slave who goes out of an Israelite household (Genesis 16; 21:8-21), instead of Israelite slaves going out of Egypt, the house of bondage. Isaac and Rebekah's deliverance out of Gerar (Genesis 26) and Jacob's departure from Laban's "bondage" along with the many possessions he had amassed in Haran also resonate with the exodus pattern (Genesis 28–32)—and the list could go on. But we turn now to explore the culminating narrative of Abraham's life, an event that however veiled within clouds of mystery forms the foundation of Passover: Abraham's binding and near sacrifice of Isaac.

Genesis 22 narrates Abraham's last recorded encounter with God. "Take now your son, your only one, whom you love, Isaac," God says, "then go get yourself to the land of Moriah and offer him up there as a whole burnt offering on one of the mountains of which I will tell you." From the start, readers of this story are made aware of the reality hidden from Abraham, namely that this divine word was a test (Genesis 22:1). Such knowledge functions literarily to take the spotlight off Isaac (for his wellbeing is safeguarded), keeping one's eyes and emotions riveted on Abraham who will offer up heartrending obedience to God, demonstrating what the Bible calls "the fear of Yahweh," true piety and Godward devotion. Necessarily leaving much unsaid, we will sound out the depths of Abraham's binding of Isaac with four observations.

[6]See John Bowker, *The Targums and Rabbinic Literature: An Introduction to Jewish Interpretations of Scripture* (Cambridge, UK: Cambridge University Press, 2008), 132.

First, God's call to Abraham is quite particular: Abraham was to offer up Isaac as a whole burnt offering. Too often this divine injunction is reduced to the notion that Abraham was asked to kill—or "murder" within more hostile views—his son. While sacrifice entails immolation, the whole burnt offering's profound theology signifies much more than the victim's death. As the entire animal was given over to Yahweh, consumed on the flames of his altar, the whole burnt offering both symbolized and solicited utter consecration unto God, and this consecration was central to the redemptive purposes of God. Having promised blessing to the nations through Abraham's seed, God here conveyed something of *how* the son of Abraham would bring about the salvation of humanity: through complete surrender and loyalty to God—that is, by a life of absolute devotion to God. Rooted within Israel's vocation—indeed, forming the kernel of the nation's being, its reason for existence—Israel had been formed by God to be the "servant of Yahweh," entirely devoted to him, for the sake of the nations. In mediating a relationship between Yahweh God and the nations living in the darkness of exile from God, Israel would be a light, living as a "royal priesthood and holy nation" (Exodus 19:6; cf. Isaiah 42:1-7). No mere symbolism, the divine test of Abraham gestures toward a path through the billows of smoke, unfolding the grave expanse of what Israel's servant role would entail.

Second, as the story progresses there is a shift in focus from Abraham's present obedience to Yahweh's future provision. The narrative turns on this point with young Isaac asking, "Where is the lamb for the whole burnt offering?" His father's response is monumental: "God will provide for himself the lamb for the whole burnt offering, my son" (Genesis 22:8). The layers of meaning in Abraham's response are difficult to capture in English. The verb translated here as "provide" derives from the root "to see" (*rā'āh*), which may be rendered as "God will see to it himself, my son." An initial fulfilment of God's provision comes when Abraham lifts his eyes and "looks" (again, from *rā'āh*) so that he sees a ram caught in a thicket by its horns. He takes the ram and "offers it up as a whole burnt offering instead of his son" (Genesis 22:13). In Abraham's concluding act, however, and in response to God's provision of the ram, he names the mountain "Yahweh will provide," from which the name Moriah derives, demonstrating his own still future-oriented expectation of

God's provision. Likewise, the editorial comment closing the same verse remarks that it was still commonly said "to this day" that "in the mountain of Yahweh, it will be provided" (Genesis 22:14). God's provision of a lamb, in other words, was still an expectation *after* God's provision of a ram for Abraham. The book of Exodus will record the ensuing divine provision, that of the Passover lamb.

Third, there is good reason for understanding the account of Abraham's binding of Isaac as a foundation story for the Jerusalem temple. Generations after Isaac's near-sacrifice, David would be led to the same mountain (1 Chronicles 21; 2 Samuel 24). God had unleashed a plague on Jerusalem due to the sin of Israel's king, so that thousands had fallen. Then, by a certain threshing floor that was elevated above the rest of the city, David saw the angel of Yahweh standing between heaven and earth, holding his sword drawn over Jerusalem. Having repented in sackcloth, calling on Yahweh for mercy, David was directed to build an altar on this threshing floor. Demanding full price, six hundred shekels of gold, he purchased the place, built an altar, and offered up to Yahweh costly whole burnt offerings and peace offerings, calling on Yahweh's name. Out of heaven, Yahweh answered by sending a flame to consume the offerings—and then by having the angel sheath his sword. David exclaimed, "This is the house of Yahweh God, and this is the altar of whole burnt offering for Israel!" (1 Chronicles 22:1), and thereafter he began to make preparations for building the temple, solemnly charging his son Solomon to build the house for Yahweh God (1 Chronicles 22:2-11). When the author of Chronicles later recounts Solomon's building of the temple, he goes back not only to Yahweh's unveiling of the site to David but to the original revelation of the mountain to Abraham: "Now Solomon began to build the house of Yahweh at Jerusalem on Mount Moriah, where he had appeared to David his father" (2 Chronicles 3:1). As Genesis 22:2 is the only other verse in the entire Old Testament that mentions Moriah, the Chronicler's reference to it here creates a theological highway between the two stories. The phrase "where he had *appeared*" uses the same root of the name Moriah and plays on the legend with which the Abraham story ends: On the mountain of Yahweh "it will be provided," which may also be read as "he will be seen" (Genesis 22:14). Just as Yahweh had once shown

Abraham the acceptable place of worship, so now Yahweh had revealed to David the same mountain.

What is relevant for our purposes is that the entire cult of Israel—that is, the temple system of priesthood and sacrifices—was built on an event, narrated in Genesis 22, where Yahweh God had provided a substitute, an animal replacement, for the seed of Abraham whose utter consecration to himself he had commanded. Far from being a subtle theological point, Isaac's near-sacrifice was widely set forth in rabbinic texts as the basis for God's acceptance of every later sacrifice at the temple, especially so of the *daily offerings*, the morning and evening sacrifices of unblemished lambs as whole burnt offerings, which formed the heart of Israel's worship.[7] Solomon's temple was founded on a theological "sleight of hand," wherein the firstborn son of Abraham and Sarah, on whom Yahweh's promise of blessing to the nations had rested, was *replaced*—exchanged, substituted—by an animal, as ordained by the One whom Abraham had declared would himself provide a lamb. Given the future orientation to the account of Isaac's binding, the expectant hope of Yahweh's own provision of a lamb opened the prospect of a reversal to the substitution, the fearfully inevitable replacement of the ram (and all sacrificial animals) with another beloved son. The Jewish authors of the New Testament had come to understand Jesus' sacrifice on a Roman cross as *the* event that, on the one hand, had given the temple system of animal sacrifices its provisional acceptance and value and that, on the other hand, has made such sacrifices obsolete ever after, having fulfilled them.

Finally, deep within the very marrow of Abraham's near sacrifice of his son lies the impress of Israel's historical exodus out of Egypt. As we will consider in a later chapter, the pivotal event of the exodus deliverance was the Passover when Yahweh brought judgment on the land of Egypt so that every firstborn son, of Egypt and Israel alike, lay under the sentence of death. The firstborn sons of Israel, however, were redeemed through Yahweh's provision of substitute lambs. Just as all Israel had been saved in the sparing of Isaac through the provision of a ram in Genesis 22, so all Israel would be saved by the sparing of firstborn sons through the provision of

---

[7] *Targum Neofiti Leviticus* 22:27; *Leviticus Rabbah* 2:11.

lambs, sacrificed in place of those sons (Exodus 11–13). Abraham's harrowing experience was in a manner relived by his descendants through the fateful night of Passover.[8] More than this, Abraham's near sacrifice of Isaac was orchestrated within the unfathomable depths of the mind of the One who dwells in a thick cloud of darkness as an ordeal that would unfold into the paschal ransom of the Israelite firstborn. The meaning of this event and its accompanying feast would form the foundation stone of the Jerusalem temple, the wellspring of Israel's hope and theology. Abraham's binding of Isaac on Mount Moriah not only foreshadows Passover, but Israel's later sacrifice of Passover would take place on the same mountain (Deuteronomy 16:2, 6; 2 Kings 23:21-23; 2 Chronicles 30:1). The awe-filled account of Genesis 22, then, is construed with Passover theology as an exodus: the ransom of Abraham's firstborn son from death through the blood of a substitute sacrifice. In the binding of Isaac, Abraham's spiritual odyssey culminates with his own experience of the figurative death and resurrection of his son—he undergoes a Passover deliverance.

A LITERARY OUTLINE OF ABRAHAM'S LIFE

Panning back now on the literary arrangement of Abraham's life in Genesis, we may observe just how deeply integrated the paradigm of the exodus is to the theological portrait of Israel's ancestor:[9]

The central pivot of the story is when God pronounces himself to be *El Shaddai* ("God Almighty") and he changes Abram's name to *Abraham*, signifying that he will be the father of many nations (Genesis 17:1-5). To be in a father-son relationship implies heritage and likeness—nations possessing the faith of Abraham will comprise his posterity (see Galatians 3:6-9). Similarly, Sarai's name is changed to *Sarah*, for she will be "a mother of nations" (Genesis 17:15-16).

From beginning to end, then, Abram's calling had the nations' plight of exile in view. Beyond a mere trek across geography, God called Abraham to

[8]Naturally, then, early Jewish interpretation linked the Passover redemption of firstborn sons with the sparing of Isaac; see Jubilees 17–18; *Mekilta de-Rabbi Ishmael, Pisḥâ'* 7; *Exodus Rabbah* 15:11; cf. Stanislas Lyonnet and Leopold Sabourin, *Sin, Redemption, and Sacrifice: A Biblical and Patristic Study*, Analecta Biblica 48 (Rome: Biblical Institute, 1970), 261-67.

[9]My outline builds on that of Gary A. Rendsburg, *The Redaction of Genesis* (Winona Lake, IN: Eisenbrauns, 1986), 27-52.

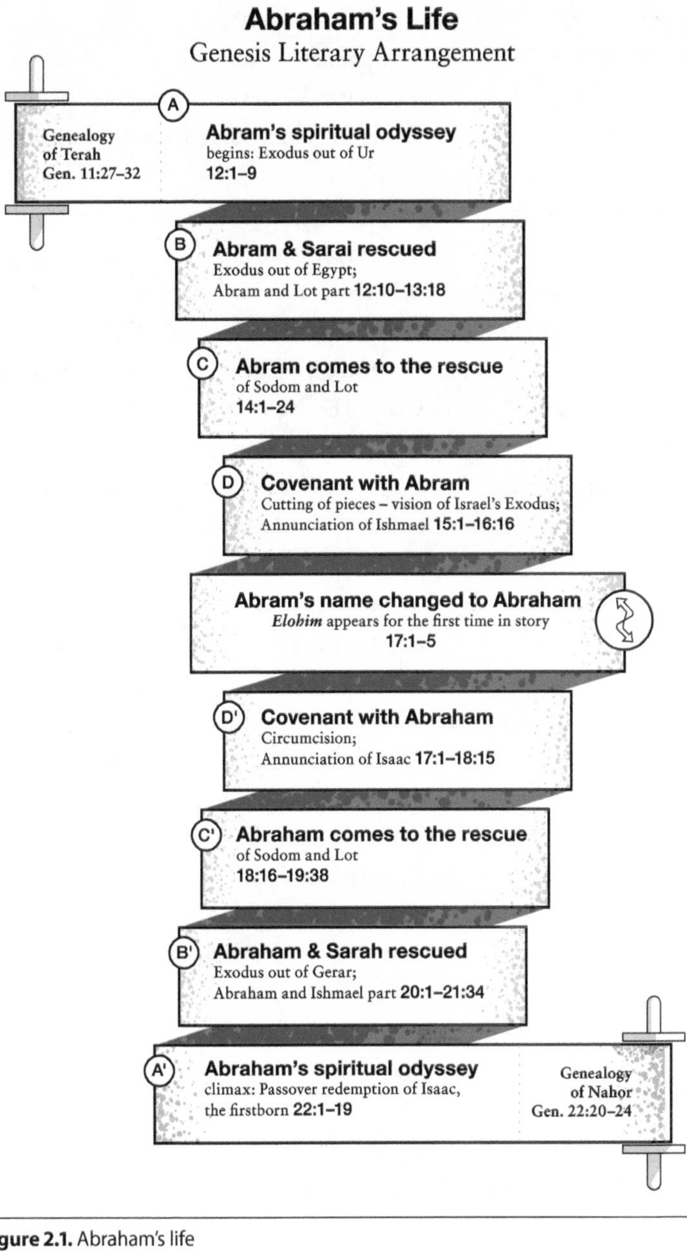
Abraham's Life
Genesis Literary Arrangement
Genealogy of Terah Gen. 11:27–32
A
Abram's spiritual odyssey
begins: Exodus out of Ur
12:1–9
B
Abram & Sarai rescued
Exodus out of Egypt;
Abram and Lot part 12:10–13:18
C
Abram comes to the rescue
of Sodom and Lot
14:1–24
D
Covenant with Abram
Cutting of pieces – vision of Israel's Exodus;
Annunciation of Ishmael 15:1–16:16
Abram's name changed to Abraham
Elohim appears for the first time in story
17:1–5
D'
Covenant with Abraham
Circumcision;
Annunciation of Isaac 17:1–18:15
C'
Abraham comes to the rescue
of Sodom and Lot
18:16–19:38
B'
Abraham & Sarah rescued
Exodus out of Gerar;
Abraham and Ishmael part 20:1–21:34
A'
Abraham's spiritual odyssey
climax: Passover redemption of Isaac,
the firstborn 22:1–19
Genealogy of Nahor Gen. 22:20–24

Figure 2.1. Abraham's life

undergo a spiritual journey of transformation, one that would excise the worldview of exile, steeped in the dark ignorance of God. Abraham's new name manifests his new identity, an identity that is also signified in this central pivot through the sign of circumcision, symbolizing the removal of sin's corruption. As such, circumcision became the sign of membership in the community of Israel.

The connection between the beginning and end of Abraham's spiritual odyssey (A, A' above) is worthy of further contemplation as these episodes comprise Abraham's first and last encounters with Yahweh. In both cases, God calls Abraham to "Go, get yourself out" (*lekh-lekha*). While at the start Yahweh had called on Abram to forsake his past (his father's house), at the climax of his spiritual journey God bid him to sacrifice his future (in offering his son, in whom all of God's promises rested). Hemmed in behind and before, Abraham's life clarifies what it means to "fear Yahweh," to rely solely and devoutly on him. Abraham's faith, his intimate knowledge of God, had matured into the awareness that the God of exodus, the Maker who delivers out of the death of exile, is ultimately the God of resurrection, able to restore Isaac to new life and so fulfill his divine promises for Abraham's seed. And indeed Abraham had told his servant-lads that he and Isaac would *both* return after worshiping God on the mount (Genesis 22:5). Such an interpretation—made plain by Hebrews 11:19 (God "was able to raise Isaac up from the dead, from which Abraham also received him in a figurative sense")—was also discerned in Judaism as integral to the Genesis account. Some Jewish traditions even suggested that Isaac had actually been sacrificed and then resurrected.[10]

Also brought out by the structural outline, the start and climax of Abraham's encounters with God are integrated with exodus-style deliverances out of Egypt and Gerar (B, B' above). Sovereignly, God stamped Abraham's spiritual odyssey with literal experiences of deliverance from a foreign land, melding these together in the crucible of providence so that the events added meaning to each other. Abraham's journey, then, as an initial reversal of exile, is an exodus journey. From the dark depths of Ur, God led him finally to ascend the summit of Mount Moriah where with nearly incomprehensible

[10]See Isaac Kalimi, "'Go, I Beg You, Take Your Beloved Son and Slay Him!' The Binding of Isaac in Rabbinic Literature and Thought," *Review of Rabbinic Judaism* 13, no. 1 (2010): 23-25.

trust and obedience Abraham, in stretching out his knife-bearing hand over Isaac, reversed Adam's self-seeking grasp of the forbidden fruit. Primal humanity's self-willed independence from God was reversed in a gesture of utter, trusting submission to the will of God—and the pathway to blessing all the nations of the earth, even through the gates of Eden's garden, was made known. Fittingly, the destiny of the nations' return to God will be the same hallowed mountain:

> Now it will come to pass in the latter days that the mountain of the house of Yahweh will be established on the summit of the mountains and will be lifted above the hills; and to it all the nations will stream. Many people will come and say, Come, let us ascend to the mountain of Yahweh, to the house of the God of Jacob. He will teach us his ways and we will walk in his paths, for out of Zion the Torah will go forth, and out of Jerusalem the word of Yahweh. (Isaiah 2:2-3)

No more will the nations exclaim, "Come, let us build a ziggurat and make a name for ourselves," but rather, "Come, let us exalt the name of Yahweh and walk in his life-giving ways." Reconciled to the Creator, and being reproved by his judgments, the nations will finally know the long-desired life of peace: "They will beat their swords into plowshares, and their spears into pruning hooks; nation will not lift up sword against nation, and they will not learn war anymore" (Isaiah 2:4). Throughout Abraham's entire life, then, from his deliverance out of the exile of Ur to the sparing of his son by God's provision, one finds the seal of God's pattern of salvation, the exodus—a movement out of death and into life.

Before concluding our look at Abraham's exodus-shaped life, it is worth reflecting once more on the call to leave his past behind, which involved a forsaking of both his country and his father's house. In divine irony, Abram's call out of exile required his forsaking of "home" and his becoming a displaced sojourner who calls on Yahweh's name. Abram's exodus out of exile was a movement *into* displacement among the nations, for Abraham, as the author of Hebrews explains, "dwelled in the land of promise as in a foreign country . . . for he waited for the city that has foundations, whose builder and maker is God" (Hebrews 11:9-10). Until the new heavens and earth appear, such is and has been the lot of all God's people: "These all died in faith, not having received the promises, but having seen them afar off were assured of them, embraced them, and confessed that they were strangers and exiles on the earth. For those who say such things declare plainly that they seek a homeland" (Hebrews 11:13-14). The exodus journey of reunion with God is a passage through death, which required Abraham to sever his bonds with a past that was, after all, a life in the land of wandering.

The same reality is true of God's people today who by spiritual union with Jesus have been crucified and raised up with him—that is, who have already died to the present world and age and have, in the Messiah, been made alive to the world and age to come. Soberingly, Jesus urged: "Remember Lot's wife!" (Luke 17:32), encouraging his people onward in their pilgrimage. Although displaced for now, we embrace the sojourning life with joy, for we serve not only the God who brought up Abraham out of Ur, not only the God who brought up Israel out of Egypt, but the God who brought up our Lord Jesus from the dead (Hebrews 13:20)—and us with him.

Chapter Three

GLORY TO GOD IN THE HIGHEST!

TO BE SURE, THE HARSH BONDAGE experienced by God's people would color their deliverance in terms of liberation. Rightly understood, liberation is being set free to serve Yahweh, the one true and living God. Typical of the Hebrew language in general, the word for "serve" (*'avad*) is open to a variety of meanings including "to slave" and "to worship," and the Exodus narrative may be read as a transition from Israel's slavery under Pharaoh to Israel's obedience and worship of Yahweh; from building cities to glorify the name of Egypt's king (whose name is quite conspicuously left out of the story) to building the tabernacle, a dwelling for the glory of Yahweh's name among his people. Liberation—not merely in the sense of political release but of a revolutionary transformation, of being freed to worship Yahweh—is expressed through multiple statements beginning with Yahweh's promise to Moses: "When you have brought the people out of Egypt, you (plural) will worship [*'avad*] God upon this mountain" (Exodus 3:12). Indeed, God's original message to Pharaoh through Moses was to be: "Let us go three days' journey into the wilderness so we may sacrifice to Yahweh our God" (Exodus 3:18; see the many similar statements in Exodus 4:31; 5:3; 7:16; 8:1,

20, 25-28; 9:1, 13; etc.). True liberation is nothing less than restoration to the right relationship between the creature and Creator. The New Testament will underscore the liberty of those who experience the new exodus accomplished by Jesus Christ, the redemption from bondage to sin and the lordship of Satan in order to glorify God with one's whole being (see Romans 6; Galatians 4).

ISRAEL'S EXILE IN EGYPT: ENTERING INTO THE PLIGHT OF THE NATIONS

The historical exodus out of Egypt was preceded, necessarily, by Israel's exile. Genesis 37–50 recounts how steadily Jacob's house ends up settled in the Egyptian land of Goshen—first through Joseph's being sold into slavery by his brothers and then through the rest of the clan's migration in response to famine. Through the cutting ceremony, God had already revealed to Abraham that his descendants would be strangers in a foreign land for four hundred years and that his people would be enslaved and harshly "afflicted" (*'anah*, Genesis 15:13). The book of Exodus opens with a description of Israel's experience of God's creation blessings amidst their exile in Egypt; the people are fruitful and multiply abundantly, filling the land (Exodus 1:7; cf. Genesis 1:28). Israel's divine growth and abundant life, however, become the very spurs that goad Egypt's king to enslave the Israelites. He sets taskmasters over them to afflict them with heavy labor, conscripting the Israelites to build cities for Egypt. Multiple uses of "afflict" (*'anah*) within the opening chapters recall Yahweh's oracle in Abraham's vision (Exodus 1:11, 12; 3:7; 4:31).

While Pharaoh is accountable to God for his actions and Egypt's king would certainly be brought to his knees in due season, God in his sovereign wisdom had ordained both Israel's exile and suffering. As a witness to the nations of God's plan for their salvation, Israel's exodus was ordained as a deliverance corresponding to the exilic situation of the nations. Israel, the servant of Yahweh, had entered into the plight of the nations, into the bitter darkness of their alienation; the bondage and harsh affliction served both to unveil the cold reality of exile and to form the cry for deliverance within their bowels. Israel's birth as a nation would be an exodus from the dark, watery womb of exile in Egypt. Only such an exodus—and such a God—could answer humanity's despair with hope.

EXILE AS SEPARATION AND IGNORANCE

More deeply, even Israel's liberty is subsumed in Exodus under a broader and higher aim, namely the glory of God, expressed by the text as the "knowledge of Yahweh." Why such knowledge needed to be published through the exodus deliverance relates to humanity's condition of exile. As noted in chapter one, Genesis 1–11 narrates humanity's ever-deepening alienation from God, described as an eastward progression away from God's Edenic presence. Implicit within this presentation of history, separation from God also leads to humanity's increasing ignorance of God, the light of the knowledge of God fading into ever-deepening darkness. Rather than an innocent lack of understanding, such gross ignorance includes the heinous perversion of truth. Although the heavens declare the glory of God, humanity, steeped in the futility of its own rebellion, suppresses the memory and knowledge of God, embracing the offspring of its own faulty and poisoned thinking, ever growing in ignorance of the living God, fashioning and re-fashioning him into humanity's own fallen image with its twisted desires (see Romans 1:18-32).

Within a plight similar to that of the nations in exile, Israel too suffered from such ignorance and blindness, if somewhat less by degree. Tellingly, when commissioned by God to deliver Israel, Moses asks: "When I come to the sons of Israel and tell them, 'The God of your fathers has sent me to you,' and they say to me, 'What is his name?' what will I tell them?" (Exodus 3:13). Clearly, Israel has not retained a knowledge of the "God of your fathers." To cross the threshold of the sea out of Egypt would be meaningless in such a condition. With inscrutable wisdom, God determined so to orchestrate Israel's deliverance that the twofold dilemma of exile—humanity's separation from Yahweh God and its utter ignorance of him—would be remedied, not only for Israel's sake but for that of the nations as well. Understood this way, the first half of Exodus restores a knowledge of Yahweh to the world through the exodus (Exodus 1-15), and the second half restores the presence of Yahweh to humanity through the covenant gift of his tabernacling presence to Israel (Exodus 16-40).

EXODUS 1–15: THE KNOWLEDGE OF YAHWEH

Before God discloses his glory through the exodus deliverance, he reveals himself to Moses through the burning bush as the One who sanctifies the ground by his nearness, the One who is "the God of your father—the God of Abraham, the God of Isaac, and the God of Jacob," and the One whose name is "I Am Who I Am" (Exodus 3:5-6, 14). He goes on to say: "I am Yahweh. I appeared to Abraham, to Isaac, and to Jacob as El Shaddai [God Almighty], but by my name Yahweh I was not known to them" (Exodus 6:2-3). Although the name Yahweh certainly appears in the patriarchal narratives (and these may simply be anachronistic references made for theological purposes), Israel's fathers had not *known* God as Yahweh; the significance of the name awaited the revelation that is the exodus. Yahweh's name, then, may only be known through the mighty acts and fatherly compassion that comprise Israel's deliverance out of Egypt. The exodus unveils the being and attributes of God as no other event thus far—to experience the exodus is to learn about Yahweh himself.

That the knowledge of Yahweh is the major issue around which the entire exodus epic turns is set forth clearly in Moses' first encounter with Pharaoh. Moses declares, "Thus says Yahweh, the God of Israel: Send out my people so they may celebrate a feast to me in the wilderness." Pharaoh's answer, one which he would live to regret, is: "*Who is Yahweh*, that I should heed his voice to send out Israel? *I do not know Yahweh*, nor will I send out Israel" (Exodus 5:1, 2-3.). Through the lips of Pharaoh himself all of the ensuing devastating acts of God—the divine signs and wonders that will soon follow—are defined as the means by which Pharaoh's arrogant challenge is answered by God: Pharaoh will come to know Yahweh in his fearsome love of his people, and so he *will* send out Israel.

Expectedly, then, the plagues—more often referred to as signs and wonders—are regularly prefaced with explicit purpose statements related to the knowledge of Yahweh. In Yahweh's opening summary statement to Moses that he would bring Israel out of Egypt "by great judgments," he says: "Egypt will know that I am Yahweh when I stretch out my hand upon Egypt and bring out the sons of Israel from their midst" (Exodus 7:4-5). Then, before the first sign of turning water into blood, Yahweh reminds Pharaoh of his previous challenge, saying through Moses that "until now you would not heed me" but by this "you will know that I am Yahweh: behold, with the staff that is in my hand I will strike the waters which are in the river and they will be turned to blood" (Exodus 7:16-17). For the second sign as well, that of frogs, Moses tells Pharaoh "that you may know there is no one like Yahweh our God" (Exodus 8:10), and the third sign, of lice, leads Pharaoh's magicians themselves to declare to Pharaoh, "This is the finger of God!" (Exodus 8:19). For the fourth sign, that of flies, God makes a distinction in not allowing the swarms to invade his own people in Goshen, to the end that Pharaoh would "know that I am Yahweh in the midst of the earth" (Exodus 8:22). In the seventh sign, of hail, Yahweh declares, "I will send all my plagues to your heart . . . so that you will know there is no one like me in all the earth." Indeed, Pharaoh afterward declares, "Yahweh is righteous" (Exodus 9:14, 27)—a confession that readily evaporates as superficial. Even when Moses later causes the thunder and hail to cease, he says, "There will be no more hail, that you may know the earth belongs to Yahweh. But as for you and your servants, I know you do not yet fear Yahweh God" (Exodus 9:29-30).

A benefit of identifying a story's major theme is that it enables one to make sense of otherwise difficult issues and sub-themes, in this case, that of Yahweh's hardening of Pharaoh's heart. To begin, Yahweh is the sovereign potter who has both the ability and the right to do all his holy will with his clay vessels so that no creature has the right to question God (Jeremiah 18:1-17; Isaiah 29:16; 45:9; 64:8; Romans 9:20-21). Making the same point in his letter to the Romans, Paul quotes from Exodus 9:16, as Yahweh says to Pharaoh: "For this purpose I have caused you to stand, to show you my power, so that my name may be proclaimed in all the earth" (Romans 9:17). Nevertheless, it is important to understand that the biblical description is mainly of God *strengthening* Pharaoh's heart, firming up his own innate resolve to defy God. Such action by God is unintelligible if one mistakes Israel's liberation as the goal of the exodus—why not, then, *soften* or change Pharaoh's heart instead? But God's agenda is to publish his own glory through signs and wonders. The king of Egypt, a mere creature, could have been reduced to ashes within moments of encountering Yahweh. Indeed, Yahweh himself tells Pharaoh: "By now I could have stretched out my hand and struck you and your people with pestilence, and you would have been cut off from the earth" (Exodus 9:15). Yet God upheld him, strengthening his heart, in order to allow further opportunity for God to display his strong arm. "I will harden the heart of Pharaoh," Yahweh says, "and (so) multiply my signs and my wonders in the land of Egypt" (Exodus 7:3); and again: "Pharaoh will not heed you, so that my wonders may be multiplied in the land of Egypt" (Exodus 11:9).

Before the eighth sign, of locusts, Yahweh reiterates his stratagem to Moses and here reveals his good purposes for his people: "I have strengthened his [Pharaoh's] heart and the heart of his servants in order to display these my signs before him, and in order that you may recount in the ears of your son and of your son's son how I dealt harshly with the Egyptians and about my signs that I displayed before them, so that you (plural) will know that I am Yahweh" (Exodus 10:1-2). By hardening Pharaoh's heart, Israel's bitter bondage necessarily had to be prolonged—their liberation too must be subsumed under the higher goal of God's glory. However, when the cries of God's people are prolonged for the sake of his glory, that agenda also includes a more lasting good for his people—even for their children and their children's children. Generations later, the great grandchildren of these Israelites would yet be nursing on the milk of God's word, recounting his glorious deeds. God's glory became the nourishment, strength, and comfort of their children.

We come now to God's final display of power after the ten signs and wonders—the splitting of the sea. More will be said about the sea crossing in the next chapter, but here we want to observe how the various lines considered so far come together. God will strengthen Pharaoh's heart yet once more so that his armies will pursue Israel into the midst of the sea to their own destruction. "I will strengthen Pharaoh's heart," Yahweh says, "and he will pursue after them, and I will gain glory by Pharaoh and all his might, and Egypt will know that I am Yahweh" (Exodus 14:4). And again, "Egypt will know that I am Yahweh when I gain glory by Pharaoh, by his chariots, and by his horsemen" (Exodus 14:18). Finally, when at the break of day the Israelites turn to see their hostile enemies strewn about the seashore dead, Moses leads them in singing the praises of God. The heart of this song by the sea declares: "Who is like you, O Yahweh, among the gods? Who is like you, glorious in holiness, awesome in praises, doing wonders?" (Exodus 15:11).

Yes, the exodus has revealed Yahweh. The people who would once have asked, "What is the name of our fathers' God?" now declare his utter incomparability, his transcendent holiness and uniqueness. They declare, to borrow Moses' previous words in Exodus 8:10, that "there is no one like Yahweh our God" and so have begun, within the context of grateful worship, to proclaim the glories of Yahweh's name throughout the earth. Pharaoh's previous mock, "Who is Yahweh?" (Exodus 5:2) has now become an ascription of praise, "Who is like you, O Yahweh, among the gods?" (Exodus 15:11).

Such incomparability, as revealed through the exodus deliverance, is vital for humanity's return to God, which must necessarily include the rejection of all other gods: "I am Yahweh your God, who brought you out of the land of Egypt, out of the house of bondage. You shall have no other gods before me" (Exodus 20:2-3). And indeed to have released Israel immediately, apart from God's mighty display of signs and wonders, would have been no true exodus at all, as the people's hearts would not have welled up in wondrous praise of his glory. Many nations, including Egypt itself, were already free politically speaking, yet nevertheless shackled in the bondage of sin and idolatry. God in his majestic wisdom ordained Israel's exile and bondage, along with the strengthening of Pharaoh's foolishly defiant heart, in order to wreak a political release that would, more deeply, form a spiritual liberation as well.

In one of his early messages to the Israelites through Moses, Yahweh had said: "I will take you for myself for a people, and I will be your God, and you will know that I am Yahweh your God, who brings you out from under the burdens of the Egyptians" (Exodus 6:7). This is who Yahweh is for his people, the God of the exodus. And yet Yahweh's self-revelation through the exodus was not for Israel's sake only, for the proclamation of Yahweh's glory was to be published over all the earth. A generation later in the city of Jericho, the Israelites would encounter a Canaanite prostitute who, having heard of Yahweh's glorious acts of deliverance, possessed the fear of Yahweh—that is, true faith. Scripture preserves her confession: "Yahweh your God, he is God in heaven above and on the earth beneath" (Joshua 2:11). With such a confession, she proves herself a genuine Israelite indeed, a daughter of Abraham. Marrying into the tribe of Judah, Rahab would become the ancestress of the

Messiah and Son of God, Jesus Christ (Matthew 1:5), at whose birth the angelic hosts would cry out, "Glory to God in the highest!" (Luke 2:14).

YAHWEH: LORD OF HEAVEN AND EARTH AND KING ABOVE ALL GODS

Israel's exodus out of Egypt, as we have seen, is associated closely with God's glory and to his being Yahweh. If Yahweh's deliverance of Israel was divinely calculated to overcome the world's ignorance of God, then what precisely did his mighty acts unveil?

In the first place, all of God's signs and wonders fall within the context of creation theology. It is stunning how often Exodus portrays the hand of Yahweh (often through Moses' hand or Aaron's rod) stretched out over the waters, the earth, the cattle, and toward heaven, a gesture of lordship over every realm and aspect of creation (see, for example, Exodus 7:19; 9:3, 23; 10:12, 21). Turning the river water into blood; smiting the region with frogs and flies; sending a pestilence among the cattle, horses, donkeys, camels, oxen, and sheep; causing boils to break out on the Egyptians and their animals; sending hail, swarms of locusts, impenetrable precreation darkness, and the death of the firstborn—all of these acts demonstrate that their author is one who possesses absolute control of nature, one who possesses all authority both in heaven and on earth. In short, the signs and wonders displayed in Israel's exodus out of Egypt demonstrate that Yahweh is the Maker of heaven and earth, the Lord over all creation. Such an understanding resonates with Rahab's confession, "Yahweh your God, he is God in heaven above and on the earth beneath" (Joshua 2:11) and includes the notion that Yahweh is utterly sovereign.

Moreover, when seen from God's culminating act of deliverance, whereby the Egyptian hosts were destroyed, submerged in the sea, it appears that God's judgment may be understood as something of a de-creation of Egypt. Without attempting, as some have, to correlate each of the plagues as a reversal of one of God's acts of creation, one may note that generally each of the signs and wonders is related to God's power over nature, but rather than progressing for the sake of life, God's acts cause the steady destruction of Egypt. Ultimately, the cosmos of the Egyptian hosts ends up submerged by the waters of chaos (Exodus 14:26-28), much like the original state of the earth before God's life-yielding acts of creation (Genesis 1:2) and much like the earth, along with Noah's generation, after God's deluge of judgment (Genesis 7:18-24). The world of Egypt comes undone, moving from cosmos to chaos, whereas the waters are separated in a new act of creation for the Israelites to walk dry-shod.

In the second place, many have also understood God's signs and wonders in relation to the Egyptian pantheon, as a defeat of Egypt's gods.[1] The notion is nearly inescapable since so many of Egypt's gods happen to be linked to nature. Turning the Nile waters into blood, for example, could hardly avoid implications for the god Khnum, the creator of water and life, or against Hapi, the god of the Nile. Similarly, the frogs plague may be seen as directed against Heket, the goddess of childbirth who was portrayed as a frog. Hathor, mother goddess of the sky, who was presented as a cow, was perhaps humiliated by the pestilence. Along these lines, the darkness may be understood as devastating those deities associated with the sun: Amon-Re, Aten, Atum, and Horus. Possibly, the death of the firstborn was directed against Osiris, the judge of the dead and patron deity of Pharaoh. While the text of the book of Exodus does not make these connections explicit, it is nevertheless conceivable that such associations would have been assumed by the original audience of Israel, to say nothing of the Egyptians themselves who endured the mighty hand of Yahweh. At least in a general manner, however, the text does make clear that God's judgments demonstrate his supremacy over the gods of Egypt. In Exodus 12:12, with particular reference to Passover, Yahweh says: "I will pass through the land of Egypt on this night and will smite all the firstborn in the land of Egypt, from man to beast, and against all the gods of Egypt I will execute judgments—I am Yahweh."

Again, in Numbers 33:4, the Pentateuch rehearses that "upon their (the Egyptians') gods, Yahweh had executed judgments," so that the exodus deliverance—especially the Passover slaying of the firstborn—must be understood as a demonstration of Yahweh's supremacy over and divine judgment on the pantheon of Egypt. By wielding creation for his own ends, Yahweh had demonstrated his supremacy over the objects of Egyptian worship, which were no gods at all. The exodus declares Yahweh to be both Lord of creation

[1]On this approach, see Ziony Zevit, "Three Ways to Look at the Ten Plagues," *Bible Review* 6, no. 3 (1990): 16-23, 42.

and king above all gods. Well did Israel sing: "Who is like you, O Yahweh, among the gods?" (Exodus 15:11; cf. Psalm 135:5). When Jethro, Moses' Midianite father-in-law, hears of God's mighty deliverance of Israel out of Egypt, he rejoices, saying, "Now I know that Yahweh is greater than all the gods!" and he worships God with sacrifices (Exodus 18:11-12). Such a revelation of Yahweh, this truth, is the chief goal and highest wonder of the exodus, and again this knowledge is for the sake of the nations. There is no true hope or sincere comfort apart from this bedrock reality—abundant life, help and restoration, begin here: Yahweh, and he alone, is God.

Humanity's exilic ignorance of God and the nations' dark perversion of his character and attributes would not have been helped by an easy, quiet release of Hebrew slaves from Egypt. Yahweh God orchestrated, therefore, the bondage of his own people and strengthened Pharaoh's pompous resolve all in order to shine the light of the knowledge of the glory of God into the darkness of exile. Through the exodus, Yahweh revealed his own matchless glory, power, supremacy, and judgments. He unveiled himself as Yahweh God, the Maker of heaven and earth, the one true and living God to whom all creation and all nations owe both homage and obedience. The salvation of his people and punishment of Egypt revealed Yahweh God to be the judge of all the earth, the one who executes judgments with a mighty arm that no gods—no powers, earthly or heavenly—can stay.

As a fulfillment of his word to Abraham, moreover, the exodus also proved Yahweh to be faithful, and as a response to Israel's groaning under bondage it demonstrated that he is near to the humble, concerned about their hardships, and willing to deliver them in his tender mercies and steadfast love. He tells Moses: "I have surely seen the affliction of my people who are in Egypt and have heard their cries because of their oppressors, for I know their sorrows" (Exodus 3:7). He sees, he hears, he knows—and he cares (see also Exodus 3:9, 16-17). Yahweh remembered the covenant relationship he had established with Israel's forefathers, including his promise to give their children the land of Canaan and to be their God. His message to Israel is personal and full of hope: "I will take you for myself as a people, and I will be your God, and you will know that I am Yahweh your God who brings you out from under the burdens of the Egyptians" (Exodus 6:7).

When the elders of Israel learn from Moses that Yahweh, having looked on their affliction, had visited to deliver them, they bow their heads and worship (Exodus 4:31), an apt response indeed. A true knowledge of Yahweh God is personal—it involves a reciprocal embrace, a claiming of the One who has redeemed us for himself. The beautiful facet of Israel's song by the sea at the culmination of the exodus is not only that the people have come to see something of the incomparability of Yahweh but that, having seen his glory and redeeming love, the people embrace him as their own: "This is my God, and I will praise him, / the God of my fathers, and I will exalt him" (Exodus 15:2). The same Israelites whom Moses had feared would not even know the name of their fathers' God now claim the God of their fathers as "my God"! Such a boast in God follows naturally from the previous line of the song: "Yahweh is my strength and my song; / He has become my salvation."

> There is none like you among the gods, O Lord,
> nor works like your works.
> All nations whom you have made will come and worship before you, O Lord,
> and glorify your name.
> For you are great and do wonders
> —you alone are God! (Psalm 86:8-10)

Chapter Four

SLAYING THE SEA DRAGON

IN THIS CHAPTER, WE WILL LOOK more closely at the creation theology of the sea crossing (Exodus 14), including how Yahweh's battle at the sea is described elsewhere in Scripture as the slaying of a sea dragon. The story of Israel's salvation at the sea is full of suspense as readers are given a view of the Egyptian pursuit with a lengthy description of the "horses and chariots of Pharaoh and his might" (Exodus 14:9) even while Israel sets up camp as yet unaware of the looming threat of destruction. As Pharaoh draws near, "the sons of Israel lifted their eyes and—look!—the Egyptians journeying after them! The sons of Israel feared greatly and cried out to Yahweh" (Exodus 14:10). Fearing the Egyptian host, the sea, the darkness—fearing death itself—the Israelites would learn to fear Yahweh in this last display of his powerful majesty: "And Israel saw the mighty hand which Yahweh worked against Egypt, and the people feared Yahweh, and they trusted in Yahweh and in Moses his servant" (Exodus 14:31).

THE PRIMORDIAL EXODUS: CREATION, RE-CREATION, AND THE SEA CROSSING

Yahweh's glorious self-revelation culminates with his final victory over the hosts of Egypt at the sea in Exodus 14, a narrative that stands as a literary masterpiece. The account contains allusions to the creation and deluge stories of Genesis, employing the imagery of darkness and light along with the passing of evening into the break of dawn, to set forth Israel's deliverance as a resurrection on the other side of death, a new creation.[1] While the exodus story follows a pattern of cosmogony, alluding to the origins of the cosmos in Genesis, the wheel may also be reversed, allowing us to understand creation and re-creation (through the flood) as exodus movements.

Creation and recreation are acts by which God brings humanity into an ordered cosmos, into life with himself, a pattern that involves his sovereign control of the sea, so that the chaotic waters (Genesis 1:2) turn into waters of life (Genesis 2:10-14). For the re-creation account of the deluge (Genesis 6–8), the exodus pattern of cosmogony is especially clear: God delivers humanity through the death-wielding waters of judgment and into an orderly—that is, life-yielding—cosmos, his wind having subdued the waters: "God caused a wind to pass over the earth, and the waters abated" (Genesis 8:1). These features of creation—splitting the sea by God's wind and the emergence of dry land—signal an exodus movement from death to life, from chaos to order, typically to Yahweh at the mountain of God. As the light of Yahweh's cloud shone into the darkness of night, as his wind clove the sea before Israel, as God's people trekked on dry land, in all these ways Israel's journey had been a retracing of the primordial exodus.

Israel's final deliverance is narrated in three sections with reference to the sea and time of day: toward the sea at dusk (Exodus 14:1-14), amidst the sea at night (Exodus 14:15-25), and on the other side of the sea at dawn (Exodus 14:26-31). The symbolism of the sea and the darkness of night, along with the impending threat of Egypt's pounding pursuit, serves to portray Israel's entrance into and emergence out of the sea as a death and resurrection that encapsulates the exodus: Israel's descent into and ascent out of Egypt, a land symbolic of Sheol, the watery abode of death. The sea, as we will observe throughout this chapter, symbolizes death. Even the alternate reference to this body of water in Exodus 15:4, *yam-suf* in Hebrew, is translated by a

[1]This section follows the fine analysis of Jean Louis Ska, "The Crossing of the Sea," *Landas* 17, no. 1 (2003): 36-50.

number of scholars as "sea of end" or the "sea of destruction," rather than Red Sea or Sea of Reeds,[2] and others insist, regardless of translation, that the sea be understood as a "theological *Sheol*."[3]

Amidst this context of darkness and death, Yahweh's first act of deliverance is to come between the camps of Egypt and Israel. Through the angel of God in the pillar of cloud, he causes darkness over Egypt while shining fiery light on Israel (Exodus 14:19-20), a separation between darkness and light that recalls God's first act of creation (Genesis 1:3-4). Then, through Moses' upheld staff, Yahweh sends a strong eastward wind (*ruakh*) to divide the sea, so that dry land appears (Exodus 14:16, 21), just as he once sent his wind (or Spirit, *ruakh*) to divide the waters covering the earth, so that dry land appeared (Genesis 1:2, 6-10). Egypt's end will be the darkness of night, "covered" (*kasah*) in the waters of chaos, just like Noah's generation was covered (*kasah*) under waters of judgment (Exodus 14:28; cf. Genesis 7:19-20). The end of Israel's enemies, like a reversal of creation, forms a return to the precreation state of the earth, submerged in both sea and darkness (Genesis 1:2). Even so, for Israel the dry land emerges as they journey out of darkness, ascending out of the sea toward the rising sun. Through the waters Israel has died to death and has been reborn, resurrected as the people of Yahweh. Salvation is an act of new creation.

EGYPT AS SHEOL

Seeing Egypt as symbolic of Sheol begins with understanding the cultural context. Skilled in the practice of mummification as well as the necessary incantations and other requisites for survival in the afterlife, Egyptians were the leading experts on death, religiously as well as scientifically. It is therefore with a biting sarcasm that the Israelites, fearing destruction at the sea, cry out: "Is it because there were no graves in Egypt that you have brought us to

---

[2]J. A. Montgomery, "Yām Sûp ('the Red Sea') = Ultimum Maré!," *Journal of the American Oriental Society* 58 (1938): 131-32; N. H. Snaith, "The Sea of Reeds: The Red Sea," *Vetus Testamentum* 15, no. 3 (1965): 395-98; Bernard F. Batto, "The Reed Sea: Requiescat in Pace," *Journal of Biblical Literature* 102, no. 1 (1983): 27-35; Nicolas Wyatt, "There and Back Again: The Significance of Movement in the Priestly Work," *Scandinavian Journal of the Old Testament* 4, no. 1 (1990): 70-72.
[3]Walter Wifall, "The Sea of Reeds as *Sheol*," *Zeitschrift Für Die Alttestamentliche Wissenschaft* 92, no. 3 (1980): 325-32.

the wilderness to die?" (Exodus 14:11). Also, the language of Scripture accords with the notion of Egypt as representing Sheol, consistently using the verb of descent (*yarad*) into Egypt and that of ascent (*'alah*) out of Egypt. As when entering the Netherworld, one always *descends* into Egypt, and the exodus of Israel out of Egypt is nothing less than an ascension.

These lines come together in the Joseph narrative, which recounts how the Israelites wound up in Egypt (Genesis 37–50). Joseph is sold to a company of Ishmaelites who are "bearing gum, balm, and myrrh, on their way to carry them down [*yarad*] to Egypt" (Genesis 37:25). Unsurprisingly, the caravan headed to Egypt, the land renowned for embalming, is laden with funerary supplies and is traveling downward. Descending to the Sheol of Egypt, Joseph has figuratively died, so that Jacob later ironically prophesies when he says, "I shall descend [*yarad*] into Sheol to my son in mourning" (Genesis 37:35), for he will indeed descend *into Egypt* to see his son—yes, and he himself will die in Egypt too. Yet God had promised Jacob: "I will go down [*yarad*] with you to Egypt and I will also surely cause you to ascend [*'alah*]" (Genesis 46:4). When God does cause Jacob to ascend out of Egypt, he is brought out embalmed (Genesis 50:1-14) just as Moses will later bring up Joseph's bones (Exodus 13:19). Indeed, the book of Genesis closes with the death of Joseph in Egypt: "So Joseph died . . .and they embalmed him and he was set in the coffin in Egypt." As with Joseph, moreover, Egypt is a place of *exile* for Israel, and exile also symbolizes death theologically. "Going down to Egypt," writes Nicolas Wyatt, "is like going down into the underworld; being in Egypt is like being in the tomb."[4] He finds an implicit symbolism in the Pentateuch whereby "Egypt signified death"—it was "a symbol of the exile, signifying the death of a people," with the sea, the *yam-suf*, serving to divide the land of the dead from that of the living.[5] Bracketed by the waters of the Nile (Exodus 2) and the sea (Exodus 14), waters of death in both contexts, the literary place of Egypt between those bookends is pervaded by the symbolism

[4]Nicolas Wyatt, *The Mythic Mind: Essays on Cosmology and Religion in Ugaritic and Old Testament Literature* (London: Routledge, 2014), 38.

[5]Nicolas Wyatt, *Myths of Power: A Study of Royal Myth and Ideology in Ugaritic and Biblical Tradition*, UBL 13 (Münster: Ugarit-Verlag, 1996), 87-88; Nicolas Wyatt, "Sea and Desert: Symbolic Geography in West Semitic Religious Thought," *Ugarit Forschungen* 19 (1987): 375-76.

of Sheol, the watery abode of death. Northrop Frye, the most influential literary theorist of the twentieth century, wrote that "the drowned Egyptian army is the continuous symbolic Egypt of darkness and death," noting that in the New Testament both the flood (1 Peter 3:21) and the sea crossing (1 Corinthians 10:2) are regarded as types of the sacrament of baptism, which symbolizes death to the old world and being made alive to the new world on the opposite shore.[6]

Literarily, it is as if Israel had been delivered from the chamber of death in the depths of the sea (and, as we will observe below, from the sea monster embodying that realm) and then conveyed to God's abode on his holy mountain. Escaping Egypt inevitably involves deliverance out of waters of death, redemption from Sheol. Justly, then, the exodus movement out of Egypt to Yahweh's presence at Mount Sinai has been likened to the movement across cosmic geography found in lament and thanksgiving psalms, as the psalmist is drawn out of the surging waters and brought to safety on God's temple mountain, a cosmogonic movement from death to life. Psalm 18, for example, describes Yahweh's deliverance of the psalmist in the following manner:

> The channels of waters were seen, and the foundations of the world
> were uncovered,
> At your rebuke, O Yahweh, at the blast of the wind [*ruakh*] of
> your nostrils.
> He sent from on high, he took me, he drew me out of great waters.
> (Psalm 18:15-16)

The language recalls Moses' own deliverance out of the waters, and "he drew me" uses the same verb from which Moses' name derives (*mashah*; cf. Exodus 2:10). Whether one suffers sickness or the attack of enemies, such threats of death lead regularly to cries for deliverance from the "great waters" (Psalm 144:7), the "waters that overwhelmed us, the torrent that passed over our soul" (Psalm 124:4; see also Psalms 40, 69, 88). Jonah's psalm of thanksgiving on his deliverance from the depth of the sea, to offer

[6]Northrop Frye, *The Great Code: The Bible and Literature* (New York: Harcourt, 1981), 147.

another example, could just as well have been sung by the Israelites after the sea crossing:[7]

I called out of my distress to Yahweh, and he answered me;
Out of the belly of Sheol I cried, and you heard my voice.
For you cast me into the deep, into the heart of the seas;
And the torrents surrounded me, all your billows and your waves passed over me.
. . . The waters closed upon me, unto my soul;
The deep surrounded me, death-reeds [*suf*] bound my head.
To the roots of the mountains I had descended;
The bars of the netherworld had barred me in forever—
But you caused my life to ascend out of the pit, O Yahweh my God. . . .
Salvation belongs to Yahweh! (Jonah 2:2-9)

Even without any reference to the historical exodus, this archetypal pattern was imbedded within the heart of ancient Israel as the theology of the exodus, of Israel's deliverance out of Egypt, the land of the dead. The cosmological symbolism serves to explain the real significance, the theology, of the historical event. Noting the parallels between the Paschal night (Exodus 12) and the sea crossing (Exodus 14–15), whereby Israel, which had been "confined to *Sheol*," is saved while the firstborn sons of Egypt and then all the Egyptian hosts are killed, Martin Hauge explains how the Song of the Sea interprets Israel's historical redemption as a sacred journey from *Sheol* (Egypt and the sea) to Yahweh's abode in the land of Canaan.[8] Precisely this theological understanding of the historical exodus out of Egypt undergirds Hosea's prophecy of a second exodus:

From the hand of *Sheol*, I will ransom them;
From Death, I will redeem them.
Where are your plagues, O Death?
Where is your sting, O *Sheol*? (Hosea 13:14)

---

[7]Also relevant, rabbinical traditions link the great fish in Jonah with Leviathan (cf. *Pirqe de-Rabbi Eliezer* 10; *Yalquṭ Shimoni*), and early Christian art portrays the fish, similarly, as a sea dragon, a reading that may be detected already in the Septuagint translation of the fish as *kētos*, "sea monster" (LXX, Jonah 2:1, 2, 11). On this topic, see Scott B. Noegel, "Jonah and Leviathan," *Henoch* 37.2 (2015), 236-60.

[8]Martin R. Hauge, *Between Sheol and Temple: Motif Structure and Function in the I-Psalms* (Sheffield, UK: Sheffield Academic Press, 1995), 113.

Emerging from the waters of the sea, Israel—God's firstborn son—emerged out of *Sheol* into resurrection life.

SLAYING THE SEA DRAGON

Israel's deliverance through the waters of death, as we have seen, was a divine act that pictured their release from Egypt as a rescue from Sheol, the watery land of death. In delivering Israel out of Egypt, however, God had also accomplished a mighty victory over the hosts of Egypt. Indeed, the account is a militaristic one, where Moses assures the trembling people that "Yahweh will fight for you!" (Exodus 14:14). As sung by Israel shortly afterward, his defeat of Pharaoh's might unveiled that "Yahweh is a Man of War—Yahweh is his name!" (Exodus 15:3). In this section, we will look at how the splitting of the sea and God's defeat of Pharaoh and Egypt was later portrayed as a slaying of the dragon associated with the sea—a mythological battle that springs out of creation theology.[9]

The account of creation in Genesis 1, while rendered with liturgical qualities like repetition, is set forth from a historical perspective and demonstrates God's utterly transcendent majesty and power, creating the world through his sovereign word without any battle whatsoever—the waters, which may represent chaos, are not personified. Similarly, in the deluge and sea crossing narratives, the waters, while surely threatening to his people, are nevertheless but a natural force wielded and sovereignly controlled by Yahweh God. In other places in Scripture, however, the theology of creation is given in more poetic ways, portraying God as a mighty warrior who conquers the waters of chaos, personified by the sea dragon that lives in those waters. As a power that humanity is unable to tame, often dark and turbulent, the sea readily came to symbolize chaos in the ancient world, the forces of darkness and the power of evil, even death. Not only was the sea itself personified, but it was

[9]On the dragon slaying myth and biblical literature, see Robert D. Miller, *The Dragon, the Mountain, and the Nations: An Old Testament Myth, Its Origins, and Its Afterlives* (University Park: Eisenbrauns, 2018); Bernard F. Batto, *Slaying the Dragon: Mythmaking in the Biblical Tradition* (Louisville, KY: Westminster John Knox, 1992); for a sound definition of "chaos" along with crucial differences between biblical imagery and the myths of the ancient world, see Sidney Greidanus, *From Chaos to Cosmos: Creation to New Creation* (Wheaton, IL: Crossway, 2018), esp. 17-49.

also embodied as a monster within the sea. Job brings the two together when he cries out to God: "Am I a sea [*yam*] or a sea dragon [*tannin*] that you set a guard upon me?" (Job 7:12). Names for mythological sea monsters include Leviathan, Yam ("sea"), Mot ("death"), Tannin ("dragon"), and Rahab. God's splitting of the seas in Genesis 1, then, may also be described as his splitting a sea dragon elsewhere:

> He stretches out the heavens—he alone,
> And treads upon the waves of the sea [*yam*]. . . .
> God will not relent his anger,
> Under him lie crushed the helpers of *Rahab*. . . .
> By his power, he churned up the sea [*yam*],
> By his understanding he smote *Rahab* in pieces.
> By his Wind, the heavens became fair,
> His hand pierced the fleeing serpent [*nakhash*]. (Job 9:8, 13; 26:12-13)

Psalm 74 also includes the slaying of sea dragons in its description of creation:

> But God my King is of ancient times,
> Working salvation in the midst of the earth.
> You, by your strength, divided (the) sea [*yam*],
> You broke the heads of the dragons [*tannin*] upon the waters.
> You crushed the heads of Leviathan,
> You gave him as food for people of the coast.
> You cleaved the springs and torrents,
> You dried up the mighty rivers.
> Yours is the day, indeed, yours is the night,
> You established the heavenly lights and the sun.
> You fixed all the boundaries of the earth,
> Summer and winter you have formed. (Psalm 74:12-17)

These few verses contain five different terms for water (*sea*, *waters*, *springs*, *torrents*, *mighty rivers*) in their manifold description of God's acts of creation.

In the ancient world, portraying creation or the establishing of divine kingship in a mythological manner as a conquest of the sea or the slaying of a monster was not unusual. In the Baal Epic (c. 1400 BC) of Ugarit, an ancient seaport city in northern Syria, the storm-god Baal slays Yam, the sea sometimes depicted as the dragon Lotan, which leads to building Baal's palace and the acclamation of his kingship. The epic also depicts Mot (death) attacking Baal, crushing him like a lamb in his mouth and swallowing him up. In biblical Hebrew, the word for "sea" is *yam*; in some contexts, as in the quote from Psalm 74 above, it may be that a reference to Yam is intended by use of "sea."[10] Indeed, when the Bible story closes with the declaration that in the new earth "there was no more sea" (Revelation 21:1), the point is theological, poetically referring to the absence of evil powers, rather than topographical.

As Ugarit was a close neighbor of Israel, Israelites were probably familiar with such popular Baal myths, and sometimes Israel's prophets echoed the language of mythology, claiming for Yahweh alone the reality of dragon slaying, that is, of creation and kingship. Yahweh himself would "swallow up Death forever" and wipe away the tears from his people's faces (Isaiah 25:8). In the most famous Mesopotamian myth, Enuma Elish (c. 1500 BC), the Babylonian god Marduk slays Tiamat, the dragon of watery darkness and chaos, and then as king of the gods uses her split carcass to create the world. Marduk's defeat of Tiamat was performed annually during the Babylonian New Year's festival and would have been experienced by the Judean exiles in Babylon (6th century BC), although it is likely that Enuma Elish was already well known to Israel before the exile. Some references to Rahab in the Bible seem to designate the same monster as Tiamat (Job 9:13; 26:12).

Yahweh's forming an orderly, habitable, and life-yielding cosmos out of a weltering wasteland (*tohu wabohu*, Genesis 1:2), when the earth had been overwhelmed by the dark primordial waters of the deep, symbolizes a conquest of chaos. His triumph in creation serves as assurance that God is always able to defeat the powers of darkness, which are ultimately anti-creational since being opposed to God means being opposed to life. As vivid metaphors for powers that oppose life, dragons are closely linked in the Bible with historical nations that oppose God and his people Israel. Ancient Egypt, represented by Pharaoh, is thereby sometimes identified with the sea dragons of chaos, Tannin and Rahab. In Ezekiel 29:3, Yahweh says, "I am against you, Pharaoh king of Egypt, the great sea dragon [*tannin*]." The names Tannin

[10]In the Hebrew text there is no definite article before "sea" in Psalm 74:13.

and Rahab are listed in poetic parallelism in Isaiah 51:9: "Was it not you who slew Rahab and pierced the sea dragon [*tannin*]?" Because of the close association between Egypt and Rahab, as well as the link between creation and redemption, it is sometimes difficult to know whether a biblical passage refers to God's triumph in creation or to his triumph over Egypt in the sea crossing. Psalm 89 declares, "Yahweh God of hosts, who is like you?" recalling the heart of Israel's song by the sea: "Who is like you, O Yahweh, among the gods?" (Exodus 15:11). The psalm then goes on to say:

> You rule over the raging of the sea,
> When its waves surge, you still them.
> You crushed Rahab in pieces, like the battle-slain,
> With your strong arm, you scattered your enemies. (Psalm 89:9-10)

While the psalm may be speaking only of God's acts in creation, with his crushing of Rahab representing his subduing of chaos, Rahab also seems to be a reference to the defeat of Egypt by Yahweh's arm, a motif of the exodus deliverance (Exodus 6:6; 15:16; Deuteronomy 4:34; 5:15; etc.). Similarly, Isaiah 51:9-10 reads:

> Awake, awake, put on strength, O arm of Yahweh,
> Awake, as in ancient days, the generations of old.
> Was it not you who slew Rahab, and pierced the Dragon [*tannin*]?
> Was it not you who dried up (the) sea [*yam*], the waters of the Great Deep [*tehom*],
> Who made a path in the depths of (the) sea for the redeemed to pass over?

While employing creation imagery, the last lines make clear that the reference is actually to the sea crossing of Exodus. Since creation and redemption (as recreation) are of a piece, we are dealing here with a false either/or. "In the primal past, it was the 'arm of YHWH' which had destroyed *Rahab* and *Tannin, Yam* and *Tehom:* ancient sea monsters all," writes Fishbane, "and it was this same 'arm' which cleaved *Yam* (the Sea personified) at the time of the exodus," and is now invoked anew for a second exodus as Israel's hope in exile.[11] Other references to Rahab clearly have Egypt in mind. Isaiah 30:7 says: "Egypt's

[11]Michael A. Fishbane, "The 'Exodus' Motif/The Paradigm of Historical Renewal," in *Biblical Text and Texture: A Literary Reading of Selected Texts* (Oxford, UK: Oneworld, 1998), 135.

help is empty and worthless, for which I call her Rahab, the one who sits still." As noted briefly already, Pharaoh, who embodies Egypt, is also described as a chaos dragon. In Ezekiel 29:3 Yahweh declares:

> Behold, I am against you, O Pharaoh, king of Egypt,
> O great sea dragon who lies in the midst of his Nile,
> Who has said, "My Nile is my own; I have made it for myself."

Later on Pharaoh is described as "a dragon in the seas, bursting forth in your rivers, troubling the waters with your feet and fouling their rivers" (Ezekiel 32:2).

Now, since elsewhere in Scripture both Pharaoh and Egypt are described as the sea dragon Rahab and God's victory over the host of Egypt in the sea crossing is described as his slaying the sea dragon of chaos, it is worth exploring if such a theological view is at play within the book of Exodus. To be sure, Pharaoh is portrayed as an anticreational foe of God's people. The book of Exodus opens with a description of Israel enjoying the blessings that God had first pronounced on humanity at creation. We read that the Israelites were "fruitful and increased abundantly and became many and grew exceedingly mighty, and the land was filled with them" (Exodus 1:7), words that echo remarkably those of Genesis 1:28: "God blessed them, and said to them, 'Be fruitful and multiply and fill the earth.'" In the Exodus narrative, Pharaoh's opposition to Israel is set forth as his direct response to their creational blessing. He says that "the sons of Israel are too many and too mighty for us" (Exodus 1:9) and then begins his various attempts at reducing them—inaugurating a battle between life and death. Within this context, two occasions especially, both in Exodus 7, resonate with the dragon-slaying motif.

In Exodus 7:8-13, Yahweh directs Aaron to cast down his staff before Pharaoh, declaring that it will become a dragon (*tannin*). Variously translated as dragon or sea monster, and used in parallel with Rahab and the Deep, *tannin* is not a garden-variety snake, writes Arie Leder, but to "the contrary, it evokes the threat of chaos."[12] When Pharaoh's magicians replicate this feat, with each of their rods becoming a dragon, then Aaron's *tannin* swallows up theirs, leading one scholar to describe Aaron's staff as a "dragon-gobbling

[12]Arie C. Leder, "Hearing Exodus 7:8-13 to Preach the Gospel: The Ancient Adversary in Today's World," *Calvin Theological Journal* 43 (2008): 97.

dragon."[13] As the only other use of "swallow" (*bālaʿ*) in Exodus describes the Egyptians being swallowed in the depths of the earth beneath the sea (Exodus 15:12), it is quite likely, as some scholars suggest, that the divine demonstration of Aaron's staff threatened Pharaoh with being swallowed up by chaos, a foreshadowing of the demise of his hosts in the sea.[14] This is precisely the trajectory that ensued with the plagues which, wreaking havoc in nature, were the steady undoing of Egypt's world, culminating with the Egyptian host submerged in the sea.

In the next scene (Exodus 7:14-25), Yahweh directs Moses to confront Pharaoh in the morning as he "is going forth into the water." Aaron is directed to bring his staff "which had turned into a serpent [*nakhash*]," and they are to confront Pharaoh at the bank of the Nile. We have already observed how Yahweh characterizes Pharaoh in Ezekiel as the "great sea dragon who lies in the midst of his Nile," claiming "my Nile is my own." Such a characterization seems to be at work in this scene as Yahweh confronts Pharaoh while he, dragonlike, wades in the river. As in Ezekiel, Pharaoh here is likened to "a huge mythical reptile wallowing in the river."[15] Through the same rod that on the previous day had turned into a dragon, Yahweh will now turn the waters of the Nile into blood, claiming sovereignty over "Pharaoh's Nile." As the first miracle and sign put before Pharaoh, respectively, the staff's transformation into a dragon and the turning of Pharaoh's Nile into blood are defining for the epic of Israel's deliverance out of Egypt.

More broadly, the first nine signs are structured in three cycles of three plagues. Within this scheme, the first sign in each cycle (the first, fourth, and seven plagues) parallel one another, and involve Moses and Aaron's approach to Pharaoh early in the morning (Exodus 7:15; 8:20; 9:13) and appear to involve confronting Pharaoh during his morning ritual bath—that is, while he wades in the Nile. For the first sign, as we have already seen, Yahweh sends Moses to Pharaoh "when he goes out to the water," with Moses standing by the bank of the river (Exodus 7:15), and the fourth sign has Moses standing before Pharaoh when "he comes out of the water" (Exodus 8:20). While the account

---

[13]Philippe Guillaume, "Metamorphosis of a Ferocious Pharaoh," *Biblica* 85 (2004): 232.

[14]Terence E. Fretheim, *God and World in the Old Testament: A Relational Theology of Creation* (Nashville: Abingdon, 2005), 115; Greidanus, *From Chaos to Cosmos*, 46.

[15]Guillaume, "Metamorphosis," 232, 235.

of the seventh sign merely indicates that Moses is to "rise early in the morning and stand before Pharaoh" (Exodus 9:13), the structural, verbal, and thematic parallels make it probable that this confrontation also takes place on the bank of the Nile. Likely, the Nile crocodile lies behind depictions of Pharaoh or Egypt as Rahab and Tannin.

A literary feature we have already noted adds further to the depiction of Yahweh's victory over Pharaoh and Egypt as his slaying of Rahab, the sea dragon of chaos. The narrative of Egypt is literarily bracketed by waters (Exodus 1–2, 14–15), which serves to portray the whole land of Egypt as a watery abode—one does not leave Egypt apart from an escape through water. In line with such an understanding, it cannot be incidental that Yahweh's first two signs are directed against the water properties of Egypt. In Exodus 7:19-20, Aaron is bidden to take the rod and stretch out his hand over "the waters of Egypt," defined as its streams, rivers, ponds, and pools of water, a sign that depicts Yahweh's "smiting the waters" (Exodus 7:17), using five different terms for Egypt's waters. Similarly, the second sign begins with Aaron taking the rod and stretching out his hand over Egypt's streams, rivers, and ponds, summarized as the "waters of Egypt" (Exodus 8:5-6), using four terms for Egypt's waters. Whereas the first sign turned those waters into blood, a sign of death, the second sign caused an innumerable horde of frogs, creatures commonly associated with the underworld, to come up out of the waters, invading the people of Egypt. Such signs not only portray Egypt as Sheol but demonstrate Yahweh's lordship over Egypt as his lordship over the waters.

Perhaps more subtly, Pharaoh is branded—identified and defined—by the raised-up serpent that donned his headdress as a crown. As an image of the goddess Wadjet, the rearing sacred cobra (or Uraeus) symbolized divine authority and supreme power in ancient Egypt. Crowning various Egyptian gods, the cobra was emblematic of Pharaoh's divine sovereignty. As his magnificent hosts, replete with horses and chariots, threaten down on Israel, Pharaoh's demise culminates within the depths of the sea in Exodus 14. How appropriate that Yahweh's final clash with Pharaoh involves both the splitting of the sea and the destruction of the hosts of Egypt as the former act of creation is undone on them. Yahweh, the divine warrior, does battle; fighting for his people, he slays the sea dragon!

These reflections on how Yahweh's victory over Pharaoh and Egypt may be understood as a divine conquest of the dragon help us to see other narratives in Exodus with new appreciation. First, when God called Moses to return to Egypt to deliver Israel, Moses had hesitated, asking, "What if the people will not believe me, and claim that Yahweh did not appear to me?" (Exodus 4:1). Yahweh responded by telling Moses to cast his staff onto the ground, which then became a serpent. Fearfully, Moses fled from its presence (literally "its face"). His fear of the serpent captures well his fear of returning to Egypt, from which he had fled. But Yahweh directs him to stretch out his hand and lay hold of the serpent by the tail; when he does so the serpent becomes a staff once more. This first of many signs, of dominating the serpent, Yahweh declares, is so that the people "may believe that Yahweh, the God of their fathers—the God of Abraham, the God of Isaac, and the God of Jacob—has appeared to you" (Exodus 4:5) and seems to summarize God's intention that he will deliver them from Egypt (the dragon).

Second, since in the ancient world locusts often serve as a metaphor for armies, it is possible that the bringing forth and vivid destruction of the locusts of the eighth sign foreshadows the destruction of the Egyptian hosts in the sea:

> So Moses stretched out his rod over the land of Egypt, and Yahweh drove an east wind on the land all that day and all night; when it was morning, the east wind had carried in the locusts. . . . Yahweh turned a very strong west wind and carried away the locusts and blew them into the sea of end [*yam-suf*]—not one locust remained in all the border of Egypt. (Exodus 10:13, 19)

The phrase "west wind" actually interprets the Hebrew "wind of sea," with *sea* representing a westward orientation in the Hebrew worldview. Although in Exodus 14 Yahweh will send a strong eastward wind all night to split the sea for his people to cross dry-shod (Exodus 14:21-22), yet those waters will return on the Egyptians so that "not one of them remained" (Exodus 14:28), and the song of the sea will describe Yahweh as casting Egypt's army into the "sea of end" (*yam-suf*, Exodus 15:4). Possibly, then, the manner by which Yahweh destroyed the locusts presages his victory over Egypt at the sea, his slaying of Rahab.

SLAYING THE DRAGON: THE LARGER NARRATIVE

Yahweh's battle against Egypt, as we have seen, is portrayed along the lines of his slaying the dragon. As opposing the people and purposes of God, Egypt however was just one historical embodiment of evil—not the evil one himself. Similarly, the book of Daniel portrays the kingdoms whose rulers would rise up against God's people as four great beasts who come up out of the sea (Daniel 7:3). As it does for the other nations, though, the Bible holds out hope for the people of Egypt, declaring that even "Rahab and Babylon" will be among those who know Yahweh and his salvation and who will be members of Zion (Psalm 87:4-6).

Ultimately, the Scriptures link the serpent with Satan, the fallen angel who along with his host of dark powers sways the nations against God and his people. Our struggle, writes the apostle Paul, is not against flesh and blood, "but against principalities and powers, against the cosmic rulers of this darkness, against spiritual hosts of evil in the heavenly places" (Ephesians 6:12). Such a sobering reality reminds us that dragon slaying is about much more than being fascinated with an adventurous *mythos*; the dragon represents true darkness, the horror of bitter tragedy and violent loss, the face of unbounded evil and hatred that threatens our lives daily. Whether as Tiamat or Yam, or the biblical Satan, the dragon is the monster who assaults life and order, beauty and goodness, light and gladness—a beast of chaos who opposes the cosmos of God. In Genesis 3 the serpent who deceives humanity is no mere snake but an embodiment of Satan. Not cursed to go on its belly until the end of the story (Genesis 3:14), the serpent (*nakhash*) should be understood as a dragon.[16] In several other places in the Bible *nakhash* is identified clearly as a dragon. Isaiah 27:1, for example, refers to "Leviathan the fleeing serpent [*nakhash*], Leviathan the twisting serpent [*nakhash*], and he will slay the dragon [*tannin*] in the sea." In Amos 9:3 Yahweh threatens that even if his rebellious Israelites hide from his judgment "at the bottom of the sea, from there I will command the serpent [*nakhash*] and he will bite them," clearly referring to the sea dragon of chaos. In the Exodus narrative, *nakhash* is used interchangeably with *tannin*, the dragon into which the staff of Moses and Aaron turns (compare Exodus 7:9, 10, 12 with Exodus 7:15; 4:3).

[16]This paragraph relies on Miller, *The Dragon, the Mountain, and the Nations*, 202-7.

Returning to the Eden narrative, Yahweh declares that he will put hostility between the seed of the serpent and the seed of the woman and that the woman's seed will crush the head of the serpent even as the serpent bruises his heel (Genesis 3:15), a prophecy that establishes a major facet of God's agenda for human history. Although the divinely established enmity applies to communities broadly, the final battle has a particular focus: between a singular seed of the woman—*he* will crush the serpent's head and *his* heel will be bruised—and the serpent itself. Within the community of his people, Yahweh's word of judgment to the serpent would bud into a hope that the Messiah would come and slay the dragon, conquering Satan definitively. Indeed, Yahweh God's victory at creation, relived, as it were, in his defeat of Pharaoh in the historical exodus, adumbrates the final conquest of the forces of darkness and death.

The ongoing story of the Bible never loses sight of this conflict, as when the opening of the Exodus narrative shows Pharaoh, an embodiment of the dragon, calling for the destruction of Israel's sons—that is, attacking the seed of the woman (Exodus 1:22). Later in Israel's history, we read of young David, already anointed to be the next king, battling the Philistine giant Goliath, whose helmet, leg armor, and javelin are of "bronze" (*nekhoshet*, the same root letters as the word for "serpent") and whose chain-mailed armor is described as having "scales" (*qasqeset*, 1 Samuel 17:5-6). While the Philistines, as enemies of God's people, stand as merely one historical expression of the dragon, this story forms a microcosm of *the* story, foreshadowing the battle of David's greater son, the Messiah, who would defeat the enemy, the power of evil behind all God-opposing forces—he will slay the dragon. The slaying of the sea dragon, as the creation theology of the exodus deliverance, serves as a paradigm for God's promised future redemption when he will defeat evil forever: "In that day, Yahweh with his sword—severe and great and strong—will punish Leviathan the fleeing serpent, Leviathan the twisting serpent, and he will slay the dragon [*tannin*] that is in the sea!" (Isaiah 27:1; see fig. 4.1 for the illustration of this verse by Gustave Doré, engraved by Hélidore-Joseph Pisan, *The Destruction of Leviathan*, c. 1865). Biblical writers, Paul Cho states, use the imagery of slaying the sea dragon to proclaim: "Today, sea dragons rage in defiance against the God of order and life; come tomorrow, God will slay the dragons and reign again, as he did in days long ago, over his creation from his stately house."[17] To be sure, God always rules sovereignly over evil, but his conquest of dragons manifests his reign and when evil is finally vanquished his kingdom will be established in its full blessedness.

Figure 4.1. Gustave Doré, *The Destruction of Leviathan*, c. 1865, engraved by Hélidore-Joseph Pisan

The Gospels narrate how Jesus first subdued (Matthew 8:23-27) and then trampled on the sea (Matthew 14:22-33), identifying him closely with Yahweh the dragon slayer (see also Mark 4:35-41; 6:45-52; Luke 8:22-25; John 6:15-21). And the book of Revelation describes Jesus the Messiah's battle with Satan in precisely these terms:

[17]Paul K.-K. Cho, *Myth, History, and Metaphor in the Hebrew Bible* (Cambridge, UK: Cambridge University Press, 2018), 10.

> And the great dragon was cast down, that ancient serpent, who is called the devil and Satan, the one deceiving the whole world—he was cast down to the earth, and his angels were cast down with him. (Revelation 12:9)

> And he grasped the dragon, that ancient serpent, who is the devil and Satan, and bound him for a thousand years. (Revelation 20:2)

In Revelation 12, we read about the dragon lying in wait, ready to devour a woman's child. This passage has been compared with the birth of Moses, Israel's first deliverer: "Leviathan lay in wait to destroy the man child of Israel when Moses was born, for Leviathan, the dragon or crocodile of the Nile, is according to Ezekiel (29:3) a type of Pharaoh and Egypt."[18] The woman of Revelation 12 likely refers to the church, while the child's birth and ascent to God's throne symbolize the Messiah's resurrection and ascension. The Messiah now reigns as King of kings over all powers and authorities and will subdue all enemies under his feet. He even sovereignly rules over the last enemy to be destroyed, namely death, which has already tasted its ultimate defeat through the resurrection—the new exodus—of Jesus Christ (1 Corinthians 15:20-28).

The story of the exodus, then, is the story of the Bible, the epic battle between Messiah—none other than Yahweh come in the flesh—and the dragon, Satan. Precisely how the dragon is slain for the redemption of God's people is wondrously unexpected—and is the next chapter's topic.

[18]Austin Farrer, *A Rebirth of Images: The Making of St. John's Apocalypse* (New York: SUNY Press, 1949), 143.

Chapter Five

THE BLOOD OF THE PASSOVER LAMB

AS OBSERVED IN CHAPTER THREE, the knowledge of Yahweh is the major theme and overarching purpose for Israel's exodus out of Egypt, revealing to the world the glory of Yahweh, his supremacy as Creator and his kingship over all gods. Turning now to the account of Passover (Exodus 11–13), we delve not only into the heart of the exodus story but also into the depths of God's self-revelation. To his people, Yahweh would reveal himself in a special way: Israel would know him as their Redeemer. Yahweh, the God of the exodus, is the One who redeems his people from slavery, who ransoms their lives from death. In this chapter we will see the exodus deliverance through the lens of Passover as the redemption of God's firstborn son from death.

PASSOVER AS THE HEART OF THE EXODUS

Passover has profound significance for understanding the theology of the historical exodus. Indeed, one cannot grasp the meaning of Israel's exodus out of Egypt without understanding the Passover ritual—the Passover *is* the exodus. Several aspects of the story bring out the crucial role of

Passover. First, while for the other signs God had made a distinction between Israel and the Egyptians (since the land of Goshen, where the Israelites resided, remained unaffected by, for example, the frogs or lice), for this tenth and final sign, the death of the firstborn son, Israel needed to be redeemed. Under the threat of death, the distinction between Egypt and God's people is made not through Israel's exemption but by the provision of a way of salvation for Israel (see Exodus 11:7). Apart from the Passover regulations, Israelites would have suffered death within their houses no less than the Egyptians.

Second, Israel's redemption from the tenth sign coincides with their redemption from Egypt itself. As the effectual event, the tenth sign would always be linked to the exodus out of Egypt. Understandably, if the Israelites had been released, say, after the fourth plague (flies) or the seventh plague (hail), then that particular sign would ever after stand as *the* sign of liberation. As it is, however, all the signs build up to the last threat of death and—for Israel—to the final wonder of deliverance from death.

Third, deliverance from the tenth sign is underscored by the elaborate Passover ritual prescribed. Not only so but through the institution of Passover, Yahweh ensures that every generation of Israel will remember the exodus out of Egypt through the lens of Passover. Again, later Israelite children will not celebrate the exodus by playing with frogs or by recounting the onslaught of hail on the land of Egypt; rather, through the ceremony they will participate in the mysterious night of Passover, partaking of the paschal meal and reliving that ominous night of redemption from death.

Fourth, the Passover redemption is so significant that God reorients time itself, making the month of Passover the first or chief month of Israel's liturgical calendar (Exodus 12:2; this month is called "Abib" in Israel's early history, then "Nisan" after the exile). Such a momentous paradigm shift served to define Israel's deliverance out of Egypt as inaugurating a new beginning, not merely in terms of a fresh start but as a new creation—a new life on the other side of their death to the old life. Indeed, every major festival of Israel was associated with the exodus, granting each generation an annual experience of Israel's redemption, intended to shape the nation's identity and vocation, and its knowledge of Yahweh, the God of the exodus.

Finally, the exodus account is framed by references to the tenth sign's death of the firstborn son, a literary feature that serves to summarize the whole epic story by the Passover event. Before Moses' first encounter with Pharaoh, Yahweh sends him with one summary message: "You will say to Pharaoh, 'Thus says Yahweh: Israel is my son, my firstborn. And I say to you, Let my son go, that he may serve me. But if you refuse to let him go—look!—I myself will slay your son, your firstborn'" (Exodus 4:22-23).

The exodus account, then, is enclosed by God's threat to Pharaoh's firstborn son in Exodus 4 and by the accomplishment of that threat in Exodus 11–13, so that the whole exodus story is summed up by the event of Passover. In fact, that frame may be broadened even further when we recall that God's threat to Pharaoh's firstborn amounts to just retribution for Egypt's treatment of Israelite sons in the opening chapters of the book, where a previous Pharaoh had commanded that every son born to the Hebrews must be cast into the river (Exodus 1:22). Understanding Israel's later deliverance through the waters, along with the destruction of the hosts of Egypt in the sea (Exodus 14–15), as poetic justice for Egypt's destruction of Israel's sons at the opening of the story, Exodus 1–2 and Exodus 14–15 provide a broader frame for the whole story that is also related to the Passover redemption of Israel's firstborn sons (see figure 5.1). It is perhaps not irrelevant here to note that those delivered through

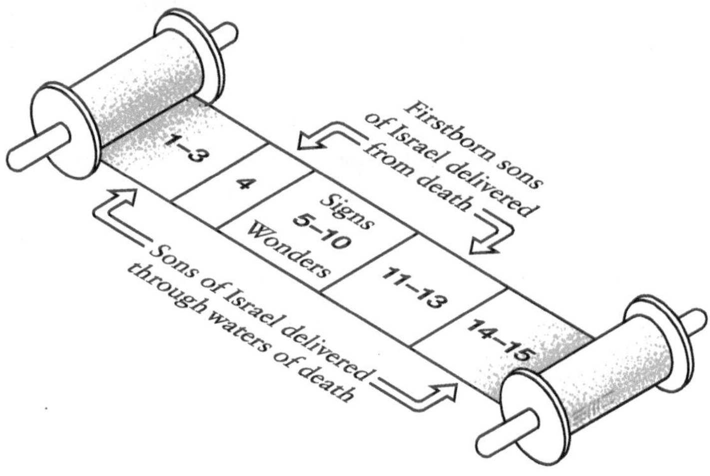

Figure 5.1. Exodus framework

the waters of the sea are "the sons of Israel" (*bene yisra'el*, Exodus 14:2, 3, 8, 10, 15, 16, 22, 29), a recurring phrase that is typically translated "the children of Israel" or "the people of Israel." Such interpretations are accurate enough since the phrase does include all the people; nevertheless, the more literal "sons of Israel" brings out more closely the relationship of the sons consigned to a watery judgment in Exodus 1–2 and the sons delivered through the sea in Exodus 14. In fact, most Old Testament passages "that refer specifically to Israel as God's son," writes Robin Routledge, "appear to be linked with the exodus."[1] The exodus story, then, is defined by Passover, and Passover signifies the redemption of Israel, God's firstborn son, from death.

A THEOLOGY OF THE PASSOVER RITUAL

Of the many important elements of the Passover ritual (see Exodus 12), we will focus on three main ones to unfold its theology: (1) the slaying of a lamb or young goat as a sacrifice, related to the idea of atonement; (2) the smearing of its blood on the doorposts of each Israelite house, understood as an act of purification; and (3) the eating of its sacrificial meat, which served to consecrate the Israelite household.[2] First, apart from the slaying of lambs the firstborn sons of Israel would have died no less than those of the Egyptian households. The Passover sacrifice therefore involved the idea of substitutionary atonement, with the animal's death being in place of the firstborn Israelite son. The lamb or young goat represented—signified—the firstborn son. While later celebrations of Passover were memorial in nature, clearly the original Passover sacrifice made atonement, sparing the firstborn son from the death threatened by Yahweh's judgment.

Second, the blood of the lamb was then applied to the lintel and doorposts of the house. Blood manipulation would become a regular practice in the rituals of the later tabernacle (and then the temple) for the sake of purification, with blood being applied to objects like the altar in order to cleanse them

---

[1]Robin Routledge, "The Exodus and Biblical Theology," chap. 10 in *Reverberations of the Exodus in Scripture*, ed. R. Michael Fox (Eugene, OR: Pickwick Publications, 2014), 190.

[2]My explanation of these three elements relies on T. Desmond Alexander, "The Passover Sacrifice," chap. 1 in *Sacrifice in the Bible*, ed. Roger T. Beckwith and Martin J. Selman (Grand Rapids, MI: Baker, 1995), 1-24, and correlates closely with L. Michael Morales, *Who Shall Ascend the Mountain of the Lord? A Theology of the Book of Leviticus* (Downers Grove, IL: IVP Academic, 2015), 80-82.

along with the worshiper (see, for example, Leviticus 4–5, 16). Consistent with this understanding of sacrificial ritual, the smearing or sprinkling of blood on doorframes for Passover would represent the purification of the household: the doorway stands for the house, and the house represents the household within. Use of the hyssop branch for striking the lintel and doorposts with blood strengthens the interpretation of Passover as a cleansing ritual for the household, since hyssop is also commonly associated with ceremonial purification in the Pentateuch (Exodus 12:22; cf. Leviticus 14:4, 6, 49, 51, 52; Numbers 19:6, 18). The need for cleansing is expressed well in the psalm associated with David's repentance: "Purge me with hyssop and I shall be clean; / Wash me and I shall be whiter than snow" (Psalm 51:7).

As a sign, not only for the Israelites but for Yahweh as well, who would see it and pass over the house, bringing no destruction on it (Exodus 12:13), the lamb's blood was the central feature of the Passover ceremony. Not without reason, many have understood the blood to have an apotropaic function, that is, the blood served to ward off harm. Such a function, however, should not be understood as a pagan notion of magic, used to ward off evil. Yahweh himself brings the judgment of destruction on this night, and the blood—by his own instruction—wards off death because the blood itself signifies that the death of the firstborn has already taken place through a substitute lamb. The household, then, is purified, cleansed, by the sacrificial blood of the firstborn son who represents that household—but the firstborn son has been replaced by a substitute lamb or young goat. Being purified by blood, Yahweh's destruction passes over the house—the household, represented by the firstborn son, has been redeemed by the blood of the lamb.

Finally, as shown by its detailed instructions (Exodus 12:8-11, 43-47), eating the lamb was also an essential part of the Passover ritual. The slaughtered lamb, for example, needed to be eaten within the house, and its bones were not to be broken. The lamb's meat was sacrificial and, as such, holy. That the meat was to be burned, roasted in fire, and not cooked by boiling in water accords with later sacrifices that would be burned on the fires of the altar of whole burnt offering. Moreover, the regulation for burning the portions that remain until morning also fits with later regulations for sacrifices, indicating that the meat was holy. Eating the sacrificial lamb's flesh, therefore, made those who ate it holy as well. The requirement that male participants in the feast be circumcised (Exodus 12:48), along with later provisions for those who were unclean to celebrate Passover on the following month (Numbers 9:1-14), underscore the sacredness of the meal. Since the household was consecrated, made holy, by partaking of the sacred flesh, the Passover feast may be understood as a feast of consecration. More deeply, as the entire household would partake of the lamb's flesh, each member thereby *identified with* the firstborn son, who was himself represented by the sacrificial lamb. As the firstborn was spared destruction, so was the rest of the household, which was identified with the firstborn son.

Ultimately, the entire Passover ceremony, along with the redemption it commemorates, had Israel's consecration unto Yahweh as its goal. Interestingly, all three of its elements make the Passover celebration remarkably similar to the consecration of Aaron's house for serving as priests in Exodus 29 and Leviticus 8. The consecration of Israel's priesthood also involved sacrificing, blood smearing, and the eating of holy meat. Through the Passover ritual, then, each Israelite household functioned in a priestly manner and Israel itself was being prepared to become "a kingdom of priests and a holy nation" (Exodus 19:6).[3]

UNLEAVENED BREAD AND BITTER HERBS

There is a fourth element of the feast of Passover, the unleavened bread with its bitter herbs, which relates to the *urgency* of the exodus. Within the biblical tradition as well as the Passover seder (or liturgy) in Judaism, the seven-day feast of Unleavened Bread is linked inseparably with Passover and given prominent emphasis. The original legislation for eating unleavened bread is explained as the result of Egypt's pressing demand to be rid of the Israelites so that God's people needed to take their dough before it was leavened, bearing their kneading bowls on their shoulders, which led to baking unleavened cakes with the dough brought out of Egypt (Exodus 12:8, 33-34, 39). Eating the Passover meal with fastened belt, sandaled feet, and staff in hand also underscored the haste with which Israel departed. The unleavened bread is

[3]T. Desmond Alexander, *From Eden to the New Jerusalem: An Introduction to Biblical Theology* (Grand Rapids, MI: Kregel, 2009), 128-29.

stressed further by the refrain that no leaven shall be eaten throughout the seven days of the feast (Exodus 13:3, 6-7) and especially by the severe punishment for those who do not participate: anyone who ate leaven throughout the feast was to be cut off from the congregation of Israel (Exodus 12:15, 19-20).

Such urgency is complemented by the addition of bitter herbs to the unleavened bread. To the seder question, "Why do we eat bitter herbs on this night?" the answer comes: "This is the bread of affliction which our forefathers ate in the land of Egypt."[4] The response betrays the liturgy's dependence on the book of Deuteronomy, where unleavened bread is called "the bread of affliction," linked to Israel's coming out of Egypt in haste (Deuteronomy 16:1-3). In Deuteronomy, Yahweh provides a recital for his people; when they are in the land and bring him of its firstfruits, they are to declare how he had delivered them from the Egyptians who "treated us harshly and afflicted us and laid on us hard labor," for Yahweh "heard our voice and saw our affliction, our trouble and our oppression," so "Yahweh brought us up out of Egypt with a mighty hand and an outstretched arm, with great fearful deeds, with signs and wonders" (Deuteronomy 26:5-8). The bitter herbs recalling the bitterness of life in Egypt complement the urgency of departure—why should Israel linger within such a bitter house of bondage?

The regular celebration of the feast of Unleavened Bread with its bitter herbs and the call to remove all traces of leaven from one's house, therefore, serves as a call for ongoing departure, for a continual forsaking of life in exile. This call to urgent departure stands in contrast to Lot's hesitancy in leaving Sodom, as we saw in our second chapter. Again, the exodus path back to abundant life with God is not accomplished with the momentary crossing of a boundary but requires a continual leaving. Rather than behaving as the Israelites who looked back on life in Egypt with desire (see, for example, Numbers 11:5-6), God's people are to recall the *bitterness* of life without God in this world, having had no hope (Ephesians 2:11-13). We are called daily to forsake the old life of futility, sin, and depravity, and to do so with urgency—the same urgency involved in our original deliverance out of darkness. Later in Israel's history, the prophet Isaiah would announce a second exodus where God's people would

---

[4]Cf. Anthony J. Saldarini, *Jesus and Passover* (New York: Paulist, 1984), 44-45.

not go out "in haste," by which he implies that there will be no pressing threat from an adversary as there was when Israel had departed out of Egypt, for Yahweh will both "go before you" and "be your rear guard" (Isaiah 52:12). Nevertheless, the Bible retains the urgent need to remove the "leaven," that is, to forsake the attitudes and behavior of our previous lives in exile. So the apostle Paul writes to the church: "Therefore purge out the old leaven that you may be a new lump (of dough), as you truly are unleavened—for indeed Christ, our Passover, has been sacrificed for us. Let us therefore celebrate the feast, not with old leaven—not with the leaven of malice and wickedness—but with the unleavened bread of sincerity and truth" (1 Corinthians 5:7-8).

Generations of Jewish people have celebrated the Passover as a way of deepening the exodus experience and identity within their souls, as the Haggadah (the traditional text recited at the Passover seder) declares that in each generation every person is obligated to see oneself as though he or she had personally come forth out of Egypt. The annual feast calls on memory as a means to shape the present time—that is, the historical exodus of one generation of Israelites is recalled for the sake of an existential exodus of Jewish people throughout the world and throughout every generation. The exodus is appropriated for an ongoing departure *today*, a continual, daily exodus whose urgency has neither waxed nor waned. In a profound sense, every person who trusts in Jesus the Messiah has indeed experienced the new exodus of his death and resurrection, having been united to him by the Spirit. Now we are called urgently to sanctification, partly defined by the Westminster Shorter Catechism as being "enabled more and more to die unto sin, and live unto righteousness."[5] Sanctification is a deepening of our own exodus, made possible by union with the Messiah, with his death to sin and with his resurrection life unto God.

THE BLOOD OF CIRCUMCISION, THE BLOOD OF PASSOVER

The Passover regulations given in Exodus 12:43-50 include the need for all males, whether Israelites or foreigners, to be circumcised in order to

[5] *Westminster Shorter Catechism* 35.

participate in the sacrificial meal—"no uncircumcised person shall eat it" (Exodus 12:48). As the sign of the covenant God made with Abraham (Genesis 17), circumcision was a sign and seal of one's membership in the congregation of Israel. Symbolizing the removal of defilement, circumcision functions somewhat similarly to the removal of leaven from one's house, except that it requires the shedding of blood. Positively, circumcision functions to seal a new identity, as Abram's circumcision came with his name change to Abraham. In the structure of the Abraham cycle of stories, we noted how the cutting ritual of Genesis 15, with its vision of Israel's exodus, was set in parallel with the covenant of circumcision in Genesis 17, bringing the two events into close relationship. The Passover regulations now accomplish something similar, inasmuch as circumcision is an integral part of the instruction for participation in the feast.

The link between circumcision and Passover is brought out in a popular Jewish notion of "two bloods." An eighth-century rabbinical interpretation of the Torah, for example, says that Israelites applied both the blood of circumcision and the blood of the Passover lamb on their door frames and lintels so when God looked on the two bloods he had compassion on Israel and passed over their houses.[6] To be sure, the application of circumcision blood is not in the exodus account, but one should nevertheless not miss the Passover themes integral to the covenant of circumcision. As with Isaac in Genesis 22, Israel's sons are put under the knife as part of their membership among the people of God. While spared from death, these sons have figuratively died to the world through circumcision, the removal of defilement, and are identified as those who belong among the congregation of Israel.

The association between circumcision and Passover surfaces in another episode of Exodus, the enigmatic account of God's attack on Moses (Exodus 4:24-26). In this "bloody bridegroom" passage, Moses is on the way to Egypt with his family when suddenly "Yahweh met him and sought to kill him." In response, Zipporah, Moses' Midianite wife, circumcises her son and "strikes" (*naga'*) his feet with the bloody skin she has removed so that "he let him go."

[6]See Gerald Friedlander, trans., *Pirke de Rabbi Eliezer* (New York: Bloch, 1916), 210-11; see also *Palestinian Targum* on Exodus 12:13 and *Exodus Rabbah* 19:5.

While several ambiguities make this text particularly difficult, the scenario appears to involve God's death threat to Moses, who is spared through the circumcision of his son, with the blood of circumcision applied to Moses' feet. In the Palestinian Targum, an Aramaic translation and expansion of the biblical text dated to the early centuries of the Christian era, Zipporah exclaims that the blood of circumcision saved her husband from the hand of the destroying angel, a clear allusion to Passover.[7] The pattern of a divine death threat avoided through the application of blood surely does bring us into the realm of Passover theology. The only other use of the verb for "to strike" within Exodus 1–15 happens to be found in the Passover instruction to "strike [*naga'*] the lintel and the two posts of the door with the blood" (Exodus 12:22). If we widen our view within the proper context, moreover, then Yahweh's seeking to kill Moses (or possibly his son) follows immediately after Yahweh's message to Moses for Pharaoh: "Thus says Yahweh, 'Israel is my son, my firstborn. I say to you, Send forth my son that he may serve me. But if you refuse to send him forth—look!—I myself will slay your son, your firstborn'" (Exodus 4:22-23).

As noted earlier, Yahweh's message to Pharaoh regarding Israel as his firstborn son summarizes the exodus deliverance in terms of redeeming God's firstborn son from death and serves as an ominous foreshadowing of the Passover destruction of Egypt's firstborn sons. Participating in the Passover redemption from such death would require Israel's sons to be circumcised. The foreshadowing of Passover, therefore, relates not only to Yahweh's message (Exodus 4:22-23) but should also include Moses' intense near-death experience with Yahweh (Exodus 4:24-26). Remarkably, then, Moses had experienced a Passover deliverance himself even before the plagues in Egypt had begun. As Israel's mediator, Moses was also Israel's forerunner in deliverance, a point we will develop further in the next chapter.

The close association between circumcision and the sacrifice of the Passover lamb finds its orienting focus on the cross of Jesus Christ, where the Lamb of God was "circumcised" in the "putting off the body of (sinful) flesh" for us (Colossians 2:11).

---

[7]See *Targum Pseudo-Jonathan* on Exodus 4:24-26.

THE PASSOVER REDEMPTION OF GOD'S SON FROM SHEOL

Through the Passover ceremony every Israelite household in the land of Egypt was reenacting the spectacle of the nation's redemption. In this way the nation's epic deliverance was itself reduced theologically to a singular household drama: the sparing of a firstborn son. That is, the Israelite firstborn son not only represented the sparing of his household, but he represented the redemption of Israel as God's firstborn son, for thus says Yahweh: "Israel is my son, my firstborn. Let my son go, that he may serve me" (Exodus 4:22-23). The question for us now is this: how does Israel's deliverance out of Egypt resemble the household redemption of the firstborn son from death? The answer is found in part through the Passover event itself. The tenth sign involved a divine judgment of death, so that Israel's deliverance out of Egypt was thereby defined as a ransoming from death, not merely a political release or a redemption from bondage.

Indeed, every Egyptian household had also experienced a national drama: "Pharaoh arose in the night, he and all his servants and all Egypt, and there was a great wailing in Egypt—for there was no house without one dead there" (Exodus 12:30). Each Egyptian house had become a house of the dead, a house of mourning, a microcosm of Egypt. As observed in chapter four, in the Bible the land of Egypt was itself thought of as a land of death, a symbol for the watery grave Sheol. Precisely here is where the theology of Passover is crucial, lest the portrayal of Israel's exodus out of Egypt as a resurrection out of the grave be reduced to a mere literary device. Israel's emergence out of Egypt really did require a ransoming from death, a deliverance from the tenth sign through the shedding of blood. From a different angle, one might ask: how is it possible to be rescued out of the watery pit of Sheol? To escape the land of death requires a death in one's place—redeemed by the blood of the lamb. Understanding Egypt as symbolic of Sheol and Israel as God's firstborn son, then, we can appreciate how the household drama of the Passover feast portrayed Israel's redemption from death.

The exodus was the redemption of God's firstborn son from death, a resurrection of Israel from Sheol. For Israel's salvation, the sea dragon was conquered by a slain lamb.

Chapter Six

MOSES THE SERVANT OF YAHWEH

IN JEWISH LORE, MOSES' NATIVITY is said to have filled his house with light.[1] Such a tradition likely derives from the language of his birth in Exodus. When Moses' mother conceived and bore a son, we are told that "she saw him that he was good" (Exodus 2:2), words that follow the creation account closely, when "God saw the light that it was good" (Genesis 1:4). Later on in his life, Moses' face would indeed radiate light, shining with the reflected glory of God (Exodus 34:29-35). Legends about his birth were one way the ancient rabbis sought to express the greatness of the historical figure of Moses, a standing that has even led some scholars to view the Pentateuch as something of a biography of Moses.

Truly, it would be difficult to underscore properly the significant role and unique status of Moses in the life of Israel. His role encompasses every conceivable office, that of deliverer and paradigm of the Messiah, lawgiver, prophet, priest, psalmist, sage, and king. Above all, no other man in the Old Testament era was nearer to Yahweh God, a relationship described as "face

---

[1]See *Sotah* 12a.

to face" (Exodus 33:11); to no one else did Yahweh God reveal himself as fully. Practically speaking, this means that for anyone else—whether Israelite or foreigner—to know God and his will and to be reconciled to God, such a person would have needed to come to God *through* Moses. "Through Moses" here means through the covenant relationship between God and Israel accomplished through Moses, including the covenant's two heavenly gifts: (1) the revelation of God, the Torah, and (2) the dwelling of God, along with its priesthood and sacrificial cult. Yahweh himself declared the utter uniqueness of "my servant Moses" who is "faithful in all my house" and "with whom I speak mouth to mouth"—who even "gazes upon the form of Yahweh" (Numbers 12:6-8).

The comprehensive role of Moses may be summed up by the designation *mediator*. In this chapter, we will look at three aspects of Moses as mediator: his being a forerunner of Israel's deliverance and encounter with God, his mediation of Yahweh's covenant with Israel, and his role as intercessor on behalf of Israel. The book of Exodus will close in a majestic manner, with the cloud of Yahweh's earthly presence descending from the summit of Mount Sinai to cover the newly constructed dwelling, filling it with the fiery glory of Yahweh. The narrative drama, especially after Israel's idolatry with the golden calf, revolves around Moses' crucial role in pleading with God to renew his original intent to establish his dwelling among Israel. So, while the infant Moses may not have filled his family's house with light when he was born, yet through his labors as Israel's mediator it may be said justly that he caused God's house, the dwelling, to be filled with the light of the glory of Yahweh.

MOSES AS FORERUNNER OF ISRAEL'S DELIVERANCE

Before Yahweh led Israel through the waters of death and rebirth by the hand of Moses their shepherd, he caused Moses to undergo such a water ordeal himself as an infant. Typically referred to as his birth narrative, Exodus 2:1-10 actually presents the *rebirth* of Israel's savior—the story begins with Moses' birth as the context for what follows, namely his deliverance through the waters of the Nile River and consequent naming. Pharaoh had just charged all his people to cast into the river every son born to the Israelites (Exodus 1:22). Not only does the river thereby come to symbolize death but the Levite mother goes through the motions of Pharaoh's edict, putting her son into these waters of death. Yet beforehand she had constructed a little ark for her son. The word for "ark" (*tevah*) appears only here and in the deluge story, where Noah constructs an ark, and seems to be an Egyptian loan word signifying a chest or coffin. Clearly, the ark encloses the babe completely for Pharaoh's daughter will need to open it in order see what is inside.

Among the treasures of the Cairo museum there is an elongated reed basket containing the body of a child from around 10,000 BC, perhaps reflecting funerary practice in Egypt, so that some have surmised the Levite mother may have put on a funeral ruse. Whether or not this is so, James Gray's understanding of the story's symbolism remains: "The Savior of Israel was laid in a coffin, and taken from a watery grave."[2] As with the flood story, however, the ark is a means of salvation from the waters of death. In Genesis 8:15-19, Noah and all his household, along with a remnant of every living creature—birds and animals and every creeping thing—emerge out of the ark's door to populate the newly cleansed earth, so that the ark functions more like a womb than a tomb. In the first half of the deluge narrative the waters represent death and destruction, prevailing over the earth so that all flesh dies (Genesis 7), only to give way to the idea of life and new creation in the second half (Genesis 8), beginning with God's sending of a wind (*ruakh*) over the waters so that dry land appears (Genesis 8:1). Similarly, the imagery in Moses' rebirth story transitions from death to life when the daughter of Pharaoh descends into the river to cleanse herself (Exodus 2:5). Her maidens, like attendant midwives, bring the ark to her and when she opens it, she sees the child. In this beautifully crafted account, the word for "child" (Exodus 2:6) is the exact center of the story, with seventy words on either side.

By use of "look!" (*hinne*) the same verse directs readers to see through the eyes of Pharaoh's daughter, giving prominent attention to what happens next: "the babe was crying." This is the first activity ascribed to the infant; previously, the baby was merely a passive object. On his rebirth, however, it is as if he is only now truly born: he cries, a wet-nurse is called for, he grows, and finally he is given a name by the young woman, the daughter of Pharaoh, who in

---

[2]James C. Gray, *The Biblical Museum* (London: E. Stock, 1876), 1:229.

drawing him out of the waters of the Nile had given him a kind of rebirth. On his deliverance through the waters, Moses is transferred out of the household of Hebrew slaves under Pharaoh's threat and enters the Pharaoh's Egyptian household as a royal son. Indeed, the narrative resolves with a stunning statement: "he became her son" (Exodus 2:10). Not only has Pharaoh's daughter claimed the son as her own, paying wages for a nursemaid, but the language of the infant's sister acknowledges the claim with a twofold use of "for you" (*lakh*): "Shall I go and call for you a nursemaid from among the Hebrews to nurse for you the child?" (Exodus 2:7). Pharaoh's daughter names him "Moses" (*mosheh*) saying, "Because out of the waters I drew [*mashah*] him." The form of Moses' name, however, is an active participle, signifying one who draws out, so that his salvation out of the waters becomes a prophetic sign of his future role in drawing Israel out of the waters of the sea.

The symbolic resurrection of Israel's savior through the waters serves as a prelude to Israel's deliverance through the sea (Exodus 14–15). In addition to their imagery of death and resurrection, the two accounts share a number of details. Moses' ark, for example, was set among the "reeds" (*sûp*) on the shore of the river (Exodus 2:3, 5), which serves as a link to the so-called Sea of Reeds (or "of end," *sûp*; Exodus 10:19; 13:18; 15:4, 22) through which Israel will be delivered (and "upon the bank" of the river is also paralleled when Israel sees the Egyptians dead "upon the bank" of the sea in Exodus 14:30). Moses' sister, moreover, is present at both the infant's deliverance through the river (Exodus 2:4, 7) and Israel's deliverance through the sea (Exodus 15:21). Her standing at a distance to know what would be done to the babe is echoed by Israel's being called to stand and see the salvation of Yahweh (Exodus 14:13).

In the Bible deliverance through water is but the first part of a wider movement: Israel is delivered through the waters of the sea then led to Mount Sinai, where the people enter into covenant relationship with God. For our purposes we may refer to this movement as an exodus pattern, although, since salvation is a new act of creation, it is really a creation pattern. In Genesis 1–3 the earth is delivered through the primal waters and Adam is brought to the Eden mount; in Genesis 6–9 Noah is delivered through the flood waters and brought to an Ararat mount; in Exodus Israel is delivered through the sea waters and brought to Sinai's mount; eventually Israel will be brought through the waters of the Jordan river for life with God in the land, centered on Mount Zion. Here we observe that Moses' deliverance through the waters of the Nile as Israel's forerunner also conforms to the broader exodus pattern.

The opening verse of Exodus 3 narrates how Moses "came to the mountain of God," where he would encounter Yahweh on holy ground. While some eighty years intervene between Moses' deliverance through the waters as an infant and his encounter with God at the mountain, literarily Moses is already in the wilderness within five verses after his rebirth (Exodus 2:15), making the pattern readily apparent. Moses' deliverance augured Israel's deliverance, a point made again by use of similar language. Moses had been delivered through the waters (Exodus 2:1-10) and brought into the wilderness where he met the fearful (*yare'*, Exodus 3:6), burning presence (*ba'esh*, Exodus 3:2) of Yahweh on the "mountain of God" (*har ha'elohim*, Exodus 3:1). Israel, after being delivered through the waters (Exodus 14), was confronted by the fearful (*yare'*, Exodus 20:20) burning presence (*ba'esh*, Exodus 19:18) of Yahweh at the mountain of God (*har ha'elohim*, Exodus 24:13). Indeed, God had earlier told Moses: "When you have brought the people out of Egypt, you [plural] will worship God upon this mountain" (Exodus 3:12), leading us to anticipate a repetition of the exodus pattern. The parallels could be developed further still: Moses spent forty years in the wilderness before returning to Egypt as Israel's savior (Exodus 7:7; Acts 7:23), and Israel, because of unbelief and rebellion, would be judged to wander the wilderness for forty years (Numbers 14:33). Also, during Moses' original entrance into the wilderness, seven daughters of a Midian priest had come to draw water from a well for their father's flock but were driven off by shepherds. Moses stood and "saved" (from *yasha'*) the daughters from the desert rogues and then watered their flock (Exodus 2:15-17), foreshadowing his later supply of water for Israel in the wilderness (Exodus 15:22-27; 17; Numbers 20:1-13).

What do we make of these parallels? Part of the point is that the mediator for God's people must first experience the journey himself for their sakes, to lead them along the same path. In a similar though infinitely more wondrous manner, the Lord Jesus went through the exodus pattern, being delivered from death and the grave and brought to the Father's heavenly presence for the sake of his people—so as to become our pioneer in salvation. This is the great message of the book of Hebrews, that the Son of God took on himself our humanity through the incarnation, becoming a little lower than the angels so that, through his atoning suffering and death and by his resurrection and ascension to God's right hand, he may now lead his flock as their shepherd and forerunner into the same resurrection glory, even to the city God has prepared for his people. Through his own journey, he has opened the way to God, and is now, by that same experience in our humanity, fully able to sympathize with our weaknesses and bitter sufferings along the way (Hebrews 2:10; 4:15; 6:20).

Returning to the dynamic between Moses and Israel, Moses' experience is given for the sake of Israel so that he might mediate the same knowledge of God to Israel. His own engagement with God, then, is often a foreshadowing of Israel's later experience. A case in point is the curious vignette recounted in Exodus 33:7-11. Israel had just committed apostasy with the golden calf. Although Yahweh had declared his purpose to dwell among his people and had already revealed the pattern for his dwelling to be set in their midst (Exodus 25–31), yet because of their exceeding sinfulness he would not be present among them. Moses, therefore, takes "the tent" and pitches it "far off from the camp" in order to continue his own "face to face" relationship with Yahweh as Israel's mediator. Intriguingly, Moses' tent is called a "tent of meeting" (Exodus 33:7), a designation that has led to much scholarly consternation, since the tent of meeting has not yet been built. Critical studies typically resolve the tension by suggesting that a variant tradition of *the* tent of meeting has been inserted in the text by an inelegant editor, out of synch with the narrative's chronology. In Jewish tradition, as with any reading of the Torah in its final form, the tent has been understood as Moses' own, which was referred to as "the tent" when last mentioned in Exodus 18:7.[3] When, therefore, one grasps the theology of Moses as mediator, particularly in his function as Israel's forerunner, then one can see this account as a ray of hope amidst a dark situation. And, indeed, Numbers 1–6 will recount the resolution to the dire state of Israel in Exodus 32–33: God will establish his own dwelling in the midst of

[3]See, for example, Umberto Cassuto, *A Commentary on the Book of Exodus*, trans. Israel Abrahams (Jerusalem: Magnes Press, 1967), 430-31; *Exodus Rabbah* XLV.2; Abraham ibn Ezra on this passage.

Israel, literally in the heart and center of the twelve tribes, and it will function as the tent of meeting between Yahweh and Israel. When God's dwelling becomes a tent of meeting *within* the camp, then the situation of Exodus 32–33 has been reversed, and we can see that Moses' personal experience in Exodus 33:7-11 was but a foretaste of Israel's later blessing. More than a foreshadowing, however, Moses' experience was the effectual basis for the later experience of Israel: he had used his own "tent of meeting" and face to face relationship with Yahweh *in order to secure* Yahweh's dwelling among his people.

MOSES AS INTERMEDIARY IN YAHWEH'S COVENANT WITH ISRAEL

While Moses' role as intermediary between Yahweh and Israel is emphatic throughout most of the Pentateuch, nevertheless that role is especially in focus as Moses mediates the covenant between Yahweh and Israel in Exodus 19–24. The distance between the two parties is displayed by use of the mountain of God, Sinai: Yahweh God is at the summit while Israel is encamped at the base of the mountain. Moses' role as mediator of the covenant is thereby portrayed by his continual ascent and descent of Mount Sinai, enabling the dialogue between Yahweh and Israel. Chapters 19 and 24 of Exodus stand in parallel, emphasizing different aspects of Moses' mediation. Exodus 19 stresses Yahweh's descent on the mountain and Moses' own descents from the summit to the people, employing the verb *descend* (*yarad*) seven times, and Exodus 24 stresses Moses' ascent of Mount Sinai, using the verb *ascend* (*'alah*) seven times. Whenever Moses *descends* from the summit to the base of the mountain, he is descending from God to Israel, bringing God's words to the people. Moses' descents, therefore, are a part of his mediatorial role in *representing God* to Israel. Whenever Moses *ascends* Mount Sinai, he does so to convey Israel's response, *representing Israel* to God.

The narrative displays the necessity of Moses' role by repeated emphasis on his singular authority to approach God by ascending the mountain. By Yahweh's intense and fiery presence on its summit, Mount Sinai had become holy—boundaries were thus set about the base and the people were warned not to approach. Yet while the people are consistently warned to keep back, Moses regularly ascends:

> Israel encamped before the mountain, but Moses ascended to God. (Exodus 19:2-3)

> Yahweh descended upon Mount Sinai, to the summit of the mountain, and Yahweh called Moses to the summit of the mountain, and Moses ascended. . . . The people are not able to ascend Mount Sinai. (Exodus 19:20, 23)

> The people stood at a distance, but Moses drew near into the thick darkness, there where God was. (Exodus 20:21)

> Now Moses alone will draw near to Yahweh, but they will not draw near, and the people will not ascend with him. (Exodus 24:2)

Moses' sevenfold ascent ever higher into the summit of Sinai is described in an especially awe-inspiring way:

> And Moses ascended the mountain, and the Cloud covered the mountain. The glory of Yahweh dwelt upon Mount Sinai and the Cloud covered it six days, and he called to Moses on the seventh day from the midst of the Cloud. (Now the appearance of the glory of Yahweh was like a consuming fire upon the summit of the mountain in the eyes of the sons of Israel.) And Moses entered into the midst of the Cloud and he ascended the mountain. And Moses was on the mountain forty days and forty nights. (Exodus 24:15-18)

Yahweh's descent on Sinai's summit was volcanic—a fiery, roaring fury that caused a great column of smoke to ascend to heaven. When he thundered forth the Decalogue from the mountain audibly, the people were utterly shaken by his voice and pleaded for God to speak to them only indirectly through Moses, confirming their embrace of his role of mediation (Exodus 20:1-21). Moses must ascend because the people cannot, else they be consumed by God's holy fire. No less certain, Moses must descend because God cannot, again else the people be consumed by his fiery glory. Nothing better exhibits Moses' role as Israel's mediator than his continual ascent and descent of Mount Sinai.

The next subsection, on Moses' intercession, will consider more deeply Moses' representation of Israel to God. But here it is worthwhile to reflect more on his role of representing God to Israel. Just as God had first revealed himself to Moses through the burning bush for Israel's sake (Exodus 3), so did he reveal himself throughout Moses' supernaturally upheld stay of forty days and nights on Sinai's summit and indeed on every occasion of engagement with his faithful servant. As the only one able to abide in such intimate fellowship with God, Moses himself became the revealer of God to his people. In one engagement with Yahweh on Sinai's summit, Moses—out of the wellspring of his own ardent desire—beseeched God to unveil more of himself: "Please, show me your glory!" (Exodus 33:18). Whereas at the burning bush, God had revealed his name, here atop Sinai's mountain, he proclaims his name, making all of his goodness pass by Moses: "I will be gracious on whomever I will be gracious, and I will be merciful to whomever I will be merciful" (Exodus 33:19). This revelation of God's sovereign dispensing of grace and mercy, or favor and compassion, stands as one of the Old Testament's deepest insights into the character of God—and this was revealed first to Moses and then to Israel through Moses.

The Torah—the divinely breathed oracles of God—was mediated to Israel through Moses and was frequently called the "Torah of Moses" (see, for example, Joshua 8:31). This means that if someone lived during the era of ancient Israel and wanted to know God, such a person would learn of God most from Moses, that is through the divine *torah*-instructions revealed through Moses. To be sure, God's glory, eternal power, and Godhead are manifested through creation (Psalm 19:1; Romans 1:20), but Moses reveals more of God than does all of creation. No one in the Old Testament era knew God as deeply and thoroughly—as intimately—as did Moses. The one occasion when Moses did not accurately represent God to Israel, when he blasted the second generation of Israelites in the wilderness, calling them "rebels," and defied God's command by striking the rock, he was punished soundly, forbidden to enter the long-awaited land of Canaan (Numbers 20).

Nevertheless, Moses' role as mediator of the old covenant points us to the glorious mediator of the new covenant, the Lord Jesus Christ. Through the wondrous incarnation, the second person of the Godhead took on himself our humanity, becoming the "God-man." As divine, equal to the Father, Jesus is able to represent God to his people more sincerely than Moses—Jesus *descended* from heaven to represent and reveal God to the world. And as the only sinless and righteous human being, as the perfect man, he is able to represent his people effectually before God—Jesus *ascended* from earth to represent his people to God. More than this, while Moses is said to have had a face-to-face friendship with God, such language is clearly figurative. Indeed, elsewhere—within the very context of God's highest self-revelation to Moses—Yahweh himself tells him, "You are not able to see my face, for no man can see me and live" (Exodus 33:20). Yet, as the eternal Son who became the God-man, Jesus comes from the very bosom of the Father and thus offers the world the fullest revelation of God (John 1:18; 14:7-11). Jesus is now the only mediator between God and human beings, thankfully, for no one could ever reveal the Father more than the Son, and no one could represent humanity more surely than he, our *perfect* mediator.

MOSES AS INTERCESSOR FOR ISRAEL

As Israel's mediator, Moses gave himself to a life of intercessory prayer, using his unique status before God to strive with him for Israel's sake, claiming his promises on behalf of God's people, often a thankless rabble. Perhaps the main lesson derived from Moses' interceding with God is that by doing so he enabled Israel to maintain its relationship with God. More pointedly, apart from Moses' prayers Israel would surely have been destroyed ever before entering the land of Canaan.

In Exodus 32, at the foot of Mount Sinai, and even as Moses was receiving from God the pattern for God's dwelling and the two tablets of the testimony, the people of Israel fell into heinous rebellion and apostasy: they commit idolatry, constructing and worshiping a golden calf. Israel sacrifices to the idol, crying out: "This is your god, O Israel, that brought you out of the land of Egypt!"—ascribing to the manufactured calf the exodus which, as we have seen, was the defining designation of God's name, Yahweh. Righteously acknowledging that the obstinate people have quickly turned aside from his way, Yahweh determines to consume them in his wrath—that is, to destroy them completely—and then to continue his plans for history by creating a new nation out of Moses (Exodus 32:7-10). The deeply grievous nature of Israel's sin is brought out further by the literary structure of this section. The golden calf incident is framed by the instructions for God's dwelling (Exodus 25–31) and the construction of God's dwelling (Exodus 35–40)—in other words, in the middle of God's fulfilling his intention to give himself to Israel, to live with and among them. Moreover, within this "God's dwelling" frame, there is a smaller inner frame related to the Sabbath day (Exodus 31:12-18; 35:1-3), highlighting the ultimate purpose for God's dwelling, namely so Israel could enjoy Sabbath-day fellowship and communion with God.

Within the context of the newly established covenant relationship, Israel's idolatry is tantamount to a bride's committing harlotry on her wedding night. In committing apostasy, turning away from Yahweh, Israel had broken the covenant, a reality reflected in Moses' breaking of the tablets of stone at the foot of the mountain (Exodus 32:19). Yahweh would have proven himself both just and good to carry out his declared intention to destroy his people. Yet while Israel deserved severe judgment, Yahweh's words actually served to solicit from Moses the intercession God himself desired of him.

Moses tells the people, "You have sinned a great sin! Now then I will ascend to Yahweh—perhaps I can make atonement for your sin" (Exodus 32:30). Thus he ascends the mountain of God in order, as we saw above, to represent Israel to God—to plea for mercy on behalf of Israel. Moses lays his own life before Yahweh, pleading, "Forgive their sin—but if not, then, I pray, blot me out of your book which you have written" (Exodus 32:32). This is true intercessory prayer, to lay one's life and self on the altar on behalf of others in a heavenward pleading that rises to God as sweet incense.

In Exodus 33 Moses continues to beseech God not only to forgive the people but to go forward with his original intent to live among his people through the dwelling. Finally, God relents (Exodus 33:12-17), which means the tabernacle can now be constructed and filled with the glory of God (Exodus 35–40). While Israel's sin is indeed framed by the sections on God's dwelling and the Sabbath day, the literary structure does not actually center on the golden-calf apostasy of Israel but rather on Moses' response of intercessory prayer (Exodus 32–34)—herein lies the crux of the drama. Part of the message is not only that without Moses' prayer Israel would have been destroyed but that without his intercessory role there would never have been a tabernacle dwelling for God—no sacrifices, no priesthood, no book of Leviticus. Through Moses' profoundly empathetic, godly striving with Yahweh—again as solicited by God himself—Israel will come to know the blessedness of Yahweh dwelling in their midst (Numbers 6:22-27).

Examples of Moses' intercession on behalf of Israel could be multiplied, especially from the book of Numbers where he regularly lessened God's wrath against his sinful, wayward people (see Numbers 11;1-3, 10-23; 12:13; 14:11-25). Although Israel would never have emerged out of the wilderness apart from Moses' intercessory prayers, this aspect of Moses' role as mediator is often neglected, especially in relation to Jesus' role as mediator of the new covenant. In the New Testament, however, Jesus Christ's role of intercession on behalf of his people is set forth as crucially important. The author of Hebrews teaches that Jesus is able to save his people to the uttermost *because* the Son "always lives to make intercession for them" (Hebrews 7:25). Similarly, the apostle Paul triumphs in the church's eternal security, saying, "Who is he who condemns? Christ Jesus is the one who died—more than this, who was raised from the dead, who is at the right hand of God, who also is interceding for us!" (Romans 8:34), rounding his argument climactically with Jesus' exalted ministry of intercession. It is now for us as the people of God to grow in our appreciation for how direly we must depend and wait upon—and rest in—the ongoing work of our all-sufficient Savior, Jesus Christ.

A NEW MOSES

In the plains of Moab before he died Moses gave Israel final exhortations and urgent pleas to remain faithful to Yahweh once in the land of Canaan. He also foretold that God would raise up for his people a new Moses: "Yahweh your God will raise up for you a prophet like me from your midst, from your brothers—to him you will listen," for Yahweh had said, "I will raise up for them a prophet like you from among their brothers" (Deuteronomy 18:15, 18). Some understand here merely the notion that God would faithfully supply his people with a line of prophets, as he certainly did throughout the history of Israel. Moreover, Deuteronomy 18:20-22 goes on to instruct Israel on how to discern true God-sent prophets from false ones. Nevertheless, there is good reason why historically Israel has understood these words to speak of a coming one who would be more than another prophet.[4] First, there is the language of this one's being like Moses ("like me," "like you"). In the last chapter of Deuteronomy, we read:

[4]On this topic, see Howard M. Teeple, *The Mosaic Eschatological Prophet* (Philadelphia: Society of Biblical Literature, 1957).

> Since then [the death of Moses] there has not arisen a prophet in Israel like Moses, whom Yahweh knew face to face, according to all the signs and wonders that Yahweh had sent him to work in the land of Egypt for Pharaoh and for all his servants and for all his land. And according to all that mighty hand and all that great dread which Moses worked in the eyes of all Israel. (Deuteronomy 34:5, 10-12)

With this epilogue, declaring that no prophet had yet arisen who may be classified as "like Moses," Deuteronomy closes by calling attention back to this one promise of God in chapter 18, underscoring its significance and turning readers' expectation to this provision especially. Here the book's closing words define for us what "like Moses" means: not simply another God-sent prophet but one who knows Yahweh face to face. The point is crucial for no other prophet in the entire era of Israel's history in the Old Testament ever surpassed Moses. Rather, every other prophet merely applied Moses' Torah to the people—they all remain, as it were, under his authority and may each be dubbed a little Moses.

The distinction between Moses, who is the fountainhead of all prophecy, and other prophets is made clear in two passages in the book of Numbers. When God supplies Israel with seventy Spirit-endowed leaders in the wilderness, he specifically distributes to them from the Spirit that has rested on Moses, demonstrating that their authority derived from and remains subsumed under Moses (Numbers 11:16-17, 25). Rather than supplying them with the Spirit directly from himself, Yahweh grants the Spirit through the conduit of Moses. Indeed, he does not even speak directly to these men, who prophesy briefly, but allows them instead to listen as Yahweh speaks to his servant Moses—they prophesy only out of Yahweh's relationship with Moses (Numbers 11:17, 25). Then in the next chapter Yahweh declares:

> Hear now my words: If there is a prophet of Yahweh among you, I make myself known in a vision to him, in a dream I speak with him. But not so with my servant Moses—he is faithful in all my house. Mouth to mouth I speak with him, neither in vision nor in riddles; the form of Yahweh he beholds—so why did you not fear to speak against my servant Moses? (Numbers 12:6-8)

Once more Yahweh makes a distinction between other prophets of Yahweh and "my servant Moses": none are like Moses because Yahweh speaks to other prophets by dreams and visions, rather than face to face as he does with Moses. Again, no one else knew Yahweh as plainly as Moses. As an aside, the Hebrew Bible is formed according to this hierarchy of revelation: Moses' Torah ("face to face" revelation) is the foundation, followed by the Prophets ("dreams and visions" revelation), which build on and apply Torah, and then the Writings (intangible "inspired" revelation). While the Spirit's inspiration and inscripturation means, of course, that all Scripture is equally God's perfect word, yet the hierarchy of revelation nevertheless establishes a logical ordering and priority.

As a second line of reasoning for why the prophet "like Moses" was understood to anticipate more than a line of prophets, the text itself defines "like Moses" quite narrowly in Deuteronomy 18:16-17 by turning to the great day of assembly before Yahweh's fiery theophany at Mount Sinai when the whole mountain fumed and quaked with his thunderous advent. The fear-struck people themselves had pleaded to be delivered from facing God's fire and from hearing his voice, embracing Moses as their mediator. References to a prophet "like me" in Deuteronomy 18:15, 18 frame this description of Moses as mediator in Deuteronomy 18:16-17. Moses defines "like me" in Deuteronomy 18:15 with "like what you all desired of Yahweh God at Horeb in the day of the assembly," using the same Hebrew particle for "like" (*ke*). Within the context of Mount Sinai, such a mediator refers to more than the function of typical prophets, priests, judges, and kings, but lies within the paradigm of the exodus redemption and the establishing of the covenant. Similarly, the closing verses of Deuteronomy define "like Moses" beyond his face-to-face relationship with Yahweh, declaring that no other prophet since has worked the signs and wonders of the exodus deliverance (Deuteronomy 34:11-12). In other words, prophets have indeed come and gone, but there has been no new Moses for there has been no new exodus.

> So Moses the servant of Yahweh died there in the land of Moab, according to the word of Yahweh...but no one knows his gravesite to this day. (Deuteronomy 34:5-6)

Chapter Seven

THE CULTIC EXODUS

GOD HAD CREATED THE COSMOS as the house in which he would dwell with humanity.[1] When this earth had been defiled by sin and polluted with death, he kept his near presence to heaven, with few exceptions. The purpose for creation, however, became the agenda for salvation: God would yet dwell with his people in fellowship. At Mount Sinai, therefore, Yahweh brought Israel into a gracious covenant relationship with himself through the mediation of Moses. One of the gifts of the Sinai covenant, along with the Decalogue, was the tabernacle, the dwelling of God, through which Yahweh gave himself, his abiding presence, to Israel (Exodus 25–40).

For our purposes it is crucial to realize that the dwelling of God was deeply connected with Israel's sacrificial cult and with the priesthood of Aaron's house. The book of Exodus ends with a crisis that illustrates the point: the glorious presence of Yahweh had filled the dwelling, but even Moses could not approach it—the dwelling could not function as a tent of meeting between God and Israel (Exodus 40:35). The resolution is narrated in the book of Leviticus: through divinely revealed sacrifices (Leviticus 1–7) and a divinely chosen and ordained priesthood (Leviticus 8), Israel may now approach

[1]See also L. Michael Morales, *Who Shall Ascend the Mountain of the Lord? A Theology of the Book of Leviticus* (Downers Grove, IL: IVP Academic, 2015), esp. 109-43 for sources.

Yahweh's presence in the dwelling and gain life-yielding blessing (Leviticus 9:22-24). In other words, the priesthood and sacrifices form the necessary mediation between God's dwelling and his people, serving to maintain Israel's relationship with Yahweh. The goal of the sacrificial system of Israel was restoration to God, the liturgy forming a journey into the heavenly presence of Yahweh God. As we will see, approaching Yahweh's dwelling through the pathway of sacrifice followed the pattern of the historical exodus out of Egypt when Israel was first restored to God at Mount Sinai.

ISRAEL'S LITURGY: A THREEFOLD MOVEMENT TO GOD'S ABODE

The tabernacle was the earthly dwelling of Yahweh, and its sacrificial system and priesthood formed the divinely ordained way for approaching his dwelling. Put differently, the sacrificial system and priesthood enabled the dwelling to function as a tent of meeting between Yahweh and his people. Israel's liturgy, then, may be described as "the way to God," as humanity's restoration to God, a sacred journey that entailed cleansing, consecration, and transformation. As the pathway to the face of God, in whose presence there is fullness of joy, the liturgy was the path of life—its end was fellowship and communion with Yahweh God.

By turning to narrative descriptions of Israel's worship, such as the inaugural ceremony of the tent of meeting found in Leviticus 9, we can observe the basic order of sacrifices and then, through this order, discern the liturgy's theology. The procedural order of sacrifices, the liturgical way to God, moved from (1) the purification offering to (2) the whole burnt offering, with its accompanying tribute offering of grain and wine, and then ended with (3) the peace offering. Although most sacrifices shared a variety of elements, nevertheless each of these three kinds of sacrifice possessed its own ritual focus from which we can derive its main significance.

The purification offering, sometimes called "sin offering," emphasized the manipulation of blood for cleansing from sin and guilt and is found, along with the closely related guilt offering, in Leviticus 4-5.[2] In the sacrificial

---

[2]The ensuing discussion on the purification and whole burnt offerings is similar to material that first appeared in L. Michael Morales, "Expiation and Propitiation" in *Tabletalk*, April 2019. https://tabletalkmagazine.com/article/2019/04/expiation-and-propitiation/. Used by permission.

system of Israel, blood was collected from an animal's severed arteries and then manipulated in a variety of ways: smeared, sprinkled, tossed, and poured out. In Leviticus, Yahweh had declared that since "the life of the flesh is in the blood," he had given Israel blood on the altar "to make atonement for your lives, for it is the blood that makes atonement by the life" (Leviticus 17:11). *Life* and *lives* here translate the same Hebrew word, *nefesh*, underscoring the idea of substitution: the shed blood of a blameless, animal substitute represented life for life.

Through the purification offering's shedding and manipulation of blood, God had taught Israel of humanity's need for *expiation*, for cleansing from sin and the removal of sin's defilement and guilt. Such purification from sin was a necessary accomplishment for making divine forgiveness possible (see Leviticus 4:20, 26, 31, 35). While displaying blood before God demonstrated that a life, albeit that of an unblemished animal substitute, had endured death, the wages of sin (Romans 6:23), atonement by blood involved purification or cleansing no less than the idea of ransoming from death. As symbolizing the life of flesh, and by the principle that life conquers death, blood was used ritually to wipe away, as it were, the defilement of sin and death. The Day of Atonement, comprised essentially of an elaborate purification offering, purified both God's house, the tent of meeting, and God's people so that God might continue to dwell with Israel. On this annual autumn day, the high priest entered with clouds of incense beyond the veil, bringing the blood of the purification offering into the holy of holies, sprinkling it before the atonement lid of the ark, Yahweh's earthly throne or footstool (Leviticus 16:12-14). Blood was also applied within the holy place and on the altar, and then a second goat, ritually loaded down with Israel's sins and guilt, was driven eastward away from the face of God (Leviticus 16:20-22)—a demonstration of expiation, that God had removed his people's transgressions as "far as the east is from the west" (Psalm 103:12).

From the purification of sin and death's defilement, the liturgy then moved on to the whole burnt offering. Israel's worship was both centered and founded on the whole burnt offering, so much so that the great outer altar, the focus of the liturgy, was dubbed "the altar of the whole burnt offering" (Exodus 30:28). The first episode in Scripture where the whole burnt offering appears is the flood story in Genesis 6–9. Early on we are told that Yahweh God, who is the main character in the narrative, was grieved "to his heart" over humanity's corruption (Genesis 6:6) and that he had determined to destroy the wicked while saving Noah and his household. The aggrieved heart of God, then, is the story's crisis. Even after the waters of divine judgment had abated, however, the situation had not changed. God had not been appeased, his just wrath had not been assuaged—not, that is, until Noah, at the dawn of a new creation, built an altar and offered up whole burnt offerings. Using instructive language that attributes human traits to God, the narrative describes Yahweh as smelling "the soothing aroma" of the whole burnt offerings so that his heart was comforted (Genesis 8:21). As a result of the soothing aroma, God spoke to his heart, avowing never to destroy humanity in such manner again, and then he established a covenant with Noah and all creation. The story of Noah's priestly act would have served to teach Israel the role of the whole burnt offering, as given by God himself, for procuring divine favor. Like fragrant incense, the smoke of the whole burnt offering ascends into heaven, the abode of God, and he, smelling its soothing aroma, is appeased—propitiated.

Such a divinely ordained impact on God leads one to wonder over the theological significance of the whole burnt offering. The one feature unique to this offering is that the whole animal, apart from its skin, was offered up to God on the altar—nothing was held back. The whole burnt offering thus signified a life of utter consecration unto God, a life of self-denying obedience to his will as expressed in the Torah. In the words of Deuteronomy, this offering represented and solicited the loving of Yahweh God with all one's heart, soul, and strength (Deuteronomy 6:5). Such a life alone, offered up to God through the flames of his altar, would ascend as a pleasing aroma to God's heavenly abode.

It is this theology of consecration that must inform our understanding of Yahweh's command to Abraham: "Take your son, your only son, whom you love, Isaac, . . . and offer him up as a whole burnt offering there on one of the mountains of which I will tell you" (Genesis 22:2). The seed of Abraham who would bring blessing to the nations must be consecrated to Yahweh and for the vocation of being Yahweh's servant—such a life would lead the true exodus back to paradise. The column of smoke, billowing up from the flames and rising to the heavens as incense, formed the biblical picture of restoration to God. Here it is important to understand the ascending smoke truly as incense, as a transformation of the sacrificed animal. Even the word for "burning" (*hiqtir*) on the altar was a technical term for cultic burning, and the same Hebrew root is used for "incense" (*qetoret*). The altar fire, in other words, did not destroy the sacrificed animal; rather, the fires transformed the blameless, vicarious substitute, causing it to ascend into Yahweh's presence in heaven. The refining fire of the Holy Spirit forms a fitting analogy, and the author of Hebrews may have this in mind when saying that Jesus offered himself up to God "through the eternal Spirit" (Hebrews 9:14). So, beyond consecration, the whole burnt offering symbolized the transformation necessary for the journey back to God. Indeed, the Hebrew designation for the whole burnt offering translates more literally as "ascension offering" (*'olah*), derived from its ritual focus: as transformed by the altar flames, the entire animal turned into fragrant smoke so that the sacrifice would ascend into Yahweh's heavenly abode as a soothing aroma.

The ascending smoke of the whole burnt offering set before the Israelite worshiper a visible representation of humanity's return to God. The transformational burning transferred the animal as a vicarious substitute from the earthly plane to the heavenly realm, Yahweh's domain. The offering, then, as Frederick Hicks wrote, "is not destroyed but transformed, sublimated, etherealized, so that it can ascend in smoke to the heaven above, the dwelling-place of God."[3] More deeply, the instructions for the whole burnt offering begin with a hand-leaning rite whereby the worshiper pressed his hand down on the animal's head, a symbolic act that declared, "This animal stands for me" (Leviticus 1:4). Recalling that the animal was required to be "unblemished" (*tamim*), which means "blameless" as applied to humans, the theology is clarified: the unworthy Israelite approached Yahweh's house *through* a vicarious, blameless substitute. In the whole burnt offering, the animal, "transformed into the vapor of smoke (but not destroyed or reduced to nothing), could ascend unto God 'in fragrant odor' (see Eph. 5:2) and thus represent

---

[3]Frederick Cyril Nugent Hicks, *The Fullness of Sacrifice: An Essay in Reconciliation*, 3rd ed. (London: SPCK, 1953), 13.

in a visible manner, as it were, the return of man to God."[4] The altar of the whole burnt offering thus existed for Israel's cultic ascent to God, ushering his people into Yahweh's presence with the clouds. Such an ascent into heaven through the flames of the whole burnt offering is found in a curious event recorded in Judges 13, in the story where a heavenly messenger announces the birth of Samson. After Manoah offered up a whole burnt offering, we read that "as the flame ascended heavenward from the altar, the messenger of Yahweh ascended in the flame of the altar!" (Judges 13:20).

The vicarious journey into God's heavenly presence through the ascending smoke of a soothing aroma explains the logic of the tribute offering, which typically accompanied the whole burnt offering, for one enters the heavenly abode with a tribute for the divine king. The cultic approach to God also explains the final sacrifice of the liturgy, the peace offering. The highlight of the peace offering was a communion meal. Some of the sacrificial meat would be returned to the worshiper who would then enjoy a sacred feast with family and friends in the presence of God. Having entered Yahweh's house, one then enjoys his unsurpassed hospitality. In the custom of the ancient Near East, Israel is amply sated by the abundance of Yahweh's house (Psalm 36:8-9), as Yahweh prepares a table for them and anoints their head with oil (Psalm 23:5). As the animal had been consecrated for sacrifice, the meat was holy—that is, it had become Yahweh's possession—so the communion meal, given by Yahweh, was a means of consecration for Israel, Yahweh's household. Humanity's restoration to God was thus portrayed as table fellowship with God and the people of God, a festive banquet in the house of God. As the *telos* of the covenant, the exodus out of the house of bondage led to a banquet of fellowship in the house of Yahweh. The journey to Yahweh's heavenly presence, as we have seen, moves from the shedding of blood, through the fires of transformation, ascending as incense, and finally to a meal of fellowship and communion with God (see figure 7.1).

In chapter two, we observed that the exodus movement to God is a reversal of the exile movement away from God. In the Passover deliverance, the lamb's blood served to ransom and purify Israel, which led to Israel's

[4]Stanislas Lyonnet and Léopold Sabourin, *Sin, Redemption, and Sacrifice: A Biblical and Patristic Study*, Analecta Biblica 48 (Rome: Editrice Pontificio Istituto Biblico, 1970), 169.

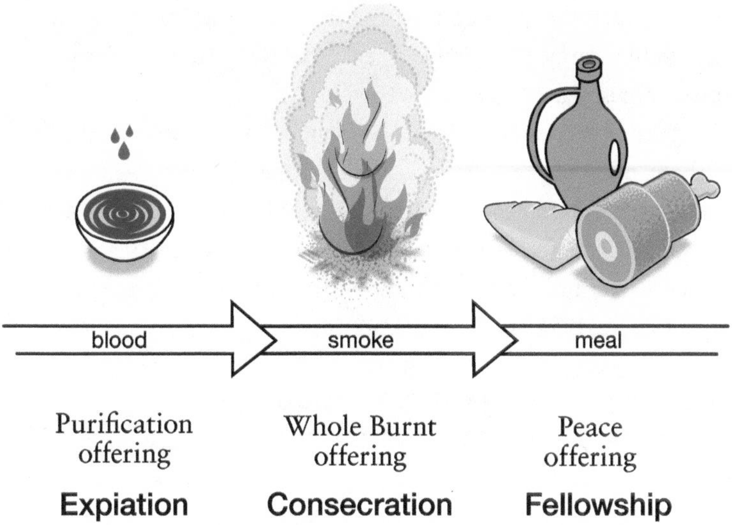

Figure 7.1. Journey into God's presence

consecration to God at Mount Sinai, a new relationship that was confirmed and experienced as a covenant meal. Then Yahweh's blessing of Israel, mediated through the upheld palms of Aaron the high priest, formed a preliminary culminating point to the historical exodus out of Egypt (Numbers 6:22-27), the conclusion to the revelation and covenant developments at Mount Sinai (Exodus 19–Numbers 6).

The cultic approach to Yahweh's house is also in line with the exodus movement. The pattern of a purification offering's blood rite, followed by the whole burnt offering's consecration and burning rite as an ascent into God's presence, this for a communion meal, may be traced historically as an exodus pattern, just as the blood of the Passover lamb was followed by Israel's ascent out of Egypt to Mount Sinai, where God's consecrated people enjoyed a meal, through their elders, in the presence of God (Exodus 24:9-11). The threefold sacrificial approach to Yahweh also culminated with a priestly benediction (Lev. 9:22). The parallel is sound, even anticipated, inasmuch as both the exodus narrative and sacrificial ritual, as movements from a profane to a sacred realm, comprise *rites of passage,* and rituals typically derive meaning by retracing a cosmic journey (in this case, the historical exodus, following a cosmogonic pattern).[5] Israel's salvation, in other words, was re-experienced through the liturgy. Worship in ancient Israel was a cultic exodus into the heavenly presence of Yahweh.

In the new exodus, Jesus' bloodshed on the cross as God's Passover lamb will be followed by his physical ascension into the Father's heavenly presence even as with upheld hands he blesses his people (Luke 24:50-53). And the worship of God's people, in union with Jesus, forms a retracing of his new exodus—a spiritual ascent to the heavenly Mount Zion through the new and living way (see Hebrews 10:19-22; 12:22-24).

THE DAY OF ATONEMENT: THROUGH THE GATES OF THE GARDEN OF EDEN

Although the fundamental liturgy as well as the annual pilgrim feasts of Israel all constituted an approach into Yahweh's presence, the Day of Atonement set the exodus pattern before God's people in a special way. On this sacred day, when all Israel was instructed to "afflict your souls" as an expression of repentance over sin (Leviticus 16:31), the divinely revealed ceremony dramatized the reversal of humanity's ultimate exile, when Adam's house—all humanity—was driven out of the Garden of Eden due to sin, exiled from the face of Yahweh God. Genesis recounts how Yahweh drove out Adam and then stationed cherubim, angelic warriors with an ever-turning, flaming sword, east of the Garden of Eden to guard the way to the tree of life found within (Genesis 3:24). Because of this primal expulsion, spiritually dead humanity now dwells on the outside, outside of abundant life and fellowship with the Creator, in exile amidst a world—within and without—deeply tainted by evil and violence, sexual perversion and brokenness, sickness and decay, by fear and worry, sadness and sorrow, alienation and death. Not merely on the outside, humanity's plight as narrated in Genesis is one of ever-deepening exile, described as an ever-eastward journey into darkness and misery (see figure 7.2).

While humanity remained banished from Yahweh's life-giving presence in paradise, Israel was given mediated access to Eden through the gift of his

[5]See, for example, Walter Vogels, "D'Égypte À Canaan: Un Rite de Passage," *Science et Esprit* 52 (2000): 21-35.

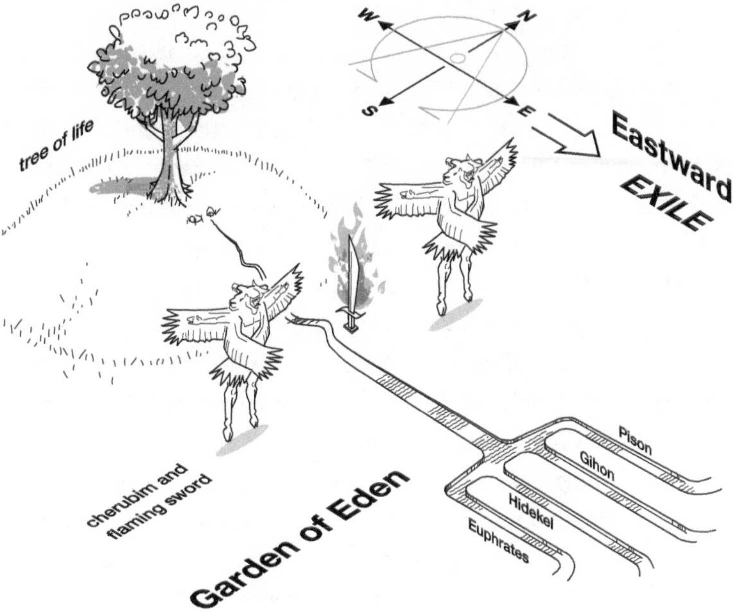

Figure 7.2. Eastward journey into exile

dwelling. Such an understanding arises from a variety of parallels between the tabernacle and Garden of Eden narratives, long noted by commentators on the Pentateuch.[6] Some have compared, for example, the lampstand, a stylized almond tree, with the tree of life. The lushness and life associated with God's presence in the holy of holies is comparable to the descriptions of paradise, and Ezekiel even sees a river of life flowing out of the temple (Ezekiel 47:1-12; compare with Genesis 2:10-14; Revelation 22:1-3). Also worth observing, the Garden of Eden's entrance was oriented toward the east, and after humanity's expulsion this gateway was guarded by cherubim. In the ancient Near East, both of these features, the eastward entrance and the celestial guardians, were readily recognized as marking the doorway of a sanctuary. The tabernacle and later temples of Israel had eastward entrances,

[6]The ensuing discussion of this subsection is similar to material that first appeared in L. Michael Morales, "The House of God" in *Tabletalk*, December 2017, https://tabletalkmagazine.com/article/2017/12/the-house-of-god/. Used by permission.

and the only other place in the Pentateuch where cherubim reappear is in connection with the curtains and atonement lid of the tabernacle.

This insight we may join to another remarkable parallel—that between Adam and the high priest. Not only is Adam's job description, best translated as "to worship and obey" (Genesis 2:15), used elsewhere only to describe the work of Levites at the tabernacle (Numbers 3:7-8) but even Yahweh's clothing of Adam and the woman reappears later in the description of Moses' clothing of the priests (Genesis 3:21; Leviticus 8:13). While it is accurate enough to call Eden an archetypal sanctuary and Adam an archetypal high priest, the theological message of the Pentateuch seems rather to focus on how the tabernacle, with its holy of holies, comprised an architectural Eden, with its garden, and how Aaron's priesthood functioned as a renewed humanity, the high priest serving fundamentally as a new Adam figure. The Eden narratives of Genesis served to explain the logic of Israel's cult, providing God's people with a narrative backdrop for understanding their divinely ordained liturgy.

On the Day of Atonement, humanity's expulsion from Eden was reversed ritually. As an Adam figure, the high priest would journey westward, through the cherubim-guarded entry into the Garden of Eden—that is, through the cherubim-embroidered veil into the holy of holies. He approached the earthly counterpart to Yahweh's heavenly throne room with the blood of atonement, the blood of ransoming and purification. Not surprisingly, the Day of Atonement came to be understood both as a judgment day as well as a new year's day, for the guilt and defilement of Israel's sins were dealt with in a dramatic manner. The separation between the blessed and the cursed on the Day of Judgment was evident in the opposite paths of the two goats used in the ceremony—exodus and exile: the one, dubbed "for Yahweh," journeyed westward into the architectural Garden of Eden through its lifeblood as a sacrifice, while the other, the scapegoat loaded with the sins of Israel, was driven eastward farther away from Yahweh's face into the wilderness as a place of chaos. The annual reentry into the Garden of Eden, the liturgy of the Day of Atonement, called on both memory and faith: it looked back to Adam's failure and expulsion from the Garden of Eden, but it also looked forward, as a prophetic ritual, to the last Adam's reopening of Eden's entrance through the blood of atonement (see figure 7.3).

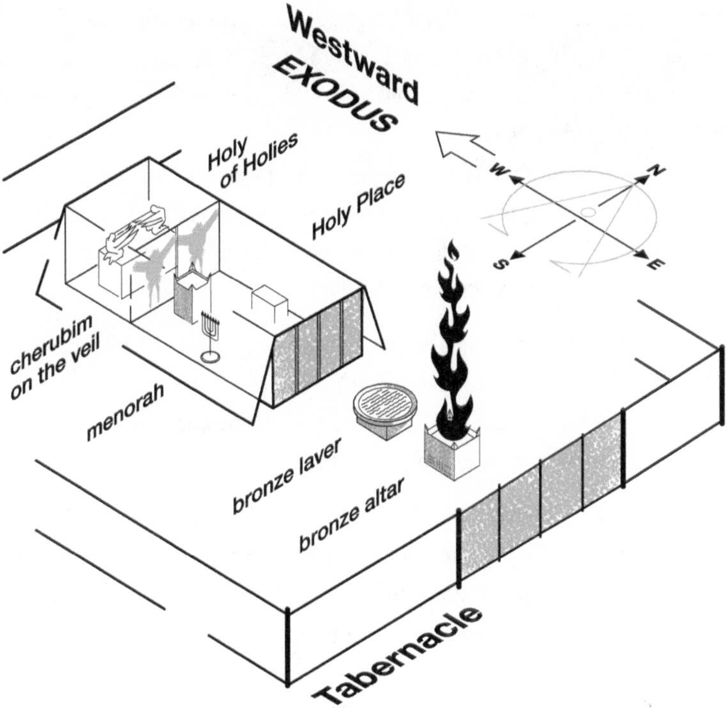

Figure 7.3. Ritual westward exodus on Day of Atonement

THE DAILY SERVICE: YAHWEH'S CONTINUAL PROVISION OF LAMBS

We have already noted the centrality of the whole burnt offering in Israel's cult. Perhaps the weightiest role established for this offering is in the divine legislation for the daily service (Exodus 29:38-46; Numbers 28:1-8). Every day, in the morning and then again at twilight, Aaron's priesthood was to offer up a yearling lamb as a whole burnt offering. This service opened and closed the functions of the tabernacle and later temple each day, subsuming all of the day's other sacrifices—along with the daily life of all Israel—within the ascending smoke of their soothing aroma. Whether plowing a field or weaving a basket, the daily life of Israel, lived within these cultic bookends, was offered up to God by the priesthood on Israel's behalf. The idea is that the altar of the whole burnt offering was to be in a state of continual offering so that Yahweh God might dwell continually with his people: "This will be a continual whole burnt offering throughout your generations at the door of the Tent of Meeting before Yahweh, where I will meet with you and speak with you there. . . . And I will dwell among the sons of Israel and I will be their God" (Exodus 29:42, 45).

The same aroma that had in the primeval era quelled the wrath of God, allowing for the continuance of the cosmos, now served to preserve Israel daily, continually. The liturgy for the daily whole burnt offering ran as follows (see Exodus 29:38-46; Numbers 28:1-8):

1. *The rite of atonement.* The priest, having slain a yearling lamb, would splash the lamb's blood against the altar of the whole burnt offering. Hereby Yahweh cleansed and pardoned his people as preparatory for meeting with them and blessing them.

2. *The rite of intercession.* After washing his hands and feet with water from the basin, the priest entered the holy place to trim the lamps and burn incense on the altar of incense. As the texts do not say, we cannot be certain that the priest would vocalize a prayer during this rite, but the ritual act of burning incense was itself an act of intercession, the high priest bearing the names of the twelve tribes on his shoulders and breastplate into the house of God, and some passages do appear to correlate incense with prayer (see, for example, Luke 1:8-13; Revelation 5:8; 8:4). With the rite of incense, Yahweh would accept his people, again as preparatory for meeting with them and blessing them. In the holy place, the priest would also pour out an offering of strong drink (*shekar*). On the Sabbath the priest's duties in the holy place also included changing the bread of the presence.

3. *The burning rite of the whole burnt offering.* The priest, garments suffused by the incense cloud's fragrance, emerged from the holy place to lay the meat and various parts of the lamb on the altar, along with a tribute offering of flour mixed with oil and a drink offering of wine, which was poured out to Yahweh in a holy place (likely beside the outer altar). The animal was transformed into smoke and ascended into Yahweh's heavenly abode with the tribute offerings offered up on behalf of Israel—the whole burnt offering signifying, once more, Israel's

consecration unto God. The pillar of smoke ascending heavenward as a soothing aroma represented humanity's restoration to God and communicated divine satisfaction, propitiation. On the Sabbath two lambs were used for each of the morning and evening services.

4. *The rite of benediction.* In Exodus 20:24, Yahweh had said that he would come to his people and bless them at the altar where they offer whole burnt and peace offerings, a promise fulfilled in the daily benediction rite.[7] The priest would stand before the altar, lift up his palms and bless the people, using the words of the Aaronic blessing to place Yahweh's name on Israel (Numbers 6:22-27; see also 1 Chronicles 23:13).

The whole approach to Yahweh through the cult, as we have seen, followed an exodus pattern, and the blood of a yearling lamb, shed every morning and evening, would surely have recalled the same message of Passover: Yahweh had redeemed Israel from destruction and for himself, through the blood of a lamb—his people were to live henceforth solely for him. And the Passover lamb, as we saw in our second chapter, evoked the sparing of Isaac, the seed of Abraham, as a whole burnt offering in Genesis 22. Israel's cultic exodus into God's heavenly presence was by way of identification with the sacrificial lamb, which represented Israel, the firstborn son of God. Israel, ritually and vicariously, underwent the cultic exodus of the sacrificial substitute, whose blameless blood was shed, whose substance was transformed by the fires of Yahweh's glory into smoke, and who ascended as a pleasing aroma into the beatific house of God. But the true lamb, who would descend into death and then be raised up into heaven, would yet be provided. Identifying with this chosen and consecrated servant, Israel and the nations would be restored to God in a new exodus.

[7]John W. Kleinig, *Leviticus*, Concordia Commentary (Saint Louis, MO: Concordia Publishing House, 2003), 219; see also the tractate *Tamid* in the Mishnah, which describes the daily offering ritual, including the benediction (chapter 7), as it was performed at the Temple.

PART 2

THE PROPHESIED SECOND EXODUS

Chapter Eight

THE PATTERN OF SACRED HISTORY

ISRAEL'S REDEMPTION THROUGH the exodus out of Egypt was but the first stage in a threefold pattern of sacred history: (1) the redemption of Israel led to (2) the nation's consecration by covenant at Mount Sinai and then to (3) the consummation of the inheritance in the land of Canaan.[1] Remarkably, the threefold cultic exodus observed in the last chapter—moving from purification by blood, to consecration, and ending with a fellowship meal in Yahweh's house—parallels this historical pattern. While the exodus tradition, broadly conceived, encompasses the full threefold movement, this book focuses only on the thematic development in Scripture of the first stage. Nevertheless, for the sake of context, it will be helpful to offer a brief word about the full movement.

The second stage of sacred history was Israel's consecration by covenant. At Mount Sinai Yahweh and Israel had entered into a covenant relationship

[1]As set forth in W. J. Phythian-Adams, "Shadow and Substance: The Meaning of Sacred History," *Interpretation* 1, no. 4 (1947): 419-35.

whereby Israel would become Yahweh's treasured people, a royal priesthood and holy nation, the firstborn son among the nations (Exodus 19:3-8). In ancient Israel, firstborn sons received a double share of the father's inheritance since they were charged with being their brothers' keeper. They were to lead and provide for the needs of the larger family, including the possibility of serving as a kinsman redeemer. The firstborn status could, however, be withdrawn due to misconduct. After he had been chastised by Yahweh, losing his firstborn status, Cain sought it back by slaying his brother. Then, to Yahweh's probing about Abel, he responded sardonically: "Am I my brother's keeper?" (Genesis 4:9). To offer another example, when Joseph was sold into slavery, Reuben alone was troubled since, as the firstborn son, he was responsible for the wellbeing of his brothers (Genesis 37:21-22, 29-30). That his real concern was for himself and his status is evident in the twice-repeated "I" of his exclamation: "The boy is no more, and I, where am I going?" (Genesis 37:30). As it turns out, Reuben will indeed lose his firstborn status for, as 1 Chronicles 5:1 explains, he "defiled his father's bed so his birthright was given to the sons of Joseph." In seeking to establish his leadership over the family prematurely by taking his father's concubine, Reuben lost his role as firstborn son (an incident explained and judged in Genesis 35:22; 49:3-4).

This dynamic of firstborn sons in ancient Israel helps us to understand Israel's calling among the nations more deeply. As Yahweh's firstborn son, Israel was set apart to be his brothers' keeper—that is, the Sinai covenant established Israel as Yahweh's servant among the nations, called to bring the light of divine redemption to the Gentiles. Chiefly, Israel was sent to live in the land for the glory of Yahweh, based on the two gifts of Sinai's summit: the Decalogue and the Dwelling, with its priesthood and sacrificial system of worship. By these Israel would possess a life of wholeness founded on God's instruction, his Torah, and of fellowship with God through the temple cult. Such abundant life was aimed at drawing the nations back to Yahweh their Creator. Yet within the clouds of God's inscrutable wisdom, veiled within the deeps of his wondrous purposes, the servant's role would finally be nothing less than the redemption of the nations—the firstborn Son would serve as the kinsman redeemer for his brothers.

FROM THE EXODUS TO SOLOMON'S TEMPLE

The third stage of sacred history was accomplished with Israel's inheritance of the land of Canaan, a life with God that reached its pinnacle in 1 Kings 8–10. These chapters narrate the building and dedication of the temple on Mount Zion by Solomon and Yahweh's response to Solomon's dedicatory prayer, affirming that he would indeed set his name on the temple. Solomon's speech during the inaugural ceremony of the temple opens and closes with references to the historical exodus out of Egypt: "Since the day that I brought forth my people Israel out of Egypt" and "when he brought them forth from the land of Egypt" (1 Kings 8:16, 21). Similarly, Solomon's dedicatory prayer concludes with a petition that Israel will be remembered in captivity since "you brought forth our fathers out of Egypt, O Lord Yahweh" (1 Kings 8:53). This chord had already been struck in the account of the temple's construction earlier in 1 Kings 6:1: "In the four hundred and eightieth year after the sons of Israel went forth from the land of Egypt . . . he [Solomon] began to build the house of Yahweh," portraying the temple as the fulfillment of Israel's exodus out of Egypt—as one purposeful movement out of the Sheol of Egypt, ascending to the heights of Mount Zion for worship at the house of Yahweh. In the narrative presentation, it was four hundred and eighty years after the exodus when Solomon began to build the temple and then it took twenty years to build the temple (seven years) and palaces (thirteen years), as noted in 1 Kings 6:38–7:1. Five hundred years after the exodus, then, Yahweh's promised rest was realized, as Solomon declares: "Blessed be Yahweh who has given rest to his people Israel, according to all that he has promised" (1 Kings 8:56)—again, the exodus has come to fulfillment with the temple.[2] The threefold pattern of sacred history culminates, therefore, with Israel's worship of Yahweh God at Mount Zion.

Two points of emphasis in the dedication of the temple (1 Kings 8) display Mount Zion as an intended theological reversal of the Tower of Babel (Genesis 11:1-9). First, the temple is built on Mount Zion for the name of Yahweh, that is, for his glory and reputation, rather than for the glory of humanity, the

[2]Cf. Amos Frisch, "The Exodus Motif in 1 Kings 1-14," *Journal for the Study of the Old Testament* 87 (2000): 5-6.

primary motivation of the tower builders who said, "Let us make a name for ourselves" (Genesis 11:4). On the contrary, Solomon proclaims: "I have built a temple for the name of Yahweh God of Israel" (1 Kings 8:20). The trajectory from Babel to Zion has several prominent junctures. Moses had guided Israel to "seek the place where Yahweh your God chooses, out of all your tribes, to put his name for his dwelling place, and there you shall go" (Deuteronomy 12:5), and this place for Yahweh's name turned out to be the last possessed by Israel (Joshua 15:63). Significantly, the role of completing the conquest was granted finally to David (2 Samuel 5:6-16), whose son would build the house for Yahweh's name (2 Samuel 7). The narrative line that began with the exodus out of Egypt now culminates with the construction and dedication of the temple, marking Israel's story as the saga of Yahweh's name.

Second, the theological reversal of the Tower of Babel also involves the undoing of the nations' exile. The house of Yahweh's name on Mount Zion was to draw back to God the nations that had been scattered—reversing their exile with an exodus movement. Solomon's dedicatory prayer is comprised of seven petitions that call on Yahweh to establish the temple as a house of prayer, the heart of Israel's relationship with him. It is the atonement ministry of the priesthood with its daily whole burnt offerings that allows the temple to function as a house of prayer. Now within this dedicatory prayer of Solomon, the temple's fundamental role in Israel's vocation among the nations is also set forth. In his fifth petition Solomon prays for "the foreigner" who hearing of Yahweh's great name comes to the temple to pray to him—the goal of the temple's construction, remarkably, being for "all peoples" of the earth to know and fear Yahweh "just as your people Israel" (1 Kings 8:41-43).

In line with the goal of the exodus, Solomon understands that Yahweh's name will be published among the nations so that even those in faraway lands will hear of his glory and seek him. Even far-flung foreigners will hear of Yahweh's great name, of his "mighty hand and outstretched arm," an expression used consistently in Scripture to indicate the exodus (see Exodus 6:6; 15:16; Deuteronomy 4:34; 5:15; 7:19; 26:8; Psalm 136:12; Jeremiah 32:21). The temple, then, will serve to publish ever more broadly the glory of Yahweh's name chiefly as it has been revealed through the exodus so that Gentiles may hear and come to know him, experiencing their own spiritual deliverance out of exile. Israel's exodus out of Egypt is shown to have continuing universal significance and becomes "a catalyst for the proclamation of God's name throughout the world."[3] The pattern of sacred history thus culminates with the prospect of the nations streaming to Yahweh's house, with Israel, as the seed of Abraham, mediating divine blessing to all the families of the earth. Even foreigners, Yahweh declared, "I will bring to my holy mountain, and make them joyful in my house of prayer . . . for my house will be called a house of prayer for all the peoples" (Isaiah 56:6-7).

Finally, as an initial fulfillment of the Davidic covenant (2 Samuel 7), to which Solomon explicitly alludes in 1 Kings 8:14-26 (see also 1 Kings 9:1-9), the temple's construction and dedication highlights the role of David's son as Yahweh's anointed king. God's program of reversing the exile of nations through Israel, in other words, focuses sharply on Israel's king, the head of Israel who functions as Yahweh's firstborn son and vice regent. Not only does Psalm 2 declare of the Davidic king, in the words of Yahweh: "You are my son, today I have begotten you" (Psalm 2:7), but Psalm 89 declares of him, again in the words of Yahweh: "Indeed, I will make him my firstborn son, the highest of the kings of the earth" (Psalm 89:27). As Yahweh's son, the Davidic king is the house builder for Yahweh's name: his reign fulfills Israel's exodus movement to God and ushers in blessing to the nations.

In summary, the path from Israel's exodus out of Egypt to Solomon's dedication of the temple on Mount Zion traces the story of establishing the mountain of Yahweh's name as a reversal of the Tower of Babel, as a place where the nations may be gathered into the light of Yahweh's uplifted face. The house for Yahweh's name is built by David's son who, as the anointed king of Israel, functions as Yahweh's firstborn son. Shortly after the dedication of the temple, on hearing of the fame of Solomon "concerning the name of Yahweh," the Queen of Sheba pays a royal visit and declares, "Blessed be Yahweh your God" (1 Kings 10:1-13)—a token episode unveiling the prospect of Israel's role among the nations. Just as Abraham's exodus out of Ur culminated with his sacrifice on Mount Moriah (Zion), affirming God's blessing of the nations (Genesis 22:18), so Israel's exodus out of Egypt culminated

---

[3]Frisch, "Exodus Motif," 11.

with the establishment of the temple on Mount Zion, again for the sake of bringing God's blessing on the nations. The movement from Moses to David, who were both shepherds of Yahweh's flock, from the exodus out of Egypt to the royal Mount Zion, is especially noteworthy. David and his role as Israel's king are inseparable from—and, more than this, are part of the consummation of—the exodus, the threefold pattern of sacred history.

FROM SOLOMON'S TEMPLE TO THE BABYLONIAN EXILE

The very next chapter after the Queen of Sheba's visit to Jerusalem, 1 Kings 11, narrates how Solomon's heart turned away from Yahweh so that he even built places of worship for the false gods of his many foreign wives. Rather than publishing the glory of his name, Israel caused the name of Yahweh to be profaned among the nations (Ezekiel 36:22; see also Isaiah 52:5; Romans 2:24). Yet the contrast before and after 1 Kings 11 is not so sharp. Amidst the narrative voyage from Egypt to Mount Zion, strong undercurrents of rebellion and sin continually threatened to pull Israel out to the dark abyss of judgment. Sadly, the story of Israel is one of dismal failure from the beginning. Even as Mount Sinai trembled with the thunderous presence of Yahweh God, newly redeemed Israel had displayed a rebellious heart given over to apostasy, worshiping a golden calf. Then there were the rebellions in the wilderness, where a generation of thousands died in unbelief for refusing to inherit the land, only to have the second generation commit spiritual harlotry with the daughters of Midian and Moab (Numbers 25). The book of Judges, portraying the first centuries of life in Canaan, narrates how as soon as Joshua and the second generation of Israelites died, the people immediately followed other gods, forsaking Yahweh to serve Baal and Ashtoreth (Judges 2:10-17).

Into the era of the monarchy, as we have already noted, Solomon, the same son of David who built the temple on Mount Zion for Yahweh's name, loved hundreds of foreign wives who eventually turned his heart away from Yahweh so that he "went after Ashtoreth the goddess of the Sidonians, and after Milcom the abomination of the Ammonites," and he "built a high place for Chemosh the abomination of Moab . . . and for Molech the abomination of the people of Ammon," burning incense and sacrificing to the gods of his foreign wives (1 Kings 11:1-13; see also Deuteronomy 17:17). As a result, God would strip away ten of the twelve tribes from the Davidic kingdom. The ten tribes would form the larger northern kingdom, who were wayward from the beginning, having set up golden calves for worship in their leading cities of Dan and Bethel. None of their kings, moreover, were entitled to the divine promises given by Yahweh to David's line. After despising and persecuting a long line of prophets, including the likes of Elijah, Elisha, Amos, and Hosea, the northern kingdom, refusing pleas to return to Yahweh, finally reaped the ultimate covenantal threat of exile in 721 BC. Yahweh sent the Assyrian armies to devastate and destroy his people, scattering them afar like so many nations from the Tower of Babel (2 Kings 17:5-23).

The southern kingdom of Judah, although enduring for another 135 years, would eventually suffer the same judgment, sieged and taken into captivity by the might of Babylon in 586 BC (2 Kings 25). The prophet Ezekiel sets forth in vivid language the heinous and steeply perverse idolatry and sexual immorality committed by the Judeans, often monstrously performed as rituals before the face of Yahweh himself—that is, within the very precincts of the temple (Ezekiel 8, 16; cf. Jeremiah 16:10-13). The story of Israel, recounted in Genesis 12 through 2 Kings, closes much like the story of humanity recounted in Genesis 1–11, with God's own people scattered in exile.

HOPE FOR A SECOND EXODUS OUT OF EXILE

As humanity's story had traversed from Eden, the mountain of God, to the scattering from the Tower of Babel ("Babylon"), so, as we have seen, Israel's story moves from Zion, the mountain of God, to the scattering of Babylonian exile. "I will scatter you among the nations" had always been the threatened judgment for rejecting Yahweh, as foretold by Moses himself (Leviticus 26:33; Deuteronomy 4:27-28; 28:64). But the symmetry between Israel and the nations in exile is also deeply theological, unfolding out of the wellspring of the infinite wisdom of God. On the one hand, Israel joins the nations in exile simply because God's people had already joined them in their hearts, straying after their false gods and plunging into their sinful ways of life. Israel had not been created simply to become one more people among the nations but to be set apart as something other—as the servant of Yahweh—for the sake of the nations. Rejecting Yahweh and joining the nations in their depravity,

Israel had forsaken its reason for existence and was judged as fit for joining the nations, scattered among the peoples of the earth. While in the land, Israel was in need of a spiritual exodus; to make this point, Yahweh exiled his people physically.

On the other hand, however, the symmetry between Israel and the nations in exile becomes a source of hope for the nations. Again through Moses, Yahweh had already promised Israel that in the end he would not give them up: "Yahweh your God will bring you back from captivity, and have compassion on you, and gather you again from all the nations where Yahweh your God has scattered you—even if you are driven out to the farthest reaches under heaven, from there Yahweh your God will gather you, and from there he will bring you" (Deuteronomy 30:3-4). Now, if there is hope for Israel, who has become like the nations both in soul and in condition of exile, then can there not be hope for the nations also? Indeed, Israel was consecrated for the sake of drawing the nations out of exile back to Yahweh God. The song of Moses, given by Yahweh as a witness against Israel, explaining the people's inevitable exile, ends with the call: "Rejoice, O nations, with his people," and declares that Yahweh will make atonement for his land and people (Deuteronomy 32:43; see Romans 15:10), intimating the prospect that Israel's atonement and restoration would lead to the fulfilling of God's purposes in bringing salvation to the nations. This, in summary, is the theology of the prophets, that Yahweh God would indeed judge his people with the scattering of exile for their wicked apostasy but that he would also restore them back to himself in such a way that the nations would be gathered in as well. The prophesied second exodus would consecrate a restored humanity comprised of both Jewish people and Gentiles. Through the exile and return of Israel, the death and resurrection of God's firstborn son, the nations would be brought forth to God.

Hosea's message, delivered to the northern kingdom in the latter half of the eighth century, is exemplary. The northern kingdom's exile is portrayed as a reversal of the exodus: "They will return to Egypt," Yahweh declares, "Ephraim will return to Egypt" (Hosea 8:13; 9:3), and the hope of Israel's restoration from exile is portrayed as a new exodus: "I will allure her and bring her into the wilderness . . . as at the time when she came out of the land of Egypt" (Hosea 2:14-15). Exile, however, means much more than Assyrian devastation of cities and the carting away of thousands of Israelites. As covenantal movements, exodus and exile are signals for the people's relationship with God, a point Yahweh makes through Hosea's own household. As a display of Israel's spiritual harlotry against her glorious God and loyal husband, Yahweh bids Hosea to marry a wife of harlotry. His wife, Gomer, first bears him a legitimate son, whom God instructs Hosea to name Jezreel, meaning "Yahweh scatters seed," as a message of judgment, signifying that God would scatter his people. The next two children are not described as "born to him [Hosea]" and are understood rather to be the fruit of Gomer's harlotry—and they are given names to reflect that illegitimate status. A daughter is born and named Lo-Ruhama, literally "No Mercy," for "I will no longer have mercy on the house of Israel" (Hosea 1:6). When Hosea looks on this girl, who does not resemble him in any way, no familial compassion stirs in his breast to care for her as his own daughter as she is the fruit of Gomer's illicit union with another man. Then a son is born and named Lo-Ammi, literally "Not My People," for "you are not my people, and I will not be your God" (Hosea 1:9), again signifying that this child does not belong to Hosea and has no claim on his fatherly love, guidance, and care, let alone blessings of inheritance. This is the initial devastating message against Israel from Yahweh.

Already the northern kingdom had come to represent a further step toward paganism, something of a midway status between Israel and the nations, having embraced the gods and culture of the nations. Hosea's prophecy declares that, though "married" to Yahweh through the Sinai covenant, nevertheless Israel's children do not derive from that relationship; they are illegitimate and have no claim on his divine mercies and will be scattered among the nations where they belong. In scattering Israel throughout the nations, they truly become "Not My People," one with the Gentiles, and as such will endure the merciless plight of the nations ("No Mercy") as "aliens from the commonwealth of Israel and strangers from the covenants of promise, having no hope and without God in the world" (Ephesians 2:12). The point is critical for understanding the theological development of God's dealings with humanity. The northern kingdom had become identified with the Gentile nations.

Lo-Ammi, "Not My People," beyond a message of somber rejection, is also a play on the covenant formula: "I will be your God and you will be my people, and I will dwell in your midst," whereby Israel is embraced as the people of God (see, for example, Exodus 29:45-46; Zechariah 8:8; Revelation 21:3). Lo-Ammi thus stands as a divine reversal of Yahweh's covenant embrace of Israel. The fully reversed formula would read: "I am not your God, you are not my people, and I will not dwell in your midst." As a covenantal movement, exile signals humanity's ruined relationship with the living God—exile, most fundamentally, means spiritual death.

And yet, even before the opening chapter of Hosea closes, Yahweh God is already promising the restoration of Israel, saying that to those of whom it was said, "You are not my people," it will then be said, "You are sons of the living God!" and to the daughter called "No Mercy" it will be said, "Mercy!" (Hosea 1:10–2:1). Again, the second chapter declares:

> Then I will sow (*zara'*) her for myself in the earth,
> And I will have mercy on her who had not obtained mercy;
> Then I will say to those who were not my people, You are my people!
> And they will say, You are my God! (Hosea 2:23)

In this profound reversal of Israel's plight, this new exodus latent with the redemptive blood of Christ and the powerful work of the Holy Spirit, the seed of the nations' hope springs. When Yahweh turns to the Israelites scattered among the nations, the people known as "Not My People" and "No Mercy," and now says, "My people!" this will include not only the "Not My People" among the scattered Israelites but also those among the scattered Gentiles—in one sense, both are in the same condition, cut off from the mercies of God (cf. Romans 3:22-24). By God's own wondrous design, even Israel's rebellion will ultimately work for the redemption of the nations; Israel will enter the dark plight of the nations so that when Israel is drawn out from the miry clay, the nations may also be drawn out as "hangers-on"—just as in the "mixed multitude" of the original exodus (Exodus 12:38). Hosea's own imagery is more powerful: although Israel as Jezreel will be scattered among the nations, yet in God's hidden plan he is rather "sowing" Israel among the nations, spreading his knowledge among Gentiles—sowing seed that will await the

Messiah's harvest in due season. The name Jezreel is based on the Hebrew verb *zara'*, which although taken in the first place as the scattering of seed in judgment, is shown ultimately to be fulfilled in the imagery of sowing seed in hope of a harvest (Hosea 2:23).

Through the prophet Isaiah, a contemporary of Hosea, Yahweh had declared the same nearly incredible message. Yahweh would make himself known even to Egypt so that Egypt will both worship and vow to him and receive blessing from him: "Blessed be my people Egypt, and the work of my hand Assyria, and my inheritance Israel" (Isaiah 19:21-25). In Yahweh's calling Egypt "my people" and Assyria "the work of my hand," Isaiah renders a vision of the nations' return to Yahweh through a deliverance patterned after Israel's exodus out of Egypt, a deliverance that will be accomplished on the day of Yahweh's visitation—note the threefold use of "on that day" (*bayyom hahu'*) in Isaiah 19:21, 23, 24—and that comprises the consecration of the nations by covenant so that they become Yahweh's people. Far from an obscure hope, Yahweh gave the same message to Zechariah a few hundred years later (c. 520 BC): "Many nations will be joined to Yahweh in that day, and they will become my people, and I will dwell in your midst" (Zechariah 2:11; see also Psalm 87:2-6). Wondrously, the nations will be embraced by Yahweh in a relationship akin to Israel's: "my people." As with Israel, the nations will experience an exodus of deliverance that will lead to a covenant relationship with Yahweh.

More than this, Yahweh's prophets declared that the whole pattern of sacred history would be repeated: There will be (1) a new exodus that will lead to (2) a new relationship of consecration by covenant, which will establish (3) a new life in the land with Yahweh—a new life for both Israel and the nations in a new creation with Yahweh dwelling in their midst. With good reason, then, Peter applies the hope of Hosea to the church, comprised already of many Gentiles along with Jewish people, writing that: "You are a chosen generation, a royal priesthood, a holy nation, a people for his own possession, that you may proclaim the praises of him who called you out of darkness into his marvelous light. Once you were *not a people* but now you are the people of God; once you had *not obtained mercy* but now you have obtained mercy" (1 Peter 2:9-10). This is precisely the understanding of God's wondrous ways that the apostle Paul had come to possess and explain in Romans 9:22-26, a section of his epistle that deals with the role of Israel among the nations and that ends with the euphoric doxology:

> O the depth of the riches of the wisdom and knowledge of God!
> How unsearchable are his judgments, and how untraceable his ways!
> For who has known the mind of the Lord, or who has been his counselor?
> Or who has first given to him that it should be repaid?
> For of him and through him and to him are all things, to whom be glory
> forever. Amen. (Romans 11:33-36)

CONCLUSION

To a people swallowed up within the darkness of captivity and exile, the prophets direct Israel's hope back to Yahweh's self-revelation through the exodus—he is the God who delivers his people from exile:

> Was it not you who dried up the Sea, the waters of the Great Deep,
> Who made a path in the depths of the sea for the redeemed to pass over?
> So the ransomed of Yahweh will return and come to Zion with singing.
> (Isaiah 51:9-11)

What God had once done for his people he would do a second time. Sacred history would be recapitulated beginning with a second exodus. Now if Israel's exile was their spiritual death, then their new exodus is nothing less than a resurrection—for what will God's receiving of them be "but life from the dead?" (Romans 11:15). The nations' hope is found, then, in the death and resurrection of Israel, Yahweh's son and servant to the world.

Chapter Nine

GREATER THAN THE FIRST EXODUS

THE SECOND EXODUS WOULD NOT be a mere repetition of the original exodus out of Egypt. A thoughtful reading of the history of Israel will leave one with a pressing question on hearing of a second exodus, namely how can a second exodus make any more difference than the first? Israel's wayward heart—along with that of all humanity—would not of itself be bent toward Yahweh, not even by the devastating agonies of exile. In the second exodus proclaimed by the prophets, however, Yahweh God would do a work *within* the hearts of his people—the deliverance would include an inward, spiritual exodus. From the beginning, since our look at the life of Abraham, we have observed that a true exodus movement toward God involves an inward dying to the old life of exile and how this had been Israel's original problem: though delivered physically out of Egyptian bondage, the hearts of God's people had remained in spiritual bondage to the world, no different from the spiritual darkness of the nations.

Such a dire reality had been prophesied by Moses who, as Israel's shepherd in the historical exodus out of Egypt, also became the first prophet of the second exodus. Moses had discerned only too deeply that Israel would end up in exile. Yahweh had affirmed that such would be the case, telling Moses that after he died Israel would play the harlot with false gods, forsaking Yahweh and breaking the covenant relationship (Deuteronomy 31:16). But Moses had already learned this truth from his own experience with Israel: "I know your rebellion and stiff neck," he said, "for if today, while I am still with you, you have been rebellious against Yahweh, how much more so will you be after my death?" (Deuteronomy 31:27). "To this very day," Moses told Israel, Yahweh has not given you a heart after him (Deuteronomy 29:4). The spiritual disease of waywardness, rebellion, and self-seeking idolatry and sexual immorality was so severe that Israel needed what only God could give. The Sinai covenant was a gracious covenant, yielding abundant blessings and comfort to God's people, but all the heavenly gifts had in large measure been squandered on an ungrateful people. Israel's obstinate heart in the face of divine grace—that is the sorrowful reality displayed in the Bible's historical narratives and prophetic literature.

Mount Sinai's gifts included Yahweh's dwelling among them, his own special presence, offering Israel a refuge and defense, abundance and fruitfulness. Included with the tabernacle was the gift of the priesthood and cult, maintaining Israel's relationship with the holy Creator through the shedding of blood and a ministry of intercession, holding out to every troubled soul a sure means of reconciliation with God, and, through the upheld hands of the high priest, the outpoured blessings of heaven. There was the gift of his Torah, the path of wisdom, wholeness, and life. There was also the gift of a good land whose regular yield was under God's care. Beyond this, he gave them the gift of Spirit-endowed leaders and judges and ultimately of divinely anointed kings. Still more, he gave them the gift of a long line of holy prophets to plead with them and with their children to turn back to God. Wretchedly, all these gifts were despised by Israel's rebellious heart. But in prophesying a second exodus, Moses also proclaimed a new and necessary—and wondrous—work of God. Not only would Yahweh gather his people from every place under heaven back to himself (Deuteronomy 30:3-5), but "Yahweh your God will circumcise your heart and the heart of your offspring, so that you will love Yahweh your God with all your heart and with all your soul—that you may live!" (Deuteronomy 30:6). In a previous chapter, we had noted the correlation between circumcision and Passover—here, in the circumcision of the heart, a *spiritual* exodus is proclaimed. The second exodus would, therefore, lead to a renewed Israel, an Israel whose heart was circumcised to love and follow Yahweh God. The reality of what Abraham's circumcision signified and sealed—his death to the old life accompanied by his new name—would be granted to God's people inwardly, a circumcision of the heart itself.

There is, then, a principle of *escalation* in the prophecies of a second exodus, for the second exodus must transcend the first if there is to be any real hope.[1] The new exodus, so the prophets proclaimed, would far surpass the historical exodus out of Egypt. Jeremiah, for instance, cried out:

> "Behold, the days are coming," declares Yahweh, "when it will no longer be said, 'As Yahweh lives who brought up the people of Israel out of the land of Egypt,' but 'As Yahweh lives who brought up the people of Israel out of the north country and out of all the countries where he had driven them.' . . . I will cause them to know my hand and my might, and they will know that my name is Yahweh." (Jeremiah 16:14-15, 21)

The second exodus will so far exceed the wonders of the old exodus that even the exodus-defined name "Yahweh" will call to mind the second exodus rather than the first. The revelation of Yahweh's being and character unveiled by the new exodus will exegete him—open him up before the world—as never before, defining and publishing his name beyond what had been accomplished in the historical exodus out of Egypt.

THE HISTORICAL RETURN FROM BABYLON

It is precisely the note of escalation that led God's people to understand that the historical return from Babylonian captivity was not—more, *could not* be—the second exodus the prophets had proclaimed. To be sure, Yahweh's good hand was on his people, causing their return to the land under the Persian ruler Cyrus, beginning in 538 BC, and even the building of a second temple. Yet only a fraction of Jewish people had actually returned to Judea,

[1]Friedbert Ninow, *Indicators of Typology Within the Old Testament: The Exodus Motif* (New York: Peter Lang, 2001), 239.

to say nothing of the northern kingdom's scattered Israelites from the Assyrian captivity. And the rebuilt temple in Jerusalem, far from surpassing the splendor of Solomon's temple, was so paltry by comparison that many of the older priests, Levites, and heads of families wept aloud, bitterly recalling the former glory (Ezra 3:12). As will become clear, moreover, several non-negotiable elements, defining features of the second exodus, were simply not realized with the return of Judeans from captivity.

First, there was no son of David sitting on the throne; rather, the Judeans continued to live under subjection to foreign powers. Second, the Spirit of Yahweh had not been poured out on his people. Based on the sins addressed by prophets *after* the return from exile, it was evident that Israel's heart had not been circumcised—the spiritual exodus still awaited fulfillment. If anything, the return from Babylon, significant though it surely was, had been but a subdued and tragic parody of the original exodus. Beyond disappointment, such a reality would have been a severe shock, to say the least, if God had not already given his people to understand that the new exodus would be a reality experienced in the last days, beyond the historical return of Jewish people to Judea. In part, the message of the book of Daniel centers on this sobering point: while some of God's people would return to Jerusalem after Jeremiah's prophesied seventy years, true restoration would await seventy "weeks" of years (some 490 years), and in the meantime they would need to be prepared to suffer, perhaps even die, under the hand of foreign powers, living faithfully and trusting patiently in Yahweh.

The physical return to the land near the end of the sixth century was but a dim foretaste of the new exodus, and the servants raised up by Yahweh after the return from exile, his holy prophets, continued to hold before Israel the still future-oriented message of past prophets: the day of Yahweh's advent would dawn. Yahweh would visit his people for a final and permanent deliverance, establishing his kingdom of life and peace among the nations.

FIVE ELEMENTS OF THE PROPHESIED SECOND EXODUS

The message of the prophets created a variety of expectations among God's people for the second exodus, and under the guidance of the same Spirit the apostles of the New Testament labored to demonstrate that such hopes had indeed been fulfilled by Jesus, even if in unexpected ways in his first advent. In this section we will focus on five elements anticipated by the prophets in their proclamation of a second exodus.

The glory of Yahweh's name. First, the second exodus would hallow the name of Yahweh, publishing his glory among the nations. In line with the major theme of the original exodus out of Egypt, the second exodus would unveil the knowledge of the glory of Yahweh's name. As noted above, Jeremiah observed that Yahweh had declared that through the second exodus "they will know my name is Yahweh" (Jeremiah 16:21). While the wayward heart of his people had caused the blaspheming of Yahweh's name among the nations (Isaiah 52:5; see also Romans 2:24), the new exodus would vindicate his name, causing the nations to know that he is Yahweh. Through Ezekiel Yahweh proclaimed that the new act of redemption would be "for the sake of my holy name, which you have profaned among the nations," for "I will sanctify my great name which has been profaned among the nations . . . and the nations will know that I am Yahweh" (Ezekiel 36:20-23). This hallowing of his name would be accomplished through the second exodus, as Yahweh redeems, cleanses, and sanctifies his people by his Spirit so that they live for the glory and praise of his name (Ezekiel 36:24-38). Yahweh's name would yet be published among the nations through Israel, and salvation blessing would finally dawn. As Yahweh declared through Malachi, the last prophet of the Old Testament: "From the rising of the sun to its setting my name will be great among the nations, and in every place incense will be offered to my name, and a pure offering—for my name will be great among the nations, says Yahweh of hosts" (Malachi 1:11).

A new David. Second, the new Moses of the second exodus will be a new David. In bringing Yahweh's rule to bear on the people, Moses was the shepherd of Israel, a leadership role that would be passed on to Joshua (Numbers 27:12-23) and later inherited by Israel's kings. The chief metaphor for kingship in the ancient world was that of shepherd. It is not so surprising, then, that the shepherd of the new exodus should arise from the house of David since Yahweh had promised him a lasting dynasty. Nevertheless, the consistency with which the prophets focus all of Israel's hope singularly on a new David is breathtaking. Two accomplishments of the new David's exodus are especially underlined in the prophets: he will, first, reunite the northern and southern kingdoms under his rule and, second, draw the nations back to Yahweh. These two motifs are so significant and widespread that they stand as distinct elements of the second exodus in themselves.

Amos, for example, proclaimed Yahweh's looming judgment of exile on the northern kingdom in the mid-eighth century. The ten northern tribes had long since separated from the house of David, saying: "What portion do we have with David? We have no inheritance with the son of Jesse! To your tents, O Israel—now look to your own house, David!" (1 Kings 12:16). Nevertheless, even after the northern kingdom's nearly two hundred years of separation from David's dynasty, Amos resolutely anchors their hope of restoration squarely on David. "On that day," Yahweh declares, "I will raise up the booth of David which is fallen and repair its damages. I will raise up its ruins, and rebuild it as in the ancient days, so they may inherit the remnant of Edom and all the nations which are called by my name—oracle of Yahweh who is doing this" (Amos 9:11-12). David's "booth" is a metaphor for his kingdom, which in losing ten of the twelve tribes through the breaking away of the northern kingdom had fallen. Moreover, Amos prophesies that when Yahweh restores David's kingdom, then Israel's vocation of bringing Yahweh's blessing to all the nations will finally be fulfilled. The nations will enjoy the Creator's blessing when they come under his rule as exercised by his firstborn son and vice regent, the Davidic king.

No less challenging, Hosea, who was sent to the northern kingdom a decade or so after Amos, declared that after God's judgment, "the sons of Israel will return and seek Yahweh their God and David their king, and they will fear Yahweh and his goodness in the latter days" (Hosea 3:5). Israel's return to Yahweh is inseparable from the northern kingdom's restoration under the rule of David. Yahweh's anointed one, the Messiah—*that* is the hope held out to the northern kingdom.

Near the end of the eighth century, after the northern kingdom's devastation and scattering at the hands of the Assyrians, Yahweh sent the prophet Micah threatening similar judgment to the southern kingdom of Judah. Once more restoration hope is focused on the advent of a new David who will lead God's people in a second exodus. Out of Bethlehem, David's hometown

(1 Samuel 16:1-13), the ruler would arise to shepherd Israel, restoring Yahweh's flock and establishing lasting peace in the name of Yahweh (Micah 5:2-5).

Jeremiah, who prophesied up to the destruction of Jerusalem in the sixth century, also proclaimed that Yahweh would restore and unify Israel (the northern kingdom) and Judah (the southern kingdom), breaking their yoke and bursting the bonds of foreign oppression, so that they may "serve Yahweh their God and David their king, whom I will raise up for them" (Jeremiah 30:1-9; see also Jeremiah 33:14-26). The second exodus will not only involve the reunion of Israel and Judah, but in a reversal of the nations' scattering from Babel will also lead to the gathering of nations to Yahweh's name:

> At that time they will call Jerusalem The Throne of Yahweh, and to her all the nations will be gathered, to the name of Yahweh, to Jerusalem. No more will they walk after the stubbornness of their evil heart. In those days the house of Judah will walk with the house of Israel, and they will come together out of the land of the north to the land that I have given as an inheritance to your fathers. (Jeremiah 3:17-18)

Several chapters later, Jeremiah, even as Judah faces the onslaught of destruction and exile by the Babylonian armies, confesses his faith in Yahweh's promise for the nations: "O Yahweh my strength and my stronghold, and my refuge in the day of suffering, to you the nations will come from the ends of the earth, and will say, 'Our fathers have inherited only lies, futility, in which there is no profit'" (Jeremiah 16:19). Such an exodus of the nations, like that of Abraham and Israel, will involve forsaking idols and turning to Yahweh, the true and living God.

Among the captive Judeans residing in Babylon in the sixth century, Yahweh called Ezekiel to deliver a message of hope that Yahweh himself would shepherd his people: "Look! I myself will search for my sheep and seek them out" (Ezekiel 34:11-16). Such shepherding imagery proclaims a new exodus. Yet even this passage, where Yahweh's role is especially underlined, culminates with a new David: "I will raise up one shepherd over them and he will shepherd them—even my servant David. He it is who will shepherd them and he will be their shepherd. And I, Yahweh, will be their God, and my servant David a prince among them: I, Yahweh, have spoken" (Ezekiel 34:23-24; see also

Ezekiel 37:24-28). Yahweh will shepherd his people in the second exodus in and through this new David.

In the late sixth century, the prophet Zechariah also proclaimed that the new David would come:

> Rejoice greatly, O daughter of Zion! Shout, O daughter of Jerusalem!
> Look! Your king is coming to you, he is just and having salvation.
> Lowly and mounted on a donkey, on a colt, the foal of a donkey.
> I will cut off the chariot from Ephraim, and the horse from Jerusalem;
> The bow of battle will be cut off, he will speak peace to the nations.
> His dominion will be from sea to sea, and from the River to the ends of the earth. (Zechariah 9:9-10)

"Your king" refers to a Davidic ruler, who rides a donkey as the son of David once did for his installment as monarch (1 Kings 1:33). Many elements are brought together in this triumphant proclamation: the new David will make peace between the northern ("Ephraim") and southern ("Jerusalem") kingdoms, restoring and reuniting them under his rule, and then he will create peace among the nations, bringing them as well under the blessings of his reign. Zechariah's prophecies resound with the theme of the restoration of David's unified kingdom, all the more remarkable not only as the kingdom by that time had been divided for nearly five centuries but because the ten tribes of the northern kingdom had remained scattered after nearly two centuries. Yet Yahweh declares: "Just as you have been a byword of cursing among the nations, O house of Judah and house of Israel, so I will save you, and you will be a blessing" (Zechariah 8:13). When restored by Yahweh, his reunited people will fulfill their vocation as the seed of Abraham and servant of Yahweh—they will be a blessing for the nations:

> Many nations will be joined to Yahweh in that day, and they will become my people, and I will dwell in your midst. (Zechariah 2:11)

> Thus says Yahweh of hosts: "Peoples will yet come, even the inhabitants of many cities. The inhabitants of one city will go to another, saying, 'Let us surely go to entreat favor from the face of Yahweh and to seek Yahweh of hosts—I myself am also going there.'" Many peoples and strong nations will come to seek Yahweh of hosts in Jerusalem, and to entreat favor from the

> face of Yahweh. Thus says Yahweh of hosts: "In those days ten men from every language of the nations will grasp the wing of a Jewish man's robe, saying, 'Let us go with you for we have heard that God is with you!'" (Zechariah 8:20-23)

> And it will be that all who remain from all the nations that came against Jerusalem will ascend from year to year to prostrate themselves before the King, Yahweh of hosts, and to celebrate the feast of Booths. (Zechariah 14:16)

Called "my people" by Yahweh, the nations will enjoy a status and relationship with God akin to that of Israel (Zechariah 2:11), this finally the fulfillment of Israel's vocation (Zechariah 8:20-23). The emphasis on every language (literally "tongue") of the nations demonstrates that the exodus movement of the nations to Zion forms the reversal of their exile movement from the Tower of Babel where they had been scattered by Yahweh through the division of languages. The prophet Zephaniah sets forth a similar picture, as Yahweh declares, "For then I will return to the peoples a pure language for them all to call upon the name of Yahweh and to serve him with one accord" (Zephaniah 3:9)—truly a thorough reverse of Babel.

In summary, the new Moses of the new exodus will be a new David: he will reunite the northern and southern kingdoms, restoring them to the praise of Yahweh's name. Through the new David, Israel will fulfill its vocation of bringing the blessings of restoration to the nations, for the Gentiles will be gathered to Yahweh under the reign of his firstborn son, the son of David—the Messiah.

While the Gospel of Luke declares that Jesus is the Messiah, who died and rose again to save his people from their sins, the book of Acts, which continues the story, demonstrates that Jesus, as the risen Lord who reigns from God's right hand in heaven, fulfills the promises of a new David. As the gospel goes forth from Jerusalem, Jesus reunites his people in Judea and Samaria, representing the southern and northern kingdoms respectively (Acts 1–8), and then he claims his inheritance to the ends of the earth as the gospel brings many among the nations under his reign (Acts 9–28). Soon the day will dawn when heavenly voices declare: "The kingdom of the world has become the kingdom of our Lord and of his Christ, and he will reign forever and ever!" (Revelation 11:15).

Elijah prepares for Yahweh's advent. Third, the second exodus will dawn with a visitation from Yahweh, whose way will be prepared by an Elijah-like messenger. Through the prophet Malachi, whose name means "my [Yahweh's] messenger," Yahweh declared that he would visit his people and that his visitation would be heralded by his messenger: "'Look! I am sending my messenger and he will prepare the way before my face. Suddenly, the Lord whom you are seeking will come to his temple, even the messenger of the covenant in whom you delight—look! He is coming!' says Yahweh of hosts" (Malachi 3:1). The term *messenger* is used twice in this passage. In the first instance, messenger refers to the one who will prepare the way for Yahweh, while in the second use the "messenger of the covenant" is equated with Yahweh himself, the Lord who will come to his own temple. This explains why the next verse asks: "Who can endure the day of his coming—and who can stand when he appears?" This second messenger, then, is likely to be understood as *the* messenger of Yahweh, typically translated as "angel" of Yahweh (since the same Hebrew word underlies both *angel* and *messenger*). Malachi's anticipation of a second exodus here forms an allusion to the original exodus out of Egypt when Yahweh had said: "Look! I myself am sending a messenger before your face to keep you in the way, and to bring you into the place which I have prepared. Beware of his presence and heed his voice; do not rebel against him, for he will not forgive your transgressions—for my name is in him" (Exodus 23:20-21). This messenger manifested Yahweh's heavenly presence on earth, appearing to Moses in the burning bush and leading Israel's exodus deliverance (Exodus 3:2; 14:19), so that he may justly be labeled the "messenger of the covenant" in Malachi.

Malachi's first messenger, then, prepares the way for a second messenger who is identified closely with Yahweh himself. In this Malachi not only alludes to the historical exodus out of Egypt but also to the new exodus that had been prophesied by Isaiah, where a messenger's voice would cry out in the wilderness: "Prepare the way of Yahweh—make straight in the desert a highway for our God! . . . And the glory of Yahweh will be unveiled, and all flesh will see it together" (Isaiah 40:3-5). Near the end of his book, Malachi adds a further detail about the first messenger, who prepares the way before Yahweh: "Look! I myself am sending you Elijah the prophet before the coming of the great and fearful day of Yahweh" (Malachi 4:5). The second exodus will dawn with the coming of an Elijah-like messenger who will prepare the way for Yahweh's visitation.

Part of the Passover ceremony in Judaism today includes leaving a cup of wine on the table designated for Elijah as an expression of hope in a future redemption when Elijah will appear to herald the arrival of the Messiah. The Gospel of Mark, which refers to Elijah in its beginning, middle, and end (1:1-6; 9:11-13; 15:33-36), especially identifies John the Baptizer as the prophesied Elijah-like messenger who was sent to prepare the way of Yahweh. Mark opens with a quotation from both Malachi 3:1 and Isaiah 40:3, and describes the Baptizer dressed as Elijah (Mark 1:1-6; see 2 Kings 1:8). Most significantly, the advent of Yahweh, with his sudden coming to his temple, is set forth in Mark as Jesus' own visitation, one that proves to be the final undoing of the temple (Mark 1:7; 11:11-20; 13:1-2; 15:37-39).

The outpouring of the Spirit. Fourth, in the second exodus Yahweh will pour out his Spirit on his people. Throughout Israel's history, the role of Yahweh's Spirit is one of enabling power. Aside from his involvement in the creation and recreation of the world (Genesis 1:2; 8:1; cf. Exodus 14:21), the Spirit enables one to perform God-given duties with wisdom, whether constructing the dwelling of God (Exodus 31:1-5; 1 Kings 5–6) or governing people wisely (Genesis 41:38-40; 1 Kings 3–4). The Spirit empowered judges to lead Israel in the way of Yahweh and to conquer their enemies in accord with the original order to drive out the inhabitants of Canaan in divine judgment (Judges 3:10; 6:34; 11:29; 13:25; 14:6, 19; 15:14, 19).

The main offices of leadership in Israel—prophet, priest, and king—involved anointing with oil, symbolizing the Spirit's consecration and enabling power for serving Yahweh's flock in his name (1 Kings 19:16; Exodus 28:41; 1 Samuel 10:1). When Samuel took the horn of oil and anointed David to be the next ruler over Israel, for example, we read that "the Spirit of Yahweh rushed upon David from that day forward" (1 Samuel 16:13). In relation to prophets, the Spirit enabled holy men to know and communicate the mind of Yahweh. When in the wilderness the Israelites demonstrated a severe spiritual depravity, God's resolution was to distribute his Spirit that was on Moses to seventy elders and scribes so that they might publish more broadly Yahweh's Torah, his will and instruction, as revealed to Moses (Numbers 11). As the one who carried the burden of leading a rebellious people, and who knew the only real remedy, Moses had exclaimed: "Oh that all the people of Yahweh were given to be prophets, that Yahweh would put his Spirit upon them!" (Numbers 11:29). Moses' plea reflected his desire that all God's people would be enabled by the Spirit to be gripped and shaped by Yahweh's word, that his people would know and do his will. In all the further rebellions and depravities of God's people, the necessity of Yahweh's Spirit for the life and wellbeing of Israel is underscored, page by page sustaining the case until one's understanding steadily matures into the original awareness of Moses, and Moses' plea becomes one's own.

Through the prophet Joel, Yahweh himself announced that the solution to Israel's wayward heart as discerned so keenly by Moses would be realized—Moses' plea had become Yahweh's promise: "And it will come to pass afterward that I will pour out my Spirit upon all flesh, and your sons and daughters will prophesy, your elder men will dream dreams and your young men will see visions. Even upon your servants and maidservants—in those days I will pour out my Spirit" (Joel 2:28-29). It is this outpouring of the Spirit that will enable God's people to cling to God in faithfulness—to repent continually over sin and to yield grateful obedience. The human, sin-stricken heart is so opposed to the character and will of God that apart from the Spirit's enablement, Israel would not remain loyal. Even within the gracious covenant relationship with Yahweh established at Mount Sinai, as we have seen, Israel was bound for judgment and exile. Here, then, is the new covenant remedy proclaimed by Jeremiah: "I [Yahweh] will put my law within them, and I will inscribe it on their hearts," with the result that "I will be their God, and they will be my people" (Jeremiah 31:33). By comparison with the words of another prophet, Ezekiel, we see that the work of inscribing God's law on the heart is the work of the Spirit:

> I will give you a new heart, and a new Spirit I will put within you.
> I will remove the heart of stone out of your flesh and will give you a heart of flesh.
> I will put my Spirit within you and cause you to walk in my statutes, and you will keep my judgments and do them. (Ezekiel 36:26-27)

Earlier in Ezekiel's prophecy, Yahweh had called on Israel to: "Cast away from you all the transgressions in which you have transgressed, and make for yourselves a new heart and a new spirit—for why would you die, O house of Israel?" (Ezekiel 18:31). Herein lies the tragic dilemma: what Israel cannot do for themselves is precisely what the people need desperately in order to live before Yahweh. Such circumcision of the heart, to use Moses' phrase (Deuteronomy 30:6), enabling one to love Yahweh with all the heart, is accomplished only by Yahweh's Spirit who will be poured out broadly on the people of God. "I will no longer hide my face from them," Yahweh says later, "for I will have poured out my Spirit upon the house of Israel" (Ezekiel 39:29). Isaiah had already focused Israel's hope on the person and work of the Spirit, prophesying how abundantly the Spirit of Yahweh would rest upon the Messiah, empowering his leadership of the second exodus (Isaiah 11), and how the outpoured Spirit would transform the wilderness of Zion, even God's spiritually thirsty people, into the garden of Yahweh (Isaiah 32:15; 44:3; 51:3).

The person and work of the Holy Spirit, more abundantly poured out upon the people of God, is the gift of the new covenant (see Acts 2:38-39), and all four Gospels single out Jesus the Messiah as the one who would baptize his people with the Spirit (Matthew 3:11; Mark 1:7-8; Luke 3:16; John 1:30-34). What his people could not do for themselves, God in his goodness and grace freely gives. This is not, of course, to say that the gift is without cost; rather, the gift of the Spirit would be purchased by the blood—the agonies—of the servant of Yahweh.

Resurrection. Fifth and finally, Israel's second exodus will be a resurrection from the dead. The consummate exodus will occur when the bodies of God's people are raised from their graves and his people are ushered into the glories of the new creation—an exodus both foretasted and accomplished with Jesus' own resurrection from the grave. While in the book of Daniel the final resurrection from the dead is asserted quite literally: "Many of those who sleep in the dust of the earth will awake, some to everlasting life, and some to shame and everlasting contempt" (Daniel 12:2), yet this hope is given to God's people within the historical context of Israel's exile. In some passages the return from exile, as a spiritual resurrection from the dead, is so deeply bound up with the final resurrection of the dead, the consummate exodus, that the two are almost inseparable, for the return from exile is the bud that flowers into the resurrection of the dead. "He will swallow up death forever," Isaiah proclaims, and "the Lord Yahweh will wipe away tears from off all faces" (Isaiah 25:8). And again: "Your dead will live, their bodies will arise. Awake and sing, you who dwell in the dust!" (Isaiah 26:19).

To be in exile from the self-existing Creator and source of all life is truly to be in a condition of death. The Bible describes eternal judgment as the second—as in, the final—death. "Then Death and Hades were cast into the lake of fire—this is the second death" (Revelation 20:14). Eternal exile from God is death in all its horrid fullness of darkness and despair. However, even within the dust of history, Israel's exile from Yahweh was a sort of death, a theological and spiritual death, so that Israel's restoration to God would be nothing short of a resurrection from the dead. Exile, writes Kenneth Turner, "is more than an historical event; it is a theological concept that signifies Israel's death," and it is not simply Israel as a socio-religious people but "Israel as Yahweh's elect son and servant, that is put to death."[2] Restoration of Israel from exile is, therefore, understood theologically as a resurrection of Yahweh's son from death—precisely, an exodus.

In the book of Hosea, Israel's second exodus is described in terms of resurrection: "After two days he will revive us, on the third day he will raise us up, and we will live before his face" (Hosea 6:2). Not without reason many understand this verse as key to the New Testament's proclamation of Jesus' resurrection on the third day—by union with the Son of God, Israel is raised up with him in his third-day resurrection. Hosea goes further:

> From the hand of Sheol, I will ransom them;
>   From Death, I will redeem them.
> Where are your plagues, O Death?
>   Where is your sting, O Sheol? (Hosea 13:14)

Even as the first exodus was a ransoming from the Sheol of Egypt through the blood of the Passover lamb, so the second exodus—the spiritual and eventually physical resurrection to God—would require a ransoming from the grave, a redeeming from death by another Passover Lamb. A similar, striking statement is found in Psalm 49:15: "But God will ransom my soul from the hand of Sheol, for he will receive me."

---

[2]Kenneth J. Turner, *The Death of Deaths in the Death of Israel: Deuteronomy's Theology of Exile* (Eugene, OR: Wipf & Stock, 2011), 224-25.

Perhaps most dramatically, Ezekiel's message portrays the restoration of Israel as a resurrection from the dead. Having been led by the Spirit to a valley filled with dry bones, a dismal picture of Israel in exile, Ezekiel is asked an intriguing question by Yahweh: Can these bones live? (Ezekiel 37:3). Ezekiel, according to Yahweh's instruction, then begins prophesying the word of Yahweh to the bones, and the bones, rattling into motion, come together, and even sinews and flesh appear. However, "there was no breath within them" (Ezekiel 37:8). *Breath* (*ruakh*) is the same word used for the Spirit: the lifeless bodies form a picture of Israel restored as a body physically in the land of Judea yet without the outpouring of Yahweh's Spirit on them—that is, a picture of post-exilic Israel still awaiting the second exodus. Ezekiel is, of course, alluding to the creation account of Genesis, where Yahweh had first formed Adam's body from the ground before breathing into him the breath of life (Genesis 2:7), the breath of Yahweh being the animating principle, the dynamic of life. Next, Yahweh bids Ezekiel to prophesy to the wind (again *ruakh*), which then enters the bodies so that Israel *lives* (Ezekiel 37:9-10).

This vivid scene becomes Ezekiel's message to the exiles, whose exodus will be a resurrection from the dead: "Thus says the Lord Yahweh: 'Look! I will open your graves, and I will cause you to ascend out of your graves, O my people! And I will bring you into the land of Israel. You will know that I am Yahweh when I open your graves and cause you to ascend from your graves, O my people!'" (Ezekiel 37:12-13). When considering the historical exodus out of Egypt, we saw that its chief aim was the knowledge of Yahweh, with "Yahweh" signifying the God of the exodus. Here, Ezekiel uses the same exodus motif for Israel's resurrection as the new exodus: "You will know that I am Yahweh *when I open your graves and cause you to ascend from your graves*"—a wondrous exodus indeed! In the next verse, Yahweh says: "I will put my Spirit within you, and you will live" (Ezekiel 37:14), linking Ezekiel's vision of resurrection with the reality expressed by Yahweh in Ezekiel 36, considered in the previous section: "I will put my Spirit within you" (Ezekiel 36:27). The Spirit is, therefore, integral to the second exodus, for he is the Spirit of life from the dead—he is the Spirit of the exodus.

Nothing less than life from the dead, resurrection—that is the prophesied second exodus.

Chapter Ten

THE SERVANT OF THE SECOND EXODUS

THE THEME OF A SECOND EXODUS unifies the message of Isaiah and is so richly developed in the central section (Isaiah 40–55) that, as one commentator wrote, it leaves the impression of being "more about the exodus than the Book of Exodus itself."[1] Near the end of Isaiah, the historical exodus out of Egypt is rehearsed simply with the remark: "So you led your people, to make for yourself a glorious name" (Isaiah 63:14). This terse summary reminds us that Israel's exodus was for the sake of Yahweh's renown among the nations, a glory that would shine the blessed light of Yahweh's face into the dark plight of humanity's exile. And yet the original deliverance of Israel out of Egypt had not resulted in the fulfillment of Israel's vocation as the servant of Yahweh, for Israel had not spread the fame of his name in blessing to the nations.

[1]John I. Durham, "Isaiah 40–55: A New Creation, A New Exodus, A New Messiah," in *The Yahweh/Baal Confrontation and Other Studies in Biblical Literature and Archaeology*, ed. Julia M. O'Brien and Fred L. Horton Jr. (New York: Edwin Mellen, 1995), 52; see also Bernard W. Anderson, "Exodus Typology in Second Isaiah," chap. 12 in *Israel's Prophetic Heritage: Essays in Honor of James Muilenburg*, ed. Bernard W. Anderson and Walter Harrelson (New York: Harper, 1962), 177-95.

Through the prophet Isaiah, Yahweh spoke to this disconnect between Israel's calling and the nation's spiritual waywardness, between the lofty ideal and the dismal reality. Having no concern for the plight of the outcast nations, from which—and *for* which—Israel had been rescued, God's people would be cast out from his face to join the nations in the darkness of exile. Because Israel "rebelled and grieved his holy Spirit," Yahweh "turned against them as an enemy, and fought against them" (Isaiah 63:10). Nevertheless, because Yahweh is the God of the exodus, the One who abounds in steadfast love and mercy (Exodus 34:6-7; Numbers 14:17-19), there is always hope. This hope is expressed as a pressing question, a question by which the entire message of Isaiah may be understood:

> Then he remembered the days of old, of Moses and his people. Where is he who brought them up from the sea with the shepherd of his flock? Where is he who set in the midst of them his holy Spirit—who caused his glorious arm to go at the right hand of Moses, who divided the waters before them to make for himself an everlasting Name? (Isaiah 63:11-12)

Such a longing builds anticipation for a new Moses and a new exodus out of exile, a deliverance that will lead to a renewed Israel. This transformed Israel will fulfill its vocation as servant of Yahweh among the nations and so bring glory to Yahweh's name.

Not unjustly, then, the message of Isaiah has been summarized as the transformation of Zion, with the city of Jerusalem here standing both for Israel as God's people and for the whole creation itself, which ultimately will participate in Israel's renewal.[2] The opening section of Isaiah (Isaiah 1:1–2:4) serves as a prologue for the book, a microcosm of its message. In the beginning, Jerusalem is defiled, profane, rebellious, disobedient, degenerate, and given over to spiritual harlotry (Isaiah 1:1-23), but Yahweh avows to redeem Zion, establishing the mountain of the house of Yahweh as the gathering place for Israel and all the peoples, who will be taught his Torah, establishing Eden-like peace (Isaiah 1:24–2:4). By the end of Isaiah, similarly, there is a new Jerusalem,

---

[2]William J. Dumbrell, "The Purpose of the Book of Isaiah," *Tyndale Bulletin* 36 (1985): 111-28; Barry G. Webb, "Zion in Transformation: A Literary Approach to Isaiah," in *The Bible in Three Dimensions: Essays in Celebration of Forty Years of Biblical Studies in the University of Sheffield*, ed. David J. A. Clines, Stephen E. Fowl, and Stanley E. Porter (Sheffield, UK: JSOT Press, 1990), 65-84.

an Israel that is cleansed, holy, submissive, and obedient, joined by many among the nations and following closely after Yahweh—indeed, there is a new heavens and earth (Isaiah 65:17-19). How can this be? How is such a transformation possible?

The key to Zion's transformation is found in the mysterious figure of the servant, who appears in the four so-called "servant songs" interspersed primarily through the second major section of Isaiah (Isaiah 40–55), although there is good reason for adding Isaiah 61 as a fifth song. While the first four servant songs present the work of the servant, in the fifth song his achievement is announced as applied and passed on to his followers, his spiritual offspring who become servants of Yahweh, a renewed people composed of Jewish people and Gentiles.

As we approach the second half of Isaiah, it will be useful to observe this section's twofold division: Isaiah 40–55, which deals with some form of Israel as the servant of Yahweh, and Isaiah 56–66, which deals with a renewed Israel who are servants of the servant of Yahweh.[3] For the sake of proper nuance, we will subdivide the first part further into two sections: Isaiah 40–48, which deals with the nation of Israel as Yahweh's failed servant, and Isaiah 49–55, which sets forth a singular embodiment of Israel as Yahweh's faithful servant. Somewhat simplified, then, the focus of the second half of the book of Isaiah moves from Israel as failed servant of Yahweh (Isaiah 40–48), to the mission of an obedient and suffering servant of Yahweh (Isaiah 49–55), to the renewed mission of the servants of Yahweh, who are disciples of the servant (Isaiah 56–66). The movement from Israel as failed servant to

[3]My treatment of Isaiah 40–66 relies closely on the following studies: Clyde T. Francisco, "The Great Redemption," *Review & Expositor* 51, no. 2 (1954): 155-67; Peter Wilcox and David Paton-Williams, "The Servant Songs in Deutero-Isaiah," *Journal for the Study of the Old Testament* 42 (1988): 79-102; Willem A. M. Beuken, "Servant and Herald of Good Tidings: Isaiah 61 as an Interpretation of Isaiah 40–55," in *The Book of Isaiah: Le Livre d'Isaïe*, ed. Jacques Vermeylen (Leuven, Belgium: Leuven University Press, 1989), 411-42; Willem A. M. Beuken, "The Main Theme of Trito-Isaiah 'The Servants of YHWH,'" *Journal for the Study of the Old Testament* 47 (1990): 67-87; Christopher Seitz, "'You Are My Servant, You Are the Israel in Whom I Will Be Glorified': The Servant Songs and the Effect of Literary Context in Isaiah," *Calvin Theological Journal* 39 (2004): 117-34; Jaap Dekker, "The Servant and the Servants in the Book of Isaiah," *Sárospataki Füzetek* 3-4 (2012): 33-45; Jaap Dekker, "The High and Lofty One Dwelling in the Heights and with His Servants: Intertextual Connections of Theological Significance Between Isaiah 6, 53 and 57," *Journal for the Study of the Old Testament* 41, no. 4 (2017): 475-91.

the renewed Israel of faithful servants, therefore, passes through the person and work of the suffering servant, an embodiment of Israel—a truer Israel in the sense of true-to-Yahweh (see figure 10.1). The servants of Yahweh in the third section are the spiritual offspring of the servant, who have benefited from his redemption and have been transformed by the Spirit—that is, they have experienced the second exodus led by the servant and are to be identified with the "survivors" and "remnant" of Israel mentioned earlier in Isaiah, the Israel within Israel (Isaiah 4:2; 11:11). They are so identified with the obedient servant of Yahweh that they become, as it were, little servants of Yahweh.

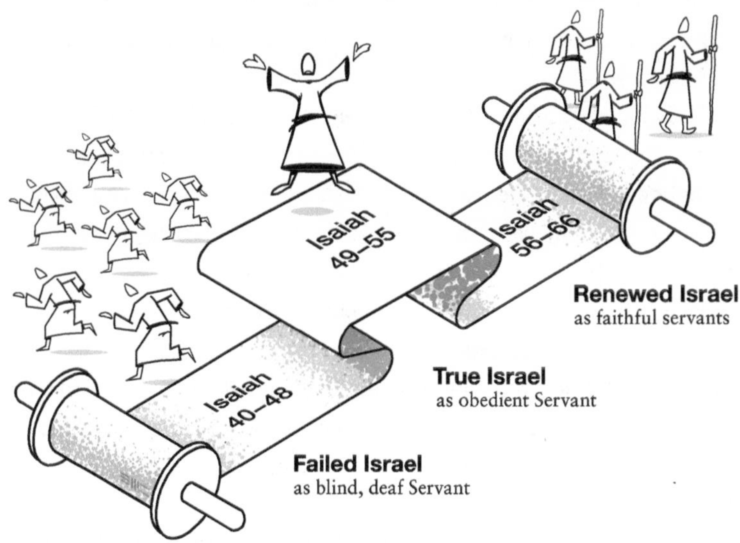

Figure 10.1. Structure of Isaiah 40–66

The failure of Israel as servant of Yahweh in Isaiah 40–48 once more not only refers to the nation's spiritual bankruptcy and lack of faithfulness but also has the nation's vocation in view, Israel's calling to publish the glory of Yahweh's name among the nations *through* Israel's own following of Yahweh's path of life, his Torah. Yahweh's original mission announced throughout the story of Abraham was to bring his salvation blessings to the nations through the seed of Abraham, Israel. In failing to follow Yahweh closely, Israel also fell short of accomplishing the nation's calling as servant of Yahweh. Yet through Isaiah, Yahweh asserts that, first, the nations will nevertheless be gathered to Zion for blessing, reversing the Tower of Babel scattering, and, second, that this divinely ordained mission will still be fulfilled by Israel as Yahweh's servant. There will be no resorting to another plan, which is precisely why the transformation of Zion, the renewal of God's people, is required.

ISAIAH 40–55: THE SERVANT OF YAHWEH

Turning now to reflect on the servant songs, we will observe that the servant portrays Israel in some form, either as the nation or as embodied by a person or group within the nation.[4] Scholars are not completely agreed as to the boundaries for each song, but we will factor in the surrounding context for each passage.

Isaiah 42:1-4: The first servant song. Within Isaiah 40–48, there is no compelling reason for understanding the servant as any figure other than the nation of Israel as set apart by Yahweh for his purposes. The servant of the first song, then, may be identified as the nation of Israel—at least in the first place. In this song, Yahweh presents his servant to the world, focusing on Israel's unique role and vocation among the nations: "Look! My servant, whom I uphold, my chosen one in whom my soul delights. I have put my Spirit upon him—he will bring forth justice to the nations" (Isaiah 42:1). The coastlands or isles (as in the farthest reaches of the world), we are told, await "his Torah," linking the servant's role with that of the Torah going forth from Zion to the nations (noted earlier in Isaiah 2:1-4).

Yahweh goes on to declare that he will guide his servant and give him as a covenant of the people for a light to the nations (Isaiah 42:6). Israel's calling and mission as a nation, as Yahweh's firstborn son and servant, was indeed to restore the nations to God. That the New Testament presents Jesus as fulfilling this text (see Matthew 12:15-21) draws us more deeply into the meaning of his life and ministry, for one aim of his advent was to fulfill the role of Israel as the true seed of Abraham. As we will see, Israel's failure as Yahweh's servant, calling for a new embodiment of Israel to fulfill the servant's vocation, is already part of the message of Isaiah.

[4]William J. Dumbrell, "The Role of the Servant in Isaiah 40–55," *Reformed Theological Review* 48 (1989): 105.

Although set apart to be a covenant for the people and a light to the nations, to open the eyes of the blind and to bring prisoners out of the dungeon and darkness (Isaiah 42:6-7), the stark reality is that Israel itself was blind, languishing in the bonds of spiritual darkness. "Who is blind," Yahweh implores, "but my servant? And who is deaf as my messenger whom I sent? Who is blind but my commissioned one, or blind as the servant of Yahweh?" (Isaiah 42:19). Throughout Isaiah 40–48, Yahweh strives with Israel, calling the nation out of its idolatry: "For the sake of my servant Jacob, and Israel my chosen, I call you by name—I name you although you do not know me. I myself am Yahweh and there is no other—no God besides me. I have upheld you, but you do not know me" (Isaiah 45:4-5). By Isaiah 48, Yahweh's frustration with Israel is apparent: "Oh that you had attended to my commandments! Then your wellbeing would have been like a river, and your righteousness like the waves of the sea! Your offspring would have been like the sand, and the descendants of your womb like its grains—his name would not be cut off nor destroyed from before my face!" (Isaiah 48:18-19).

Israel's failure as Yahweh's servant recurs throughout these chapters without relenting. Although Yahweh had chosen Israel to be his servant for a great worldwide purpose, his soul had not delighted in the nation, which was blind and deaf (Isaiah 42:19), had burdened him with its sin (Isaiah 43:24), questioned his ways (Isaiah 45:11), and in short had been rebellious since before its birth, dealing treacherously (Isaiah 48:8).[5] Nevertheless, Yahweh promises to redeem "his servant Jacob" (Isaiah 48:20), a redemption that will indeed lead to the transformation of Zion.

Intriguingly, one of the last lines of Isaiah 48 reads: "But now Lord Yahweh has sent me and his Spirit" (Isaiah 48:16). For the first time in all of Isaiah 40–48 one finds a first-person ("I") voice who is not Yahweh. Because the new servant who speaks in the second song just a few verses later also speaks in the first person singular, it is likely that Isaiah 48 marks a transition from Isaiah 40–48 to Isaiah 49–55, from the nation of Israel as servant to the figure of a new embodiment of Israel as servant.[6] Here possibly the new figure steps

[5]Francisco, "Great Redemption," esp. 158-60.

[6]Other features link the voice of Isaiah 48:16 with the new servant of Isaiah 49–55, like the use of "but now" (Isaiah 48:16; 49:4), along with the phrase "Lord Yahweh" (*ʾadonay yhwh*), which recurs throughout the third song (four times in Isaiah 50:4-9).

forward who, in the second servant song (Isaiah 49:1-6), will be appointed as the new Israel and servant for the sake of both Israel and the nations. On this reading, Isaiah 48:17-22 may be taken as something of a summary of the new servant's message to Israel.

Isaiah 49:1-6: The second servant song. Although the vocation of the servant presented in Isaiah 42:1-4 must ultimately fall on the new embodiment of Israel as well, it is in Isaiah 49–55 that the servant songs may be said to apply directly, first and foremost, to the *new* Israel as servant of Yahweh. Indeed, not a few scholars understand the second song as serving to designate the new servant figure as Israel, translating Isaiah 49:3, "And he [Yahweh] said to me, 'You are my servant, [you are] Israel, in whom I will be glorified.'" According to this reading, which is equally as valid as the typical vocative translation ("O Israel"), the person addressed is declaring that Yahweh has now appointed him to be his servant—he is now Israel, called to fulfill Israel's mission of glorifying Yahweh's name among the nations. The servant does not replace corporate Israel but is himself an Israelite who embodies Israel.

Yet, since the old Israel suffers the same plight as the nations, this new Israel—Yahweh's servant—also has a mission *to* Israel as a nation, "to restore Jacob" to Yahweh (Isaiah 49:5). This servant will lead Israel in a new exodus greater than the first. Yahweh declares that such a deliverance will surpass the historical exodus out of Egypt for it will be an exodus for all the nations (Isaiah 49:6): "And he [Yahweh] said, 'It is too light a thing for you to be my servant to raise up the tribes of Jacob, and to restore the preserved of Israel—I will give you for a light to the nations, so you will be my salvation to the ends of the earth!'" While there is a note of discouragement as the servant's labors among God's people appear to be in vain, a theme developed in the next two songs as well, the servant nevertheless commits himself to Yahweh, trusting in him for the wages of his labor (Isaiah 49:4). Reassuringly, the servant is "honored in the eyes of Yahweh" and God is his strength (Isaiah 49:5). As said of Israel in the first song (Isaiah 42:6), the new Israel, this true servant, will be given as a covenant of the people, calling prisoners out of darkness (Isaiah 49:8-9).

Isaiah 50:4-9: The third servant song. In the third song, the servant is presented as a devoted student and teacher of Yahweh's instruction, whose ears are open to God and who neither rebels nor turns away from him—even when made to suffer by those who reject Yahweh's will. He declares his willingness to suffer disgrace as an essential facet of his vocation: "My back I gave to those who strike, and my cheeks to those who wrench the beard—my face I did not hide from shame and spitting" (Isaiah 50:6). Once more, as in the previous song, the servant commits himself to Yahweh amidst temptation to discouragement. With Yahweh God strengthening him, he sets his face firm, determined to fulfill his mission and to await his vindication from Yahweh (Isaiah 50:7-9). Clearly, this servant has been justly dubbed the "suffering servant" based not only on the fourth song (Isaiah 52:13–53:12), where his agony and sorrow are nearly unbearable, but on the whole trajectory of his role, beginning with the second song, intensifying in the third, and welling up out of the fourth. Moreover, as will become evident, the servant's ill-treatment and rejection derive not merely—and perhaps not even primarily—from his vocation among the nations but from his mission to the nation of Israel. As Israel had long defied Yahweh himself, spurning his messengers beginning with Moses, so Israel now resists and opposes his servant. Israel is, however, exhorted to follow the servant, and obedience to the servant becomes the test of fearing Yahweh (Isaiah 50:10-11), a message that already has renewed Israel as servants of the servant in view. The language echoes that of the expected new Moses promised in Deuteronomy—whom, Yahweh declared, Israel must heed (Deuteronomy 18:18-19).

Isaiah 52:13–53:12: The fourth servant song. Coming to the fourth song, we enter through the veil of divine mystery and onto hallowed ground—we behold the servant led like a lamb to the slaughter, despised by men and crushed by Yahweh. Here the eternal plans of divine wisdom—infinitely vast—for the redemption of Israel and the nations unfold, like so many rungs of a celestial ladder unrolling down onto the earth-and-dust of human history. While Isaiah 49–52 resounds with the anticipation of Israel's salvation, and Isaiah 54–55 comprises a divine invitation for people to participate in Yahweh's salvation, Isaiah 53 forms the bridge from anticipation to invitation. This servant song sets forth the *means* of redemption, the unexpected, divinely orchestrated way of humanity's restoration to God—namely atonement through the sacrificial suffering of the servant of Yahweh.

Structurally, the song has five stanzas, beginning and ending with the servant's exaltation. Enveloped by this frame his rejection is described, with the heart and center of the poem unfolding the significance of the servant's suffering (Isaiah 53:4-6). "My servant," Yahweh declares in the song's opening verse, "will be high and lifted up and very exalted," using terms of glory by way of contrast to the depths of lowliness his servant has endured. In the last stanza the servant's exaltation is presented as his seeing his offspring, obtaining life, and succeeding in his mission, with Yahweh's will prospering in his hand. After his suffering, death, and burial, he is raised up, living and victorious, and "will divide the spoil" with the strong. The servant, therefore, fulfills the hope prophesied of the Messiah earlier in Isaiah, when the people are said to rejoice as when they "divide the spoil," a joy ushered in with the kingdom of the child who is born for us, the son who is given for us (Isaiah 9:3, 6). What a son given *for us* means finds an awe-inspiring answer in this fourth song.

The servant's rejection and suffering is described with language both unrelentingly brutal and intensely sympathetic, describing him as despised and rejected, acquainted with grief, a man of sorrows who was smitten, stricken, afflicted, wounded, and bruised, who bore chastisement and was lacerated with stripes. Surprisingly, aside from the servant's rejection by people, the ultimate actor against the servant—the one who planned the smiting, afflicting, wounding, and striking—is none other than Yahweh God himself, for it was "the will of Yahweh to crush him, to make him grief-stricken" (Isaiah 53:10). Nevertheless, the servant was thoroughly rejected by many among Israel. Yahweh had judged Israel for its rebellion, hardening the people in their blindness and deafness (Isaiah 6:10) so that the servant's rejection is understood as an outworking of Israel's own spiritual blindness (Isaiah 53:1) but also as the ordained means for Israel's remedy. God's own judgment on Israel, having given them over to their willful blindness, led to the despising and abuse of the servant, which in turn opened up the channel of divine forgiveness for Israel. The severe hammer-blow of justice cleft open the fissure through which heavenly mercy would flow, for the servant is God's own sacrificial provision, the promised Lamb of God given as Abraham's seed, Israel.

Just here it is crucial to understand how the servant as new Israel relates to his servants as the renewed Israel. Aside from Yahweh's speeches in the frame, the fourth song is written from the later perspective of this renewed Israel. We hear, as it were, the confession of Israelites who had once despised and rejected this servant, assuming him damned of God. They have since discovered to their shock that this same one, from whom they had hidden their faces, has been exalted, vindicated, and set forth by Yahweh as his faithful servant, the One through whom Israel would be raised up—even the seed of Abraham through whom the nations would be restored finally to God. That is the incredible proclamation of the central stanza as it unfolds the significance of the servant's life (Isaiah 53:4-6). With the awe-filled understanding of hindsight, through the lens of the servant's divine vindication and exaltation, these Israelites turn their faces to look once more, fully on the sufferings of the despised One. Healed of their blindness by the servant's exaltation, they are enabled now to see clearly the wonders of Yahweh's profound wisdom and provision: it was, in fact, *our* sorrows that he bore, it was for *our* transgressions that he was wounded! Although we had all gone astray, each one of us to his own way, yet Yahweh has laid on him all our iniquity. The scorned servant was actually born for us; he was the Son given for us. No mere substitution, the servant dies for Israel to die with him; he is raised up for Israel to be raised up with him—herein lies the *crux* of Zion's transformation.

Ultimately, it is Israel's sacrificial system that illumines the theology of the servant's suffering, that provides the categories for Israel to understand that Yahweh has redeemed his people through the Servant, by making "his soul a guilt offering" (Isaiah 53:10). The guilt offering, like the purification offering, was a sacrifice given by Yahweh for cleansing Israel from sin, making divine forgiveness possible (see Leviticus 4–5; see also the discussion in chap. 7 above). Beyond purification from sin, the guilt offering also included the notion of making restitution for one's offence against God—it brought in more fully the idea of restoration along with purification. Signifying atonement and cleansing from sin, the purification and guilt offerings focused especially on the blood rite of the ritual—the collecting and sprinkling or smearing of blood. As Yahweh declared in Leviticus, he had given Israel blood on the altar as life for life (*nefesh*), or soul for soul, to make atonement for the sins of his people (Leviticus 17:11). In Isaiah 53, Yahweh, having laid on his blameless servant the iniquity of his people, crushes him, making "his soul [*nefesh*] a guilt offering" (Isaiah 53:10).

The servant suffers, then, as a vicarious substitute for the people of God, claiming for himself the depth and fullness of Israel's judgement—this is the new revelation that dawns on the "we" who speak from within Israel and who now form the servants of Yahweh, disciples of the servant. In seeing the significance of the servant's suffering, these Israelites come to discern themselves and their own sinfulness more deeply. Indeed, the Israelites say as much about themselves, by way of confession, as they do about the servant:

> However, it was our griefs that he bore and our sorrows he carried,
> Yet we ourselves had thought him struck, smitten by God, and afflicted.
> But he was pierced for our transgressions, he was crushed for
> our iniquities.
> Upon him was the chastisement for our peace, by his wounds, there is
> healing for us.
> All we like sheep had gone astray, we had each one turned to his own way,
> But Yahweh himself laid upon him the iniquity of all of us. (Isaiah 53:4-6)

Through the servant, through his suffering and exaltation, they have come to see their own blindness and to condemn their own self-justification. In the light of his suffering, they are enabled to see the darkness of their own condition and, with profound humility, confess their own guilt, completely absolving the servant as blameless: our griefs, our sorrows, our transgressions, our iniquities, our need of chastisement and healing, our waywardness from Yahweh's paths of righteousness—our iniquity. And in the darkness of their need, they see the light in his suffering, that by his chastisement they find peace, that by his wounds they find healing. The servant's suffering as a vicarious, sacrificial substitute is inescapable, for he "will bear their iniquities," he "carried the sin of many" (Isaiah 53:11, 12). His soul serving as a guilt offering, he was "led as a lamb to the slaughter" (Isaiah 53:7).

Here Yahweh's own lamb undergoes the *cultic exodus*. What was once said even of the scapegoat's role on the Day of Atonement—that it would "bear (*nasa'*) upon him all their iniquities" (Leviticus 16:22)—is echoed in the labor of the servant who "bore [*nasa'*] the sin of many" (Isaiah 53:12). The servant has been sent to deal with the ultimate problem of Israel and of all humanity, sin, which makes exile from God absolutely and unalterably necessary. Sin separates humanity from God and leads to death—to an eternal exile from the only fountain of life. True restoration to God, a definitive exodus, must raise humanity up from sin and death and not only cleanse but finally transform—sanctify and glorify—human beings into true children of God, a path that will be pioneered and opened by the servant for Israel's sake. The summation of the servant's labor, for it was a God-ordained mission, is that he made *intercession* for transgressors (Isaiah 53:12). For this reason, many have likened the servant to the figure of Moses, whose entire life was an act of intercession on behalf of Israel.

As those who have benefited from his redemption, the servants are given to penetrate to the profound reality that this servant's suffering and vindication are the very means of God whereby both Israel's restoration and Israel's vocation among the nations will be fulfilled. But the servant must indeed suffer and die and then be raised again—the suffering and the exaltation fill each other with significance and power, and it is only from his royal exaltation that the servant leads his people through the new exodus of his own suffering and glory. By the New Testament's illumination, we see that as a function of the servant's exalted glory, so emphasized in Isaiah, he is enabled to pour out the Spirit upon the peoples for whom he was made an atoning sacrifice, uniting them to his own death and resurrection. The servants of the servant who speak in the fourth song do so from the vantage point of their own spiritual resurrection. With the eyes of the old creation, as it were, they had only looked with loathing and scorn on the servant. But now, having their sight healed and enlightened by the outpoured Spirit, their eyes see him as their Lord and Savior, who with unsearchable love laid down his own life to ransom them from the grave and redeem them from death. All the streams of heavenly blessings converge through the one unifying sieve of this servant, the Messiah. He is the Rock through whom every divine promise pours out as a rushing river, transforming the wilderness of this age into the paradise of a new creation.

ISAIAH 56–66: THE SERVANTS OF THE SERVANT

In a book that traces the theological inversion of Zion—transformed from a wicked and rebellious people blaspheming the name of Yahweh among the nations to a holy and faithful people glorifying his name among the nations—the suffering and exaltation of the servant forms the pivot, the corkscrew turn at the center. The servant descends in divine judgment into suffering and death and then ascends in divine vindication, raised up and exalted into glory—and he does so in order to pull humanity and all creation through with him. After pouring out his soul unto death as a blameless and righteous one in whose mouth no deceit was found, and in utter submission to the will of God, the servant is raised up from the dead and exalted, and he makes many righteous, blessing them with lasting peace.

As his disciples, the righteous followers of the servant form the "servants of Yahweh" and take up his role—Israel's vocation—to be a light to the nations, drawing humanity to the blessings of Zion. Significantly and beautifully, *after* the suffering servant song of Isaiah 53, God's people, the followers of the servant, are called for the first time "the servants of Yahweh" (Isaiah 54:17). Based on the remnant principle, the nucleus of true-to-Yahweh Israelites form a renewed Israel that will also incorporate true-to-Yahweh Gentiles, the remnant of the nations also redeemed by the blood of the servant who was led as a lamb to slaughter. They too experience the outpouring of the Spirit. Remarkably, the opening chapter of Isaiah 56–66 identifies the servants of Yahweh not merely as the pious among Israel but as including foreigners who join themselves to Yahweh—neither the son of a foreigner nor the socially outcast eunuch has any reason to despair of divine mercy. Indeed, anyone who loves his name and serves him will be included under the designation "his servants" and will be brought in joy to Yahweh's holy mountain, for his house will be called a house of prayer for all peoples, and he will gather others beyond the outcasts of Israel (Isaiah 56:6-8).

In Isaiah 61, the servant proclaims that he has been anointed by the Spirit to be a herald of glad tidings, to bring healing and liberty, joy and beauty in place of mourning and ashes, for God's people who are "the planting of Yahweh," called "the servants of your God." Yahweh had promised, "I will pour my Spirit on your descendants, and my blessing on your offspring"

(Isaiah 44:3), and now that reality begins to unfold through the servant whose preaching yields spiritual offspring. The goal is a new community who are servants of Yahweh, a righteous offspring formed through the labors of the servant. These servants, then, are those who have benefited from the servant's mission: through his self-offering for their sins and guilt, they enjoy reconciliation with Yahweh God. The servants enjoy peace through the servant who bore the chastisement for their peace; they obtain righteousness through "my righteous servant," who, bearing their iniquities, makes many righteous (compare Isaiah 53:5, 11 with Isaiah 54:13, 17).

Although Yahweh is "the high and lofty One who dwells in eternity," although his "name is holy" and he dwells on high in holiness, yet he will condescend to dwell with the "crushed [*dakka'*] and lowly of spirit" for the sake of reviving the heart of "the crushed ones" (*dakka'*; Isaiah 57:15)—and this because the servant himself "was crushed [*dakka'*] for our iniquities," for "it pleased Yahweh to crush [*dakka'*] him" (Isaiah 53:5, 10). In these humble and faithful servants, the servant sees his promised offspring (Isaiah 53:10), and all who see them will finally acknowledge: "Surely they are the offspring whom Yahweh has blessed!" (Isaiah 61:9; see also Isaiah 65:23). The new Jerusalem belongs to the servant and his offspring. Indeed, the exaltation of Zion—her people established in holy joy and perfect peace, dwelling in the fiery glory of God—this is both the fruit and the function of the servant's exaltation and vindication as divinely promised in Isaiah 53. The servant is exalted for the sake of his servants. His transforming exodus from suffering and death to resurrection glory is the kernel of the second exodus for Israel and the nations.

Chapter Eleven

WHO IS THE SERVANT OF YAHWEH?

THE SERVANT OF YAHWEH, as observed in the last chapter, is Israel in some form. Israel was called to be Yahweh's servant among the nations, but on Israel's deeply tragic failure Yahweh designated a person, a true Israelite, to embody Israel, commissioning this servant both to restore his people and to fulfill Israel's vocation. The message of Isaiah, as we have seen, makes the servant's mission in history the utterly necessary accomplishment for the final exaltation of Zion as a new Eden, for the putting away of Israel's sins and defilement, and for the drawing of the nations to the light of Yahweh's face. No mere ideal figure, who is the servant of Yahweh?

THE SERVANT AS THE ESCHATOLOGICAL NEW MOSES

There was only one person in the history of Israel of whom much that is said about Isaiah's servant can be said, if by degree, and that was Moses.[1] Bearing all the characteristic features of the figure called the Messianic eschatological

[1]Claude Chavasse, "The Suffering Servant and Moses," *Church Quarterly Review* 165 (1964): 156; cf. Klaus Baltzer, "The Book of Isaiah," *The Harvard Theological Review* 103, no. 3 (2010): 267.

prophet-like-Moses in early Judaism, the suffering servant of Yahweh is the Moses of the new exodus.[2] Indeed, since the servant of Isaiah is the agent of the second exodus, one would anticipate finding parallels between him and Moses. Plainly, Moses is the preeminent servant—the one without equal—in the Old Testament. He is called *servant* some forty times, claims eighteen of the twenty-three occurrences of the phrase "servant of Yahweh," and all four occurrences of "servant of God" refer to him.[3] Others who are designated servants of Yahweh serve him in some way after the manner of Moses.

Perhaps the main point to consider when approaching the figure of the servant in Isaiah is that each of the servant songs is set within the context of the prophesied second exodus.[4] While exodus imagery pervades the whole book of Isaiah, this is especially so around the four servant songs. Surrounding the first song (Isaiah 42:1-4), we read that God will make the wilderness a pool of water (Isaiah 41:17-20) and that he will lead the blind on paths they had not known (Isaiah 42:13-16). The second song (Isaiah 49:1-6) is directly preceded by Yahweh's call to go forth from Babylon and recalls the original exodus when he led them through deserts and caused waters to gush from the split rock (Isaiah 48:20-21) and then is followed by further exodus imagery (Isaiah 49:8-12).

Similarly, the third song (Isaiah 50:4-9) is preceded by an allusion to the original exodus as Yahweh declares: "Is my hand severely shortened that it cannot redeem? Do I have no power to deliver? Look! By my rebuke I dry up the sea—I make the rivers a wilderness" (Isaiah 50:2). Isaiah 51, which forms the context for the fourth song, portrays the exodus theme through dragon-slaying imagery:

> Awake, awake, put on strength, O arm of Yahweh!
>   Awake, as in ancient days, the generations of old.
> Was it not you who slew Rahab, and pierced the dragon?
>   Was it not you who dried up the Sea, the waters of the Great Deep,

---

[2]Edward Schillebeeckx, *The Collected Works of Edward Schillebeeckx: Interim Report on the Books "Jesus" and "Christ,"* vol. 8 (New York: Bloomsbury Publishing, 2014), 56.

[3]G. P. Hugenberger, "The Servant of the Lord in the 'Servant Songs' of Isaiah: A Second Moses Figure," chap. 6 in *The Lord's Anointed: Interpretation of Old Testament Messianic Texts*, ed. P. E. Satterthwaite, R. S. Hess, and G. J. Wenham (Grand Rapids, MI: Baker, 1995), 26.

[4]On this point, see Chavasse, "Suffering Servant," 152-63. Hugenberger, "Servant of the Lord."

> Who made a path in the depths of the sea for the redeemed to pass over?
> So the ransomed of Yahweh will return and come to Zion with singing.
> (Isaiah 51:9-11)

Isaiah 52 continues the exodus imagery—and note here the parallel use of "Awake, awake" (Isaiah 52:1). There are references to when Yahweh's "people descended into Egypt at the first to dwell there" (Isaiah 52:4) and to the baring of his holy arm (Isaiah 52:10). The section culminates immediately before the fourth song with an urgent call to "Depart! Depart! . . . For Yahweh will go before you, and the God of Israel will be your rear guard" (Isaiah 52:11-12).

The literary context of the songs, setting forth the servant as Yahweh's agent for a second exodus, leads one to anticipate similarities between the servant and Moses. Here we will only mention two parallels. First, as Moses was a Spirit-endowed servant of Yahweh who had pleaded, "Oh that Yahweh would put his Spirit upon all his people!" (Numbers 11:29), so the servant is portrayed as abundantly endowed and empowered by Yahweh's Spirit (Isaiah 42:1), a forerunner—and even conduit—of the Spirit's outpouring upon the people of Israel (see Isaiah 32:15; 44:3; compare Numbers 11:16-17, 24-26). A second point of comparison with the servant, Moses endured with meekness Israel's rejection and rebellions. From the beginning he was rejected by his brothers—"Who made you prince and judge over us?!" (Exodus 2:14)—and was ever the subject of their bitter complaints (Exodus 15:24; 16:2; 17:2; Numbers 12:1; 16:3, 41; 20:3). Israel contended with Moses violently, questioned his authority repeatedly, desiring to replace him on various occasions (Exodus 14:11-12; 16:3; 17:3; 32:1; Numbers 14:4), and was even ready to stone him to death (Exodus 17:4). All such abuse he not only received meekly, often without opening his mouth in response, but, prostrating himself before Yahweh, he interceded on behalf of Israel, pleading for their forgiveness, calling for an easing of their punishment, petitioning for their daily needs, and even interposing his own life for their sake (Exodus 15:25; 17:4; 32:11-14, 30-32; 33:15-16; Numbers 11:2; 14:13-19; 21:7; cf. Hebrews 11:25-26). Small wonder, then, the Talmud, a central text of rabbinic Judaism, explains the life of Moses, including his travails as Israel's savior, by turning to the servant's description in Isaiah 53.[5]

---

[5]See *Sotah* 14a; *Berakhot* 32a.

"Moses," writes James Plastaras, "is presented as the type and prefigurement of the servant of the new exodus,"[6] and unsurprisingly so for it was Moses himself who had directed Israel's expectations to "a prophet like me" (Deut. 18:15; cf. Acts 7:35-37; 3:22, 26). The servant, as Christopher Seitz explains, "is the culmination of hopes associated with the prophet like Moses."[7]

THE SERVANT AS NEW DAVID, THE MESSIAH

Hopes for a new Moses are ultimately Messianic hopes—the anticipation of a new David. In the book of Revelation, the redeemed sing "the song of Moses, the servant of God, and the song of the Lamb" (Revelation 15:3), a description that identifies Moses as servant and connects him closely with the Messiah, the Lamb who leads the second exodus. A recurring motto by the ancient rabbis captures the thought well: "Like the first redeemer [Moses], so will the final redeemer [Messiah] be."[8] Understanding the servant as the long-awaited Messiah—the new David—has been the traditional view within both Judaism and Christianity, although the suffering described in Isaiah 53 is generally construed in Jewish literature to be endured by others, whether Israel or the Gentiles, rather than by the Messiah himself.

Necessarily, significant points of comparison between David and the servant, both within and outside of the context of Isaiah, will need to be bypassed. To offer one example alone, David is often presented as a righteous sufferer in the book of Psalms, which calls him the "servant of Yahweh" (Psalms 18:1; 36:1). In Psalm 89:3, Yahweh declares, "I have made a covenant with my chosen one, I have sworn to David my servant," using the same two terms together, "my servant" and "my chosen one," that Yahweh uses in Isaiah for the servant: "Behold my servant . . . my chosen one" (Isaiah 42:1). Psalm 22 in particular moves through the persecution of a David figure and, after his divine deliverance and vindication, into the renewed praises of Israel, led by this David, ushering in the knowledge of Yahweh among the families of the

[6]James Plastaras, *The God of the Exodus* (Milwaukee, WI: Bruce Publishing, 1966), 309.
[7]Christopher Seitz, "'You Are My Servant, You Are the Israel in Whom I Will Be Glorified': The Servant Songs and the Effect of Literary Context in Isaiah," *Calvin Theological Journal* 39 (2004): 133.
[8]Judah J. Slotki, trans., *The Midrash Rabbah: Numbers Rabbah I*, vol. V (London: Soncino Press, 1951), 413; (*Numbers Rabbah* 11:2); see also *Ruth Rabbah* 5:6; *Song of Songs Rabbah* 2:22; *Pesikta Rabbati* 15:10 (72b); *Ecclesiastes Rabbah* 1:9.

nations. As with Isaiah 53, Psalm 22 entails a newly gained perspective on the figure's suffering, the realization that Yahweh "has not despised or abhorred the affliction of the afflicted one," that he "has not hidden his face from him" (Psalm 22:24). Strikingly similar to the language in Isaiah, the suffering and vindication of David leads to the fear and praise of Yahweh by the "offspring" of Israel (Psalm 22:23, 30)—an offspring that "will serve" Yahweh as his generation of servants (Psalm 22:30). Both Psalm 22 and Isaiah's songs share the theological insight that Yahweh will accomplish his purposes—the restoration of Israel and the glory of his name among the nations—through the suffering and vindication of a righteous Israelite who embodies the nation. The shape of lament and thanksgiving found in the psalms, of affliction and deliverance, suffering and glory, death and resurrection, forms an *exodus pattern* engraved deeply on the soul of God's anointed one, the Messiah and shepherd of Israel. While we cannot here explore the thematic message of the Psalter, one recent study concluded that the Psalter presents David as a new Moses-like suffering servant and leader of a new exodus.[9]

For our purposes and within the book of Isaiah, the Messiah's most significant link with the servant is found in the anticipation that he will lead a second exodus. As a subdivision, Isaiah 1–12 ends with a transformed Zion as the result of an eschatological exodus led by a new David. Just as the Spirit is later said to rest upon and empower the servant for his mission (Isaiah 42:1), Yahweh's Spirit will rest on and empower the Messiah completely (Isaiah 11:1-2), enabling him to establish justice, conquer the wicked, and usher in Eden-like peace and harmony, filling creation with the renovating knowledge of Yahweh (Isaiah 11:3-10). A proclamation of the second exodus culminates the oracle of the Messiah: a "second time," Yahweh declares—there will be another deliverance "just as it was" in Israel's exodus out of Egypt (Isaiah 11:11-16). Many of the elements of the second exodus are found in this passage: the reunion of Israel and Judah, who will no longer strive against one another, and the drawing of the nations to Yahweh. Then, just as the first exodus was crowned by a song of praise to Yahweh for his deliverance (Exodus 15:1-19), so the second exodus is crowned by a song of praise to Yahweh in Isaiah 12.

[9]Adam D. Hensley, *Covenant Relationships and the Editing of the Hebrew Psalter*, LHBOTS 666 (New York: T&T Clark, 2018), 262.

The last verse of Isaiah 11 tells of an exodus "highway" for the remnant of God's people to traverse, just "as it was for Israel in the day he ascended out of the land of Egypt" (Isaiah 11:16), and the opening verse of Isaiah 12 begins by declaring: "On that day, you [singular] will say, 'I will praise you, O Yahweh!'" Given that the singer is an individual, it may be that the new David leads the redeemed, as Moses once did, in singing the praises of God. The song of Isaiah 12 echoes the original song of the exodus beautifully, including similar phrases like "Yah is my strength and song, and he has become my salvation" (Exodus 15:2; Isaiah 12:2), and "sing unto Yahweh" (Exodus 15:1, 21; Isaiah 12:5). Isaiah 1–12 culminates, then, with the Messiah's new exodus, capped by a doxology where Yahweh's redeemed people sing praise to his name—led by a new Moses-like David, the Messiah.

Later in Isaiah, the divine invitation to participate in the renewed creation that is the heritage of Yahweh's servants, based on the servant's accomplished mission, is elaborated in terms of the Davidic covenant: "I will make an everlasting covenant with you, even the sure (*'aman*) loving-kindnesses (*khesed*) of David" (Isaiah 55:3). The language is intriguingly close to the poignant question of Psalm 89: "O Lord, where are your former loving-kindnesses [*khesed*] which you swore to David in your surety [*'aman*]? Remember, O Lord, the reproach of your servants" (Psalm 89:49-50). Yahweh's covenant faithfulness to David, then, is for the good of God's people, "your servants." In becoming disciples of the servant, who is a royal son of David, these servants enjoy the benefits of Yahweh's faithful loving-kindness to him, participating in David's role among the nations.

The new David, *the Messiah*, will be a Moses-like suffering servant who takes up and fulfills the vocation of Israel among the nations, who makes atonement for his people and leads them in a wondrous eschatological exodus. The servant's vindication after his sacrificial suffering will inaugurate a glorious kingdom and everlasting reign, fulfilling prophecies for David's house and covenant (see Isaiah 9:7; cf. 2 Samuel 7).

THE SERVANT AS A MANIFESTATION OF YAHWEH

We have seen that the Moses figure of the second exodus is one and the same as the anticipated new David, the Messiah. Yet the book of Isaiah offers hints of still another layer of significance for the servant. In the fourth song, for example, the servant is identified with the "arm of Yahweh" (Isaiah 53:1; cf. 51:9), that is, with Yahweh's power and glory as revealed through the exodus. "I will redeem you with an outstretched arm and with mighty judgments" (Exodus 6:6), language ever after used of his self-revelation in the deliverance of Israel out of Egypt (see also Exodus 15:6; Deuteronomy 4:34; Psalm 136:11-12). The Israelites would thus later sing, "You crushed Rahab like a carcass, by your mighty arm you scattered your enemies" (Psalm 89:10). Identifying the servant with Yahweh's arm, therefore, gives cause for reflection.

Other language in Isaiah, also arresting, connects the servant with Yahweh. In each of the three major sections of the book, Yahweh is described in the loftiest of terms:

> I saw the Lord sitting upon a throne, high [*ram*] and exalted [*nissa'*]. (Isaiah 6:1)

> Now I will rise, says Yahweh, now I will lift myself high [*ram*]—now I will be exalted [*nissa'*]. (Isaiah 33:10)

> Thus says the high [*ram*] and exalted [*nissa'*] One, who dwells in eternity, and whose name is holy: In the high [*ram*] and holy place I dwell. (Isaiah 57:15)

Along with these declarations of Yahweh's majesty, there is also the definitive assertion: "I am Yahweh—that is my name—and my glory I will not give to another" (Isaiah 42:8; see also Isaiah 48:11). Twice Yahweh declares that while arrogant humanity will be brought low, Yahweh alone will be exalted (Isaiah 2:11, 17). Yet, after the servant's suffering and death endured in submission to Yahweh's will, the servant himself is exalted—and this with language otherwise reserved exclusively for the glory of Yahweh: the servant "will be high [*ram*] and lifted up [*nissa'*], and greatly elevated" (Isaiah 52:13). Especially within a book that proclaims and guards the glory of Yahweh, such an association with the Holy One of Israel—the Sovereign king whose glory fills the whole earth—is not only the highest acclamation conceivable but also a deeply profound wonder.

Such language in turn bids us to pause and think more deeply on the awaited Messiah's fourfold name, which undulates with divine attributes

(Isaiah 9:6). The new David is called "Wonder of a Counselor" (*pele' yôʿēṣ*). The term *wonder* or *wonderful* is usually reserved for Yahweh: "Is anything too wonderful for Yahweh?" (Genesis 18:14); "I will stretch out my hand, and smite Egypt with all my wonders" (Exodus 3:20); "Who is like you, O Yahweh, among the gods . . . doing wonders?" (Exodus 15:11); "Why do you ask my name, seeing it is wonderful?" (Judges 13:18). More than this, within Isaiah the same two words are used of Yahweh of hosts who is "wonderful in counsel" (*hiplî' ʿēṣāh*, Isaiah 28:29). In the same way, Isaiah 10:21 declares that the remnant of Jacob will return to "Mighty God" (*'el gibbor*)—and yet this, too, is one of the titles of the Messiah (Isaiah 9:6)!

It is possible to explain these titles as merely pointing to God and his deliverance, as with Joshua's name, which means "Yahweh saves." Yet while Joshua and other names like Elijah ("My God is Yahweh") make statements about God, the titles for this son of David resonate more with divine names like El Shaddai ("God Almighty"), which unfold his attributes. The prophetic mist, blurring the boundaries between Yahweh and his servant, gathers volume and depth in Isaiah 11 where the new David is presented not merely as a shoot springing forth from the stump of Jesse, that is, as a descendant of Jesse, but also as "the root" of Jesse—he is both in the line of David and the origin and wellspring of that line (Isaiah 11:1, 10). Through the haze and out of the pages and prophecies of Isaiah, the figure of the servant emerges as in some way a manifestation of Yahweh.

WHO IS THE SERVANT?

Along a desert path outside of Jerusalem in the first century, a high court official, a eunuch, was reading the scroll of Isaiah while sitting in his chariot on the homeward journey to Ethiopia (Acts 8:26-35). When he learned of the suffering servant, who was led like a lamb to the slaughter, he too wondered: "Of whom does the prophet speak?" The answer he received, from a messenger sent by the Holy Spirit, is the same answer proclaimed by all disciples of the servant, the name cherished by the servant's spiritual progeny. "Then Philip opened his mouth and, beginning with this Scripture, he preached to him Jesus" (Acts 8:35). Who is the servant? His name, his beautiful name, is Jesus. He is the one, the only one:

who committed no sin, nor was deceit found in his mouth;
who, when he was reviled, did not revile in return;
when he suffered, he did not threaten, but entrusted himself to him who judges justly;
who himself bore our sins in his body on the tree,
that we, dying to sins, would live to righteousness
—by whose stripes you have been healed.
For you were as sheep going astray,
but have now returned to the Shepherd and Guardian of your souls.
(1 Peter 2:22-25)

As son and servant, Jesus summed up the mission of Israel in his own person and, gathering a remnant around himself, he became the center and stem of a renewed Israel constituted by his resurrection from the dead.[10] Sung with one voice, the whole New Testament heralds Jesus as Isaiah's servant.

Stricken, smitten, and afflicted,
See Him dying on the tree!

'Tis the Christ by man rejected;
Yes, my soul, 'tis He, 'tis He!

'Tis the long-expected prophet,
David's Son, yet David's Lord;

By His Son, God now has spoken,
'Tis the true and faithful Word.[11]

[10]A. Michael Ramsey, *The Resurrection of Christ* (Centenary Press: 1945), 89-90.
[11]Thomas Kelly, "Stricken, Smitten and Afflicted," 1804.

PART 3

THE NEW EXODUS OF JESUS THE MESSIAH

Chapter Twelve

THE NEW EXODUS IN THE GOSPEL OF JOHN

THROUGH THE SPEECHES OF John the Baptizer, the Gospel of John introduces Jesus in a twofold manner, exposing the book's main biblical-theological arteries: Jesus is God's Passover Lamb of the New Exodus (John 1:29, 36), and the Son who will baptize God's people with the Spirit of the New Creation (John 1:30-34). The glorified Son will renew creation by pouring out the Spirit, but the Spirit must first be given the effectual basis for that renewal, culminating with the shed blood of Jesus: first the blood, and then the water (John 19:34). This twofold work of Jesus relates to his two estates, of humiliation and of exaltation: first, as sacrificial Lamb, to shed his blood unto death for the redemption of the world; then, as glorified Son, to pour out the Spirit of life for the recreation of the world. More deeply, his twofold work relates to Jesus' own participation, first, in the old creation, and then in the new creation: through the Incarnation, the Son entered into and became a part of the old creation, which must die with him; through the resurrection, the Son entered into and became a part of the new creation, which rises with him. The pattern of his life, first unto death and then unto indestructible life, not only unveils the paradigm of renewal for creation, but is the dynamic source and basis of that renewal.

In this chapter, we will look at Jesus' crucifixion as Passover Lamb of the new exodus, endeavoring to understand more deeply how his resurrection forms the new exodus. Then in chapter thirteen we will turn to Jesus' role as Giver of the Spirit of new creation. Since life with God in a new creation, reversing the exile out of Eden, is the goal of the new exodus, Jesus' gift may also be called the Spirit of the new exodus.

JESUS' CRUCIFIXION AS PASSOVER LAMB

One of the most dominant motifs in the New Testament, the new exodus serves as an organizing principle and explanatory key for many of its narratives and teachings. The new exodus also provides the theological lens for understanding the central historical event of the New Testament's message, the crucifixion and resurrection of Jesus. On the eve of his death, as the first three Gospels narrate, Jesus instituted the Eucharist as the Passover meal of the new exodus, bidding his disciples to eat his flesh and to drink of the cup, his blood of the new covenant, shed for the forgiveness of sins (Matthew 26:26-29; Mark 14:22-25; Luke 22:14-23). In partaking of his body and blood, the disciples were identifying with the firstborn Son—of God's household, the firstborn of a new humanity. The apostle Paul declared that "indeed, Christ our Passover was sacrificed for us" (1 Corinthians 5:7), and Peter wrote that God's people were redeemed "with the precious blood of Christ, as of a lamb without blemish and spot" (1 Peter 1:18-19). Of all the writings of the New Testament, however, it is in John's Gospel where one finds the deepest meditation on the new exodus, especially in its use of Passover theology: Jesus the Son of God is the true Passover Lamb.

As the theological context for Jesus' words and acts, the feast of Passover is mentioned in the Gospel of John more than in any other Gospel, some ten times (John 2:13, 23; 6:4; 11:55 twice; 12:1; 13:1; 18:28, 39; 19:14), and appears simply as "the feast" another nine times (John 2:23; 4:45 twice; John 5:1; 6:4; 11:56; 12:12, 20; 13:29). In this way, the narrative of Jesus is not only unified by the Passover theme but may be read as having something of a Passover storyline. Various allusions to the exodus also contribute to the Gospel's rich Passover symbolism.

By way of example, John 2–4 as a unit begins and ends with a glory-manifesting sign by Jesus in Cana (John 2:1, 11; 4:46, 54). The first sign takes place on "the third day," linked to Jesus' resurrection (see John 2:1, 19), and the concluding sign apparently also on a third day (John 4:43, 52). Jesus' first sign of turning water into wine at a wedding recalls Moses' opening sign of turning the Nile water into blood—and also anticipates the blood and water that will pour forth from Jesus' pierced side in his passion (John 19:34), the only other scene where his mother is present. The concluding sign at Cana involved the granting of life to the son of a royal man (*basilikos*) and perhaps forms a reversal of the death of Egypt's firstborn sons. (It may not be insignificant here that forms of *basileus* are used for Pharaoh throughout the Greek version of Exodus.) Jesus, in this second sign, ardently repeats: "Your son lives" (John 4:50, 53). The unit closes, then, in a way that adumbrates the sixth sign of raising Lazarus from the dead (John 11:1-53), itself a foreshadowing of Jesus' own death and resurrection, the seventh sign. In this new exodus, then, the former signs of death have been transformed into life-giving deeds, and, more than this, as Murray Rae writes, "are concerned unmistakably with the redemptive transformation of the old creation and the ushering in of the new."[1]

Also unique to John's Gospel are seven "I am" sayings, such as "I am the bread of life" and "I am the resurrection and the life" (John 6:35; 8:12; 10:7; 10:11; 11:25; 14:6; 15:1). Along with the more emphatic "I am" declarations by Jesus (see John 18:5-8), these sayings resonate with the burning bush revelation of Yahweh (Exodus 3:14; 6:2), also found in Isaiah's prophesied new exodus, where Yahweh declares that his people will know that "I am he" (Isaiah 41:4; 43:13; see also Deuteronomy 32:39). As the Son who reveals God the Father, Jesus prays, "I have manifested your name to those you have given me out of the world" (John 17:6, 11-12). Other exodus motifs abound: within the context of the Passover feast, Jesus declares that his flesh, given for the life of the world, must be eaten (John 6:53); and later portrays his mission as bringing judgment upon Satan, "the ruler of this world" (John 12:31; 14:30; 16:11), and

---

[1]Murray Rae, "The Testimony of Works in the Christology of John's Gospel," in *The Gospel of John and Christian Theology*, ed. Richard Bauckam and Carl Mosser (Grand Rapids, MI: Eerdmans, 2008), 304.

salvation as freedom from bondage to slavery, a redemption accomplished within God's household by the Son (John 8:31-38).

Jesus as Lamb of God. John's Gospel is structured with what may be called paschal bookends, passages that introduce Jesus and portray his death in terms of the Passover lamb. In the opening chapter of the Gospel, Jesus is presented for public ministry by John the Baptizer with the appellation "Lamb of God": "The next day John saw Jesus coming to him, and said, Look! The Lamb of God who takes away the sin of the world! . . . And looking at Jesus as he walked, he said, Look! The Lamb of God!" (John 1:29, 36). There have been many suggestions as to what "Lamb of God" means here, including the lamb of Isaac's sacrifice (Genesis 22), the Passover lamb (Exodus 12), the lambs of the daily whole burnt offerings (Exodus 29:38-46), as well as the suffering servant who is portrayed as a lamb led to the slaughter (Isaiah 53)—ideas that are far from being mutually exclusive. Together with the parallel ascription for Jesus, the "Son of God" (John 1:34), also called the "only" Son of the Father (John 1:14, 18; 3:16), the title "Lamb of God" unfolds a rich theological tapestry. The Greek word for "lamb" in John's Gospel is *amnos*, used in the Greek version of the Old Testament about a hundred times in connection with sacrificial lambs and is also used for the suffering servant of Isaiah 53.[2] Outside of the Gospel of John (John 1:29, 36), *amnos* occurs only two more times in the New Testament: once with reference to the suffering servant (Acts 8:32) and once with reference to our Passover redemption by the blood of Christ, "as of a lamb," who is identified shortly afterward with the suffering servant (1 Peter 1:19; 2:22-25). In John's Gospel as well, the Passover Lamb is inseparable from the righteous Davidic servant who must suffer for the sake of the many. Indeed, the Passover lamb, founded on the near sacrifice of Isaac and reimaged through the daily offering of lambs, was not only a cultic substitute for Israel but the prophetic solicitation of the righteous servant—notions that are linked profoundly by the theology of the firstborn son. Just as the Passover lamb represented Israel as God's son, so John's Gospel uses "Lamb of God" and "Son of God" to mark Jesus as the sacrificial firstborn—the sacrifice provided by God.

---

[2]Norman Hillyer, "'The Lamb' in the Apocalypse," *Evangelical Quarterly* 39 (1967): 228-29.

As God's Lamb, Jesus is Son of God in a special sense that goes beyond a mere human designation. John the Baptizer functions as Isaiah's voice "crying in the wilderness, prepare the way of Yahweh" (John 1:23; cf. Isaiah 40:3). His voice signals the advent of Yahweh. Thus the Baptizer declares that one "is coming [*erchomenos*] after me" who is greater, one who was before him (John 1:27). Both ascriptions of Jesus as the Lamb of God declare him to be such meaningfully while he is walking—in the first instance, as he is "coming" (*erchomenon*) to John (John 1:29) and is followed immediately by the testimony that this is whom the Baptizer meant by one who comes (*erchetai*) after him (John 1:30). This association flows into Martha's confession: "Yes, Lord, I believe you are the Christ, the Son of God, who is coming [*erchomenos*] into the world" (John 11:27). The Elijah-like Baptizer has prepared a way in the wilderness for the coming of Yahweh, the only Son of God. This Jesus, the *divine* Son of God, "is the Lamb of God, that is, the Lamb which God himself furnishes for sacrifice (Genesis 22:8)."[3] From a literary perspective, such an introductory labeling of Jesus means he continues to function as Lamb of God throughout the ensuing narrative, a point that becomes especially clear when we turn to the other Passover bookend that together with this one serves to frame the Gospel of John.

The Lamb of God sacrificed at Passover. The "Lamb of God" in the opening of the Gospel finds its counterpart in the crucifixion, when God's Lamb is sacrificed at Passover (John 19:31-37). The scene of Jesus' death brings together a number of details that mark the cross as the ultimate Passover sacrifice.[4] First, the chronology of the crucifixion is minutely detailed so as to manifest its correlation to Israel's paschal feast—Jesus was crucified as the Passover lambs were being slaughtered (John 18:28, 39; 19:14, 31, 42). That Jesus' body was not allowed to stay on the cross until the next morning has also been understood as paralleling the rule that the vestiges of the Passover meal were not to remain until the next day (John 19:31, 38; Exodus 12:19). More clearly, the presence of a hyssop branch at Jesus' crucifixion, noted by John's Gospel alone, forms a strong echo of the use of hyssop branches for

[3]T. F. Glasson, *Moses in the Fourth Gospel* (London: SCM Press, 1963), 100.
[4]See Stanley E. Porter, *Sacred Tradition in the New Testament: Tracing Old Testament Themes in the Gospels and Epistles* (Grand Rapids, MI: Baker Academic, 2016), 127-51.

spattering lamb's blood on the lintels and doorposts on the original night of Passover (John 19:29; Exodus 12:22)—the cross on which Jesus shed his blood has become the doorpost of the world.

Furthermore, the Fourth Gospel alone offers the detail that, since he was already dead, the soldiers did not need to break Jesus' legs (John 19:31-37). This took place, John instructs the reader directly, in order to fulfill the Passover legislation, that "not one of his bones will be broken" (John 19:36)—in the slaying, roasting, eating, and burning of the remains of the firstborn's substitutionary lamb, the animal's bones were not to be broken (Exodus 12:46; Numbers 9:12; cf. Psalm 34:20). To this scriptural quotation another is added in the next verse, which fuses once more the Passover lamb imagery with that of the Davidic righteous sufferer: "They will look upon him whom they pierced" (Zechariah 12:10). Along with the quotation from Psalm 22 (in John 19:24), this word from the prophet Zechariah points to the sufferings of the Messiah as servant, which leads to mourning for him as for a beloved son, a firstborn. In Zechariah this piercing is followed by the opening of a fountain for cleansing from sin (Zechariah 13:1), a reality that finds fulfillment in the blood and water that flow from Jesus' side (John 19:34).

Through the theological lens of Passover, in summary, John's Gospel presents Jesus as the Lamb of God who by his crucifixion takes away the sin of the world. Questions over the atoning value of the later *memorial* Passover celebrations aside, no other sacrifice is so deeply associated with redemption from death, along with the cleansing and sanctification of Israel, than the original Passover sacrifice of the exodus out of Egypt.[5] Just as the blood of the Passover lamb, substituted for Israel as God's firstborn son, had stayed the death-threat of God's judgment, redeeming Israel from bondage and ransoming them from the grave, so the crucifixion of Jesus, the perfect paschal sacrifice, delivers God's people from death and bondage to sin—fully and finally.

Jesus' death as departure. Even as the original Passover formed the rite of departure, so too Jesus' sacrifice opened the doorway of the new exodus—

[5]Paul M. Hoskins, "Deliverance from Death by the True Passover Lamb: A Significant Aspect of the Fulfillment of the Passover in the Gospel of John," *Journal of the Evangelical Theological Society* 52, no. 2 (2009): 285-99.

namely his resurrection from the grave. In the historical exodus of Israel, there had been no way out of Egypt apart from the sacrificed Passover lamb—its shed blood was the only means of departure. The resurrection life of the new exodus is likewise found only through the new Passover Lamb, through the crucifixion of Jesus.

Jesus' advent is presented in the Fourth Gospel in terms of descent and ascent: the Son descends from the bosom of the Father, who sent him through the incarnation, and then he returns to the house of the Father through his resurrection and ascension.[6] Within this scheme, Jesus begins his return to the Father through his paschal crucifixion, which is bound up with his resurrection and ascension as their basis. This, in John's Gospel, is the glory of Jesus' death. The cross is the means by which he departs, by which he accomplishes an exodus for himself out of this world and returns to his Father's heavenly abode. Jesus' crucifixion not only begins but is the means of his return to the Father. To be more precise, and in the words of Susan Humble, "Jesus' crucifixion was the means by which he departed from the world, and his resurrection, and particularly his ascension, was the means by which he returned to God," so that "the resurrection results in a condition where Jesus has departed from the world, though not yet returned/ascended to God."[7]

By analogy one may suggest that the Passover sacrifice was for the sake of Israel's departure out of Egypt (death to the old life), and the sea crossing symbolized Israel's rebirth (or resurrection), with the ascent to God's presence at Sinai corresponding to Jesus' ascension. Such an exodus is all the more wondrous when it is firmly grasped that Jesus was transformed through his crucifixion-death, burial, and resurrection, that is, his exodus was *out of* the old creation, under the judgment of God, and *into* the new creation of glory. In chapter seven, we observed a similar exodus pattern for the daily whole burnt offering: the lamb was offered to God through the altar fire and taken up to God's heavenly abode, having been *transformed* into a pleasing aroma.

---

[6]On Jesus' descent and ascent in John's Gospel, see Godfrey C. Nicholson, *Death as Departure: The Johannine Descent-Ascent Schema* (Chico, CA: Scholars Press, 1983); S. E. Humble, *A Divine Round Trip: The Literary and Christological Function of the Descent/Ascent Leitmotif in the Gospel of John* (Leuven, Belgium: Peeters, 2016).

[7]Humble, *Divine Round Trip*, 109-10.

For this function the whole burnt offering was more properly—and literally—called the "ascension offering." Just as the altar of the whole burnt offering was the means for Israel's cultic ascent into God's heavenly presence, so in John's Gospel the cross was the means for the Son's ascent, for his exodus return to the Father's side in heaven—and, through spiritual union with Jesus, for the ascent of all God's people.

The Spirit, who had descended as a dove and remained on Jesus (John 1:32), recalling the recreation of the earth through the floodwaters (Genesis 8:8-12; see also 1:2), is the one who makes the crucifixion, burial, and resurrection a cycle of transformation so that the Son becomes a new creation through this passage. The risen Jesus, before ascending to the Father, has indeed departed from the world, being part of the new creation. Jesus' crucifixion is thus his being lifted up, not merely literally on a wooden stake but in the sense of being the catalyst for his exaltation and return to God. The primary definition for the Greek term underlying *lifted up* (*hypsoō*) is "to exalt," and John's usage of it for Jesus often has the exaltation of the Son's return to the Father in view. Jesus must be lifted up, *exalted*, that whoever looks to him may have life (John 3:14; see also John 8:28; 12:32-34). Likely, in these "lifted up" sayings, we are meant to hear an echo of the suffering servant who would be "lifted up [*hypsoō* in the Greek version] and glorified exceedingly" (Isaiah 52:13).

JESUS' RESURRECTION AS THE NEW EXODUS

Jesus' crucifixion is inseparable, as we have seen, from his ascended lordship and exaltation; it is only through that lordship, through the exaltation of which the cross partakes—and inaugurates—that the Son will become the source of eternal life for his people, leading them in the new exodus out of the old creation. Through his crucifixion as Passover Lamb of God, Jesus departs this world. Astonishingly and wondrously, Jesus' resurrection out of the grave, anticipating his return to the Father, is the new exodus.

The new exodus as new creation. By his death, burial, and resurrection, Jesus departed the old creation and entered into—or better, both became and ushered in—a new creation. Allusions to the book of Genesis seal the Gospel's theology of creation which, culminating with Jesus' resurrection as a new creation, is inseparable from its exodus theme. The opening verse of John, "In the beginning," draws the reader to the creation account of Genesis, and when from the cross Jesus cries out, "It is finished" (John 19:30), he is declaring the end of the old creation—an end for which he has been working. His "it is finished" is followed immediately by a notice of the great Sabbath in the next verse (John 19:31). Significantly, the seventh-day Sabbath is not only the goal of the old creation but also the sign of the Mosaic covenant (Exodus 31:13), which was linked deeply with God's purposes for the old creation. When on the Sabbath Jesus' body rests in the grave, he has taken both the old creation and the Mosaic economy to their destined end.

The whole Gospel works toward this fulcrum, demonstrating that creation, along with the Jewish temple cult and feasts of Moses, awaited Sabbath-day fulfillment in the Son. Typically, this theology is built on through use of the numbers six and seven. The sixth day is not only the day on which humanity was created, but it represents creation *before* the spiritual consummation of the Sabbath. John's Gospel anticipates the true Sabbath-day fulfillment, with its object of communion with God—a goal for creation which, due to Adam's sin, was never consummated. Throughout the narratives, the number six symbolizes this lack of fulfillment, for both the old creation and the Sinai covenant inseparably bound up with it. There are six stone water jars (*hydriai*) for Jewish ritual purification (John 2:1-11), just as the Samaritan woman has known six men in her life (John 4:1-30). Completion comes through Jesus, in his transformation of water into wine as the true bridegroom of Israel, and as he—the seventh man—becomes the object of faith for the Samaritan woman, who leaves her water jar (*hydrian*) at the feet of Jesus, the seventh (and final) use of water jar in John's Gospel. Jesus met with the Samaritan woman at "about the sixth hour" (John 4:6) and told her of "an hour that is coming, and now is" (John 4:23), that is, the seventh hour. It is also at "about the sixth hour" when Jesus is presented before the crowds by Pilate with the words, "Look, your King!" (John 19:14)—paralleled with, "Look, the Man!" (John 19:5), indicating that Jesus stands as the last Adam.

Shy of the approaching Sabbath hour, Jesus understands his labors as six-day labors: he explains his life-giving acts of mercy—on the Sabbath no less—with, "My Father until now is working, and I am working" (John 5:17). Indeed, the Son had come *to finish* (*teleiōsō*) his Father's work, to bring it to completion, to its destined goal (John 4:34; see also 9:4; 17:4). The work of the Son, then, is the work of creation, the work of renewing creation. As with the water changed into wine (the first of six signs—with the seventh being Jesus' own passion and resurrection), Jesus' fulfillment brings about transformation, pointing to his work of bringing about a new creation, true Sabbath rest. The royal man's son is delivered from death and brought into life on "the seventh hour" (John 4:52), just as many of Jesus' acts of restoration are performed on the Sabbath Day (John 5:8-10).

This creation theology also accounts for John's use of both "first day" and "eighth day" as the context for Jesus' resurrection and his subsequent resurrection appearances (John 20:1, 19, 26). Through his own humanity, as a single seed that has died to yield the fruit of life for many, he has brought the destined judgment and end of the old creation, ushering in its transformation into a new creation. The first, or eighth, day signifies new creation, a symbolism built on the creation week and informing the theology of the circumcision rite (aligned with Abraham's new identity and name) performed on the eighth day (see Genesis 17:9-14) and which led the servants of Jesus to worship on the first day of the week (Acts 20:7). The first day is not the first day of the old creation but the eighth day—that is, the new first day *after* the final seventh day of the old creation. For this reason, Jesus cries out from the cross, "It is finished [*tetelestai*]!" Echoing the completion of creation, where we read that the heavens and earth were finished (*synetelesthēsan*) and that God on the seventh day finished (*synetelesen*) his work that he had done and then rested from all his work that he had done (Genesis 2:1-2), Jesus' declaration of completion is, again, followed immediately by the notice that the ensuing Sabbath was a "great Sabbath" (John 19:31)—Jesus' death has completed the old creation, ushering the cosmos into its destined Sabbath end and *renewal* in himself. This is no mere symbolism but the reality and cosmic significance of what the Son has experienced. His death and burial were the death and burial of the old creation *in himself*; his resurrection dawns the new creation in himself—he, body and soul, is the new man, the last Adam, a new-creation humanity treading on the ground of the as-yet old creation.

Jesus' resurrection as reversal of the expulsion out of Eden. Jesus' crucifixion, burial, and resurrection are situated more deeply within the Gospel's creation theology by allusions to the Garden of Eden. Before his crucifixion, we read that Jesus and his disciples "entered a garden" (John 18:1). The particular name *Gethsemane* supplied by Mark and Matthew is left out in John's Gospel, which offers *garden* as something of a type-scene echoing Eden. The garden locale is mentioned throughout this section of John's Gospel, as a contextual backdrop to the narrative (see John 18:1, 26; 19:41; 20:15), a usage all the more notable when we realize that the word "garden" (*kēpos*) is not used whatsoever in any of the other three Gospels, with one exception (in a parable in Luke 13:19). Later we discover that "in the place where he was crucified there was a garden, and in the garden a new tomb wherein no one had ever been laid" (John 19:41). Within this setting of the garden, John's Gospel adds the detail that Jesus was crucified "in the middle," that is, between two others (John 19:17-18). As Mary Coloe explains, the phrase "in the middle" (*meson*) "echoes the phrase in Genesis where God plants 'the tree of life in the middle of the garden' (Genesis 2:9). The evangelist depicts the Crucifixion with the iconography of Genesis 2: there is a garden, and in the middle of the garden is the cross, the tree of life."[8]

As a supporting argument, John uses similar Eden motifs in his Apocalypse, but in a more obvious manner. We read that a pure river of life flowed out from the throne of God and the Lamb, and "in the middle (*mesō*) . . . was the tree of life" (22:1-2). Grasping the Gospel's layered depths, early church fathers understood the opening of Jesus' side after his death in relation to Adam's "sleep of death" within the Garden, when Yahweh had opened his side to create the woman for his bride (Genesis 2:21-25)—Jesus' blood and water were poured out for the creation of the church as his bride.[9] Such Adam typology is evident already in the writings of the apostle Paul (Roman 5:12-21; 1 Corinthians 15:21-22; Ephesians 5:25-33) and, as we have observed, informs John's depiction of Jesus before his crucifixion when, robed in purple and wearing a crown of thorns, he is presented by Pilate with the words, "Look! The Man!"

[8]Mary L. Coloe, "Theological Reflections on Creation in the Gospel of John," *Pacifica* 24 (2011): 5.
[9]Jean Daniélou, *From Shadows to Reality: Studies in the Biblical Typology of the Fathers* (Westminster, MD: Newman, 1960), 48-56.

(John 19:5), alluding, as Jeannine Brown observes, "to that first man, Adam, in the first creation story."[10]

This creation theology also explains Jesus' use of "woman" (rather than their names) for the various women that appear throughout the Gospel of John, including his own mother. As the last Adam, he has come to redeem his bride: Jesus calls his mother "woman" within the context of a wedding in Cana (John 2:1-12); his encounter with the "woman" in Samaria takes place at a well, a familiar locale in Scripture for betrothal (John 4:1-26; see Genesis 24:10-28; 29:1-30; Exodus 2:15-22); and finally Jesus the "gardener" and a "woman" are found within a garden on the first day of the week (John 20:11-18). "He who has the bride," John the Baptizer had said, "is the bridegroom" (John 3:29)—indeed. That Jesus' mother is called "woman" (John 2:4; 19:26) and designated "mother" (John 2:1; 19:25) may allude to the names given to the first woman: "She shall be called Woman" (Genesis 2:23); "The man called his wife's name Eve because she was the mother of all the living" (Genesis 3:20).[11] In any case, the mother of Jesus, the Samaritan woman, and Mary Magdalene, and possibly the woman caught in adultery as well (8:2-11), each being called "woman" by Jesus, likely serve to recall Eve as archetypes—theological portraits—of the church, the bride of Adam, the only Son of God.[12] Jesus even compares his disciples' sorrow at his death to *the* woman (*hē gynē*) in birth pangs, who finally rejoices with the birth of a "man" (*anthrōpos*, John 16:21), an image strikingly similar to that found in John's Apocalypse where the Eve-like "woman" who represents the church cries with labor pangs and gives birth to a child, the risen Jesus, who ascends to God and his throne (Revelation 12:1-6). Then in glory the church is described "as a Bride prepared" for the marriage and wedding supper of the Lamb, a "Bride adorned for her husband" (Revelation 19:7-9; 21:2). Jesus is the last Adam; the church is both the children of God and the last Adam's bride, the new Eve.[13] Since the true exodus forms a reversal of the exile from Eden and a passage from the old

[10]Jeannine K. Brown, "Creation's Renewal in the Gospel of John," *Catholic Biblical Quarterly* 72 (2010): 281; several of our own observations are also made by Brown in her fine essay.

[11]Coloe, "Creation in the Gospel of John," 5; see also Addison Hodges Hart, *The Woman, the Hour, and the Garden: A Study of Imagery in the Gospel of John* (Grand Rapids, MI: Eerdmans, 2016), 77-90.

[12]Similarly, see Hart, *The Woman, the Hour, and the Garden*.

[13]Hart, *The Woman, the Hour, and the Garden*, also acknowledges these connections.

creation to the new, this creation imagery is especially relevant to the Gospel's message about Jesus' new exodus.

The Eden imagery is developed even more richly for Jesus' resurrection and appearances to his disciples (John 20). Early on the first day of the week, Mary Magdalene, having approached the garden tomb, sees Jesus standing before her and supposes him to be "the gardener" (John 20:15), an allusion to Adam within the Garden of Eden (Genesis 2:8-9; 9:20)—and he calls her "woman" (John 20: 15). Then, for the first and only time, Jesus calls a woman by name, "Mary!" (John 20:16). As the Greek form of Miriam, the name of Moses' sister who rejoiced over the original exodus out of Egypt (Exodus 15:20-21), the use of her name at just this point—the new exodus of Jesus' resurrection—may be part of the Gospel's exodus motif. Later in the same chapter, Jesus breathes the Spirit on his disciples (John 20:21-22) just as Yahweh had once breathed the breath of life into the nostrils of the first human in the Eden narrative (Genesis 2:7).

A garden, a tree in the middle, two angelic beings, a gardener, and a woman—these aspects of the Eden narrative are equally present in John's telling of Jesus' passion and resurrection.[14] Perhaps most telling, even the tomb is located "within the garden," and described as "new, wherein no one had ever been laid" (John 19:41)—the tomb, in other words, is not associated with death at all but with newness and life, ultimately with the indestructible resurrection life of the Lord Jesus in the garden. The Garden of Eden allusions with which John's Gospel concludes enable readers to grasp the theological reality of Jesus' crucifixion death, burial, resurrection, and ascension as the new exodus out of the old creation and into the new creation, out of this world and into the heavenly reality of the Father's presence—all from the angle of the Bible's main plotline: *an exodus out of the primal exile and into paradise with God.*

In chapter seven we observed the same plotline in how the Day of Atonement ritual portrayed the high priest as an Adam figure who once a year reentered the cultic Garden of Eden (the holy of holies) through the cherubim-laden veil with the blood of atonement. One may discern a similar

[14]Coloe, "Creation in the Gospel of John," 5, notes the same parallels, except for the angels.

theological portrait in the Fourth Gospel: an allusion to the atonement lid of the holy of holies within John's presentation of the garden tomb.[15] Mary looks within the tomb and sees two angels sitting "one at the head and one at the feet" of where Jesus had lain (John 20:12), perhaps symbolizing the two cherubim positioned at the two ends of the atonement lid, with "one cherub at one end and one cherub at the other end" (Exodus 25:18-19). Outside the tabernacle texts, the only other place where cherubim are found in the Pentateuch is at the entrance to the Garden of Eden (Genesis 3:24). Because the cherubim on the tabernacle's veil and on the atonement lid of the ark are themselves allusions to Eden's gateway, it seems probable that John's Gospel also has both in mind: Jesus' resurrection from the grave fulfills the Day of Atonement, for Jesus as a new Adam has reentered the garden of paradise. It is perhaps not too much to say, then, that for John's Gospel the taking away of the stone from the tomb forms the theological parallel to the rending of the temple veil in the other Gospels.

In sum, through allusions to Eden the Gospel of John presents the reality of Jesus' new exodus as a reversal of humanity's exile and an entry into the new creation. The first day of the week signifies the theological reality of the new creation and finds a man and a woman (back) inside a garden. As with the historical exodus of Israel out of Egypt, the new exodus is the deliverance of God's firstborn Son from death. And even as the sea crossing was narrated with creation imagery to convey that Israel had become a new people (Exodus 14), John's Gospel uses creation imagery to convey the reality of the new creation ushered in with Jesus' resurrection as a new humanity.

Jesus, we have seen, has himself entered into and become a new creation, but now how is it that anyone else can be made partakers of the new creation with him? How can we experience the new exodus as well? The answer relates to Jesus' gift of the Spirit, the topic of our next chapter.

[15]See Raymond E. Brown, *The Gospel According to John XIII-XXI*, vol. 2 (Garden City, NY: Anchor Bible, 1970), 989; more recently, Nicholas P. Lunn, "Jesus, the Ark, and the Day of Atonement: Intertextual Echoes in John 19:38–20:18," *Journal of the Evangelical Theological Society* 52, no. 4 (2009): 731-46.

Chapter Thirteen

THE SPIRIT OF THE NEW EXODUS

IN MANY WAYS JOHN 20:22 CONVEYS the message of John's Gospel within a single gesture in time: Jesus "breathed on them and said to them, 'Receive the Holy Spirit.'" Jesus himself, as we will explore in this chapter, has become the wellspring of the Spirit for his people and for all creation. Through his gift of the Spirit, the Son renews humanity and creation and brings his people into his Father's household, leading them in a new exodus.

JESUS POURS OUT THE SPIRIT OF NEW CREATION

The Eden imagery that pervades the account of Jesus' resurrection in John's Gospel points to the theological realities of the hoped-for new exodus of Isaiah—that Yahweh would make Zion's "wilderness like Eden, and her desert like the garden of Yahweh" (Isaiah 51:3). In Isaiah also, it is the outpouring of the Spirit that *effects* Zion's transformation: when "the Spirit is poured out upon us from on high," then "the wilderness will become a fruitful field" (Isaiah 32:15). As we will see, Isaiah's theology is embedded deeply within the Gospel of John. After the prologue, John's Gospel begins with the wilderness and, as we have seen, ends with the Garden of Eden. The key to the transformation from wilderness to paradise may be traced throughout John's narrative, as with the message of Isaiah, as the gift of the Spirit, regularly portrayed in Scripture with water imagery. Hope begins within the wilderness, as an Elijah-like voice proclaims Jesus to be the coming one who will baptize with the Holy Spirit (John 1:32-33), for it is this pouring out of the Spirit of life that will transform Zion's wilderness into Eden.

The Gospel of John, written from the perspective of the Son's exalted glory, manifests him as the giver of the Spirit. The one on whom the Spirit descends and remains, John the Baptizer confessed, this is the one who will baptize with the Spirit—this is the Son of God (John 1:33-34). Whether Jesus is instructing Nicodemus that he must be born from above, of water and the Spirit (John 3:3-5), or urging the Samaritan woman to ask him for the gift of living water, the Spirit, that springs up into eternal life (John 4:10-14), teaching his disciples that it is the Spirit who gives life (John 6:63), or at the feast of Tabernacles inviting all who thirst to come to him and drink for from within him the rivers of living water will flow (John 7:37-39), he is everywhere set forth in John's Gospel as the one who at his exaltation gives the Spirit.

The feast of Tabernacles in Jerusalem centered on a water-pouring ritual whereby priests, having drawn water from the pool of Siloam, would pour out those waters upon the altar. As a prayer for abundant rainfall to make Zion fertile and fruitful, the ritual symbolized the outpouring of the Spirit upon God's people. The imagery, once more, derived from Isaiah:

> For I will pour out water on the thirsty land, and streams on the dry ground;
> I will pour out my Spirit upon your offspring, and my blessing on your descendants. (Isaiah 44:3)

Noting the parallelism between water and Spirit, and between the *thirsty* land and God's people, the later divine invitation of Isaiah, in terms of thirst, is clarified: "Come, everyone who thirsts, come to the waters!" (Isaiah 55:1). Israel's liturgy, the psalms, also uses the imagery of dry land for a person's spiritual thirst for God—"my soul thirsts for you, my flesh yearns for you, in a dry and thirsty land where there is no water" (Psalm 63:1), "my soul is as a thirsty land for you" (Psalm 143:6)—a motif that uncovers the deep significance of the feast of Tabernacles for Israel.

Other prophets also proclaimed the blessings of the outpoured Spirit as life-yielding waters, flowing into the symbolism of the feast. "On that day," declared Zechariah, "living waters will flow out from Jerusalem" (Zechariah 14:8). So, too, Joel announced "a fount will come forth from the house of Yahweh" (Joel 3:18), and Ezekiel described waters issuing forth from the house of Yahweh, eastward, and wherever the river flows, it brings life and healing to creation (Ezekiel 47; note also Psalms 36:8; 46:4; 65:9). Indeed, the imagery is traced back, ultimately, to the Garden of Eden, for a river went forth out of Eden to water the garden, and then, as four branches, to give life and fruitfulness to the rest of the land (Genesis 2:10-14; cf. 13:10). These images all signal the life-giving nature of the outpoured Spirit of Yahweh. This was the hope integral to the feast of Tabernacles, underscoring Jesus' action on the last day of this feast, as he stood up and cried out, inviting all who *thirst* to come to him and drink, for from within him—out of the Messiah—the rivers of living water would flow.

Throughout the narrative the reader almost gets the impression of Jesus being so Spirit-indwelled that to puncture him is to release the Spirit from within. Yet the context of Jesus' atoning death, his crucifixion as sacrifice, is utterly fundamental for the theology of the Fourth Gospel, which presents Jesus "as divine Servant and Lord, possessor and giver of the Spirit, who takes away the world's sin not simply by giving the Spirit but by doing so through his expiatory and sacrificial death (as Suffering Servant and Paschal lamb)."[1] Even before the blood and water flowed from his pierced side, Jesus had said, "It is finished," and then bowed his head and "gave up his spirit" (John 19:30), better translated as "delivered over the Spirit." The Greek term *paredōkev* ("deliver over") is used elsewhere in the New Testament for a centurion who delivered over prisoners to the captain of the guard (Acts 28:17) and is not attested in Greek literature as a euphemism for death. Moreover, the text does not say he delivered over "his" spirit but "the" spirit (*to pneuma*), leading us to understand the Spirit of God. Probably intended as a *double entendre,* we are dealing with a false choice—although the Gospel always leads from the surface-level reading to its theological interpretation, to the spiritual

[1]Thomas Barrosse, "The Seven Days of the New Creation in St. John's Gospel," *Catholic Biblical Quarterly* 21 (1959): 509.

reality. Just as earlier he had thirsted and then promised the Samaritan woman the life-giving water of the Spirit, so from the cross he cries, "I thirst!" and then delivers over the Spirit (John 19:28).

When his side is pierced so that blood and water flowed, we are given a vision of Zechariah's declaration that Yahweh would "pour upon the house of David and on the inhabitants of Jerusalem the Spirit of grace and mercies—then they will look on me whom they have pierced," for the crucifixion is "that day" when "a fountain will be opened" to cleanse from sin, a fountain described as "living waters" flowing from Jerusalem (Zechariah 12:10; 13:1; 14:8). The blood and water flowing from Jesus' pierced side are the same living waters, both cleansing and healing, that transform the wilderness into the garden of Yahweh, the old creation into the new, which Ezekiel saw flowing from the side of the new temple (Ezekiel 47)—identified with Jesus' own body in the Gospel (John 1:14; 2:21). The living waters that renew creation, the rivers of life that transform the barren wilderness of Zion into the garden of Yahweh, derive from the opened side of the Son—from his sacrificial blood and his sending forth of the Spirit as living water.

Through his finished old-creation work, culminating with his death on the cross as the Passover Lamb of God, Jesus "delivers the Spirit" of the new creation to his people. The Gospel's description of Jesus' death points to this theological reality and functions as a symbolic gesture to be complemented by another at the Son's resurrection. We are thus brought to the crowning verse of the Gospel of John, a verse that may well be the culmination and climax of the Gospel's narrative and theology, when Jesus breathed on his disciples and said, "Receive the Holy Spirit" (John 20:22). The word "breathed" (*enephysēse*) is used only twice in the Greek translation of the Old Testament. First, alluding to when Yahweh breathed (*enephysēsen*) into the nostrils of Adam so that he became a "living soul" (Genesis 2:7), the glorified Son is presented as the author of the new creation—a new humanity. The "In the beginning" of the old creation now gives way to this "Receive the Spirit" of the new.

The second occasion the term is used in the Greek Scriptures is when the prophet Ezekiel himself echoes Genesis 2:7 in describing the resurrection of Israel out of exile: "breathe (*emphysēson*) upon these slain, that they may live!" (Ezekiel 37:9). The spiritual condition of Israel in exile had been likened to that of a graveyard, for God's people had been spiritually dead for a long time—an estate of utter hopelessness, dry bones. But Yahweh told Israel, "I will put my Spirit within you, and you will live!" (Ezekiel 37:14)—yes, he promised, "This land that is desolate will be as the garden of Eden" (Ezekiel 36:35). And so we read: "O Spirit, *breathe* on these slain that they may live! . . . And breath came into them, and they lived and stood on their feet, an exceedingly vast multitude" (Ezekiel 37:9-10). The restoration of God's people would be life from the dead—by the Spirit. Jesus' breathing on his Jewish disciples, then, is also an act of restoration. In breathing out the Spirit, Jesus is raising old creation Israel up from the dead so that here stands not only the new humanity, but the renewed Israel of God—the new creation Israel. How clearly, from this vantage point, does one see that the glorified Son is the source of the church's life. The resurrected Son, the new creation Adam within the sphere of the old creation, is like the rock in the wilderness out of which the waters of life flow for the people of God (Exodus 17:6; Numbers 20:11; Psalms 78:16; 105:41; 1 Corinthians 10:4). In this way John's Gospel builds the transformation from wilderness to garden by use of an exodus motif: Jesus supplies water in the wilderness—he, the Rock, pours out the Holy Spirit.

In presenting Jesus' act of breathing out the Spirit, the narrative comes full circle to where the prologue began, unveiling the depths of who the Son is, for who is able to send—*to breathe out*—the Spirit? It was Yahweh who had breathed into the nostrils of Adam, giving him life. Indeed, "By the word of Yahweh the heavens were made, and all the host of them by the breath of *his* mouth" (Ps. 33:6), "You [Yahweh] send forth your Spirit, they are created, and you renew the face of the ground" (Ps. 104:30), "The Spirit of God has made me, and the breath of *Shaddai* gives me life" (Job 33:4). More than the Adam of the new creation or the Moses of the new exodus or the Messiah of David's new kingdom, the resurrected Jesus is God the Son pouring out the waters of new creation life upon the old creation people of God, this through his own lips—waters that transform the wilderness into the garden of Yahweh. What the prologue had asserted concerning the Son and the old creation, that "all things were made through him" (John 1:3), here *we see*—we see all things being remade through him. Higher still, we see the Godhead, the Fountain of Life, pouring forth the waters of life.

The gesture is profound: the Spirit, although a distinct Person of the Godhead, is intimately connected with the Son. The Spirit is not simply an object given from the Son's hand but breathed out from within him. In other words, the Spirit is a gift only the Son, who is one with the Father, gives. The Holy Spirit, who rested on and remained with the Son, is given by the Father through the conduit of the Son. The Spirit is the one whom God "poured out upon us richly *through* Jesus Christ our Savior" (Titus 3:6). In this sense, the Spirit is the Spirit of Christ, the Spirit who has been stamped and sealed with the Son, but also as the One who brings the Son, and with him the Father, to dwell within believers. All intellect must fall, at last, before this wondrous mystery, surrendered unto praise: The Son is sent by the Father, and the Spirit is sent by the Son, who is one with the Father, and then the Son is brought by the Spirit, and the Father is brought with the Son. Thus, the Father sends the Son who sends the Spirit, and the Spirit brings the Son who brings the Father—through the One to the Three, and through the Three to the One!

Here, in the context of his sending the disciples on mission, the Son, as the Sent One who is in union with the Father, sends the Spirit. In presenting this marvelously iconic act, John's Gospel draws us toward the deep mystery of the inner and eternal life of the triune God, revealing a glimpse of infinite glory in time, even the eternal processions of the Son and the Spirit from the Father. Incredibly, these processions flow into mission and into the sending of God's people who have been brought into union with God. The new exodus must be defined within this marvel of the workings of the triune God. The outpoured Spirit who unites God's people to the Son, ushers them into a new household, making them partakers of divine fellowship—casting them upon the infinite ocean of eternal, reciprocal love that is the blessed, holy Trinity. Well does the church sing:

> For your gift of God the Spirit, pow'r to make our lives anew,
> pledge of life and hope of glory, Savior, we would worship you.
> Crowning gift of resurrection sent from your ascended throne,
> fullness of the very Godhead, come to make your life our own.[2]

Jesus, then, not only experienced the transformation from the old to a new creation by the Spirit, but the new creation is itself his own work and

---

[2]Margaret Clarkson, "For Your Gift of God the Spirit,"

accomplishment through the Spirit. As the divine *Logos*, the Son is the one through whom all the former things had been made—without him not one part of the old creation was made (John 1:3). By his sacrifice and consequent sending forth of the Spirit, inseparable realities, Jesus is the restorer of creation, the one through whom all things will be made new. And this new creation, we begin to understand more deeply, refers to a new Spirit-pervaded reality of communion and fellowship with God.

THE SPIRIT OF GOD'S HOUSEHOLD

Another image, as pervasive as that of creation, is used by John's Gospel to convey the wonders of the Spirit's role in the new exodus: that of the household of God. The Gospel begins with a bold statement, that through the Son many will "become children of God," being born "not of blood, nor of the will of the flesh, nor of the will of man, but of God" (John 1:12-13), and this birth into the household of God forms a major unifying theme of the book. Such a prospect requires that people be born "from above" by the Spirit, for just as the Son was sent from heaven, so all who would belong to God's house must be from heaven as well (John 3:1-21; see also John 17:14-19; 20:21-22). While Nicodemus misunderstood the words of Jesus as meaning merely "born again," that is, a second time, Jesus means "born from above [*anōthen*]," just as Jesus himself is designated the one "who comes from above [*anōthen*]" (John 3:31; see also 8:23). The Son, who reveals God as his own Father, is able to set people free from bondage to sin and death and make of them children in God's house (John 8:13-59). For he is the one who at his exaltation will send the Spirit to his own, uniting them to himself, the Son, and thereby bringing them into his Father's house as children (John 14:1-3).

Just as Moses had been sent by God from Mount Sinai only to return to him with thousands of Israelites, so John's Gospel presents the Son as the one sent by God only to return to his Father's house, bringing many brothers and sisters, sons and daughters of his Father, back with him in a new exodus. While the first half of the Gospel of John focuses on his descent from heaven as sent by the Father (John 1–12), in the second half the Son's return to the Father by way of ascent is stressed (John 13–21). Although both where Jesus comes from and where he is going are concerns found throughout the Gospel, there is a notable shift in the second half to where Jesus is going (see, for example, John 13:1, 33, 36; 14:3-5, 28; 16:5, etc.). The disciples, having finally embraced where Jesus is from—that he was sent by God from heaven—then begin struggling through a new lesson, namely where Jesus is going—that he needs to ascend, returning to the Father. To Jesus' declaration that he had come forth from the Father into the world and must soon depart the world and return to the Father, the disciples respond only with "we believe you came forth from God" (John 16:28, 30), omitting any reference to his return. Yet, as the new exodus, the resurrection has his return to the Father as the crucial goal.

John 13 opens with a reference to Jesus' third and final Passover, the one during which he would make his exodus, and describes that exodus in terms of his return to the Father: "Now before the feast of Passover, as Jesus knew that his hour had come that he should depart out of this world unto the Father, having loved his own who were in the world, he loved them to the end" (John 13:1). Jesus' exodus is not only out of the old creation and into the new but out of this world and into heaven, an ascent back into his Father's house. He will go on to comfort his disciples saying that he goes to prepare a place for them in his Father's house and that he would return to bring them there (John 14:1-4). His exodus, in other words, is for the sake of his disciples' exodus, to bring them back with him into the Father's house—through the gift of the Spirit.

Profoundly, the Son's bringing his people into the Father's house signifies spiritual union. Even though he has descended from the Father's bosom, nevertheless Jesus remains in union with his heavenly Father while on earth. Precisely this pattern he will replicate with his followers: while God's people remain on earth, they will nevertheless be in union with the Son through the Spirit, and through union with the Son they will also be in union with the Father—a blessed household (John 14; 17:20-26). In this way, the Father's house may be understood as the Father's bosom, or simply as heaven, the place of communion and fellowship with the Godhead. Anticipating this reality, Jesus washes his disciples' feet, a gesture of hospitality, welcoming them to the Father's house, and then he refers to them for the first time as "little children" (John 13:33), a designation John will use frequently in his first epistle with reference to the church (1 John 2:1, 12, 28; 3:7, 18; 4:4; 5:21). Jesus thereby signals the welcome of his followers into the household of God, an entry that requires his own crucifixion as the Son, the firstborn, the Passover Lamb of God whose blood must atone for the household.

From the cross Jesus forms the household: turning his mother's gaze on his beloved disciple, he says, "Woman, look! Your son!" And to the disciple, he says, "Look! Your mother!" From that point on, we read, the disciple took her unto his own (John 19:26-27). It was for this act of creating a new household, announced already at the beginning of the Gospel, for which the Son had entered the world. "After this," the Gospel states, Jesus knew "that all things were now accomplished" (John 19:28). Here at the cross God's household is born, the new family stands with Jesus, like the tree of life "in the middle." Jesus' later appearances to this household on the first (or eighth) day will be portrayed similarly with Jesus standing "in the middle" (*meson*) of them (John 20:19, 26, the only other uses of this term in John's Gospel). "Go to my brothers," he tells Mary, saying, "I am ascending to my Father and to your Father" (John 20:17). Believers have become both the house and household of God, brothers and sisters of the Son, with God as their Father. "Look, what kind of love the Father has given us," John elsewhere exclaims, "that we should be called the children of God!" (1 John 3:1).

THE SPIRIT OF ISRAEL'S NEW EXODUS

The wonders of Jesus' ascent into the Father's house are profound—he bears our own humanity as the last Adam into paradise. This is only well and good for him alone, however, apart from our union with the Son by the Spirit. The household must be identified with the firstborn, with the Passover Lamb of God. This, to be sure, is the whole point of the Fourth Gospel—not merely to tell the story of Jesus' own experience but to proclaim Israel's new exodus, how by believing in Jesus people become children of God and a new creation. Because Israel is raised up only through union with the Son by the Spirit, Jesus' teaching on the Spirit intensifies during his final Passover (John 14–16).

Why is the Spirit so indispensable? The Spirit is necessary because it is only through the doorway of Jesus' *own* crucifixion and resurrection that one is enabled to experience the transforming exodus out of the old creation and into the new, out of spiritual bondage and death and into the household of the living God. Jesus descended—sent by the Father—and then ascended through his paschal crucifixion, burial, and resurrection, *in order* to open this passageway, this new exodus, for his people. The point is not simply that Jesus had to die and be resurrected in order to open a door for us; rather, *his* crucifixion and resurrection form the only exodus out of the old creation and into the new—Jesus himself is the doorway, his torn flesh and shed blood the new and living way (Hebrews 10:20). The question is, how may Jesus' exodus become mine, my own experience? To clarify, the question is not how can Jesus' exodus count for me, but how can I experience his death and resurrection? He is the Son born for us (Isaiah 9:6)—the death he dies, he died for us, and his resurrection life is life for us. To be raised up, Israel must be spiritually united to Jesus' own death and resurrection, which means the person and work of the Spirit, uniting us to the Son, are essential.

Because we need to be united to Jesus by the Spirit, because we need to experience *his* exodus, then clearly without the death and bodily resurrection of Jesus Christ there would be no hope of eternal life in a new creation for anyone else. Not only the spiritual rebirth as a new creation but the bodily resurrection to glory of all God's people on the last day is only possible through the narrow entry of Jesus' own crucifixion and resurrection—this is the *only* Spirit-wrought passage, the only doorway of departure from the old creation into the new. The unrepentant dead, "the unjust" (Acts 24:15), will certainly be raised up but in shame and only for the sake of judgment. Scripture gives no reason for considering their raised bodies as anything more than grotesque vessels fit to endure an eternal death of judgment. But Jesus' crucifixion was itself an endurance of divine judgment as the sacrificial, wrath-bearing Lamb of God. He links the hour of his lifting up with "the judgment of this world" and the casting out of the "ruler of this world" (John 12:31-32)—in being slain, the Lamb has slayed the dragon. Jesus endured and absorbed the thunderstorm of judgment looming over the old creation and sinful humanity, and the Spirit, through whom Jesus offered himself up to the Father, renovated his lowly body, transforming him into a glorious new creation.

Now for anyone to experience the new exodus, Jesus' own Passover death, his departure from the world, and his resurrection out of the grave as a new creation, need to become one's own. For this very purpose—praise God—Jesus, as the exalted Lord, sends the Spirit to lead his own through the way he has opened, uniting them to himself, to his own crucifixion, burial, resurrection, and ascension. Again, it is precisely for this reason that Jesus, knowing he must soon depart to the Father (John 13:1), begins teaching the disciples and praying to the Father about the person and work of the Holy Spirit: he must explain to them that his departure is for their sakes, for their exodus, for their comfort and eternal good—through the gift of the Spirit. Apart from the Spirit's uniting God's people to the Son, Israel cannot experience the new exodus. The disciples had been grieved and confused by the announcement of his going away. But if the Son does not depart to the Father's house, then they cannot depart to the Father's house; if the Son remains a part of the old creation, in Egypt, in this spiritual Sheol, then so too must Israel. By his descent through the incarnation, the Son clung—forever!—to our humanity that by his ascent he would bring us up, in and with him, before the face of God, bearing us up into the Father's house by the Spirit. This is the new exodus. Even so, it is only its budding.

Our spiritual regeneration will eventually flower into our physical resurrection from the grave, an utterly thoroughgoing transformation by the Spirit of God, ushering us into the life of the newly regenerated cosmos—the culminating exodus of glory accomplished by the Son. In the book of Revelation, Jesus is exalted as the true Passover Lamb: "for you were slain and have redeemed us to God by your blood out of every tribe and tongue and people and nation" (Revelation 5:9). Here Jesus' crucifixion is celebrated as the new Passover of the prophesied exodus for the redemption not only of Jewish people but also of the nations out of the misery of their long and dark exile. The nations thus stream into the New Jerusalem of a new creation to know the life of blessing and joy before the face of the Lamb (Revelation 21:22-27). In this way, the full vision of the prophets will be realized. While Jesus himself has already entered into the glory of the new creation and his people taste that reality now spiritually by the gift of his heavenly Spirit, yet the full glory—and consummate exodus—is yet to come at the Son's return.

As with the Gospel of John, so Revelation ends with an Edenic garden, with a tree of life and a pure river of life-giving water flowing out from the throne of God and of the Lamb (Revelation 22:1-5), from the God who says, "Look! I am making all things new! . . . To the one who is thirsty I will give freely of the fountain of the water of life" (Revelation 21:5-6). Fittingly, the Bible then closes with an invitation to this paradise—to enter eternal life through faith in Jesus the Lamb: both the Spirit and the bride, the church, say, "Come! . . . Let whoever thirsts, come! Whoever desires, take the waters of life as a gift!" (Revelation 22:17).

Come, you faithful, raise the strain
of triumphant gladness!
God has brought forth Israel
into joy from sadness,
loosed from Pharaoh's bitter yoke
Jacob's sons and daughters;
led them with unmoistened foot
through the Red Sea waters.

'Tis the Spring of souls today:
Christ has burst his prison,
and from three days' sleep in death
as a sun has risen.
All the Winter of our sins,
long and dark, is flying
from the Light to whom we give
laud and praise undying.[3]

[3]John of Damascus, "Come You Faithful, Raise the Strain," trans. J. M. Neale, 1859.

Chapter Fourteen

THE ONLY HOPE

IN SENDING THE SPIRIT to unite his people to himself—to his crucifixion death as the Passover Lamb of God, to his resurrection from the grave and ascension into the heavenly presence of the Father as the new exodus—Jesus leads God's people in a great redemption. We experience his new exodus first spiritually then bodily when he returns to usher us into the glories of the new heavens and earth. The Messiah's deliverance, as we have seen throughout this work, was foreshadowed in a variety of ways throughout the Old Testament. Our chapter on the life of Abraham began with Abram's exodus out of Ur, a sort of resurrection from the life of paganism, and culminated with the near-sacrifice of Isaac, which also formed a kind of resurrection as Abraham's beloved son was restored back to him. So the author of Hebrews understands that Abraham had acted by faith, reasoning that God was able even to raise Isaac from the dead (Hebrews 11:17-19). Even Israel's historical exodus out of Egypt is portrayed as a symbolic resurrection through the waters of death, out of Egypt as a figurative Sheol inhabited by the sea dragon, Pharaoh. The return of Jews from exile too is likened to a resurrection out of death and the grave, a prophesied second exodus. Time and again the concepts of exodus and resurrection are united deeply.

WHY THE RESURRECTION?

One may well ask why it is that so many theological roads appear to converge on the doctrine of the resurrection. And yet, is not the answer obvious? Is not death, as the wages of sin and doorway to everlasting judgment, the great problem that faces us all—whether rich or poor, African or Asian, male or female, educated or ignorant, young or elderly, Buddhist or Jewish? Do not all our strivings and sought-after comforts—the numbing noise of our music and incessant entertainment, the leaning for luxury and accumulation of possessions, the tiresome chasing after health and attractiveness, the hollow assurances of political power and financial investments—do they not all fall prostrate inevitably before that final enemy, death? No doubt, we have tasted something of the joys of escaping the monster's clutches in the past, like recovering from cancer or surviving a treacherous crash, but we must surely sense within ourselves the gnawing reality that all such deliverances amount to nothing more than temporary reprieves—the grave will not be denied our bodies, death will make no exceptions. No, we cannot, like the tower builders of Babel, set empty hope on overcoming the curse of death through science and human ingenuity.

Science will not resolve the problem of death. The gains of medicine will never surpass technological advances in warfare and weaponry, nor the violent impulse gestating in the human heart, the profound evil and cruel inhumanity that ever cast the threat of death like a shadow over the world. History is an open book: daily tragedies of violence and depravity scorn the pleas of enlightenment—to say nothing of the chronic ideologies that justify and spur such brutality. Even so, within the unrelenting sorrows and shallow revelries of human civilization, the fear of death continues to hold sway over every living soul. How plainly, from within the house of mourning and before the cold stare of the gravestone or amidst the turmoil of nations and the violence in our streets, we see that apart from the resurrection of the dead all our hopes and human endeavors are vain, and resolutely so. Death, according to the Bible, is not the result of physical frailty; death is a judicial verdict, the consequence of human rebellion against the Creator.

The real problem, which is more encompassing than death, is sin. The entire world has become a place of exile from God dominated by the enslaving power of sin within, a Sheol inhabited by the dragon. Through the principle and power of sin within fallen human nature, the Evil One sways people by their own corrupt desires, as they sink into lusts and passions—and into despair. Sin, which has separated the human race from God as its source of life and wholeness, darkening cultures with futile thinking and boundless depravity, has also affected the rest of creation deeply. As Adam was inseparable from the world in which he was made (indeed, responsible for all creation on Yahweh's behalf), so the curse of God for his sin came upon all creation. But though it pervades creation like cancer, sin cannot be eradicated like cancerous cells—there is no education, technology, or program that can rid the world of its corruption, of all that stands in the way of a life of peace. Rather, the whole creation must be redeemed and remade anew; the old creation must be transformed through judgment—through death, burial, and resurrection—into a new heavens and earth. This, as we considered in our last chapter on the Gospel of John, is the work of God, in the Son and through his Spirit.

Why, then, do so many scriptural paths lead to Jesus' empty grave at the dawn of the first day? In short, the Bible holds out resurrection life because divine wisdom knows our deepest need—from God's own action in history in raising Jesus from his judgment-enduring death, we are shown the problem by its remedy. Biblically, the word *death* refers to a destiny that is especially connected with sin and separation from God, while the word *resurrection*, when applied to the Messiah, means an act of divine victory over both death and sin as the means for humanity to live in unbroken fellowship with God in a new creation.[1]

The reality of Jesus' resurrection, with its resolution to both sin and death, alone offers a bedrock within the thrashing sea. Resurrection alone offers genuine hope and deep peace in the face of our own death, amid our battles with sickness and suffering, broken relationships and loss—and in the face of the evil within ourselves. Rabbi Adin Steinsaltz writes,

> The basic attitude of Judaism to death, which, it is said, was ushered in with Adam's expulsion from the Garden of Eden, is that it is not a natural,

[1]Michael Ramsey, *The Resurrection of Christ: An Essay in Biblical Theology* (London: The Centenary Press, 1945), 20-21.

> inevitable phenomenon. Death is life diseased, distorted, perverted, diverted from the flow of holiness, which is identified with life. . . . The world's worst defect is seen to be death, whose representative is Satan. The remedy is faith in the resurrection.[2]

While I would change the last sentence to read "the remedy is *the Messiah's* resurrection," nevertheless his overall sentiment is profoundly true and must inevitably lead one to the Son's empty tomb. In raising Jesus from the dead, our God and heavenly Father has supplied his people with an unshakable living hope and unfading cause for rejoicing. By enduring our judgment himself and clothing us with his righteousness, the Messiah has reconciled us to the living God, removing the sting from death. Any solution short of resurrection as we undergo the travails of life in a broken world would be of no use at all—an insulting opiate. By contrast, confessing the Apostles' Creed with the historic church, with its "I believe in . . . the resurrection of the body and the life everlasting," floods the soul with the radiance of dawn.

Even the resurrection of our bodies, however, does not embrace the full majesty of the Messiah's new exodus, which has the whole cosmos in its scope—as far as the curse is found (Romans 8:18-22). All things were created both through and for the Son, who is before all things and in whom all things hold together, and by him all things will be reconciled to God the Father, whether things on earth or in heaven (Colossians 1:17-20; John 1:1-3). The place of exile, the wilderness of the old creation, will be transformed into paradise, a new creation. By the Spirit, the whole cosmos will undergo the new exodus. Every fiber and molecule of the new creation will have been led through the passage of the crucifixion, burial, and resurrection of the Son—*in whom* they hold together—into new life. As all living things emerged out of the ark with Noah, so an entire new creation emerges out of the tomb in the resurrection of Jesus Christ.

PAUL: THE APOSTLE OF RESURRECTION

Such hope through the resurrection of Jesus, the heart of the church's proclamation, forms the light that illumines every page of the New Testament,

---

[2]Rabbi Adin Steinsaltz, "Death Shall Be Defeated" *Shefa Quarterly* 1, no. 3 (1978): 6.

and especially the life and letters of the apostle Paul, who summarized his faith with the words: "I have hope in God . . . that there will be a resurrection of the dead" (Acts 24:15). Again, in Acts 26, as a prisoner testifying before a magistrate, Paul further underscores his foundational hope, with a threefold use of "hope" (*elpis*): "Now I stand and am judged for the hope of the promise made by God to our fathers. To this promise our twelve tribes, earnestly serving God night and day, hope to attain. For this hope's sake, King Agrippa, I am accused by the Jews. Why should it be thought incredible by you that God raises the dead?" (Acts 26:6-8). Here Paul summarizes the patriarchal promises and entire prophetic expectation, the heart of the Old Testament's message of hope, with God's raising up of the dead—this is what the people of God "hope to attain." The apostle's final question delves into the heart of the matter and rebukes our own lack of faith: Why should we think such a hope—that God raises the dead—so incredible? God is the fountain of life and being, the God of the living, who flung forth the galaxies out of nothing, who has directed the course of history so that his original intentions for creation should be fulfilled in a new creation. He has sent his Son through the incarnation—Jesus Christ, born of the virgin Mary—to die and be raised, this precisely so that his people may die and be raised up with him.

Indeed, death is the first threat Paul dismisses when he declares his conviction that nothing can separate us from the love of God in Christ Jesus (Romans 8:38-39)—no, not death! Elsewhere, he cries out triumphantly, "Where, O Death, is your sting? Where, O Grave, is your victory?" (1 Corinthians 15:55). In this Paul is but quoting the hope expressed through the ancient prophet Hosea, where the return from exile and the resurrection swirl into one awaited exodus: "From the power of Sheol (the grave) I will ransom them, from death I will redeem them: O Death, where are your plagues? O Sheol, where is your destruction?" (Hosea 13:14). Paul's own rhetoric sings with the brilliant apprehension that in Christ's redemption these words have been fulfilled. Jesus' resurrection from the grave was God's way of bringing his people out of exile. Michael Ramsey writes: "Finally a day comes when Jesus Christ, identifying himself with Israel, bears the destiny of Israel with him to the Cross and the grave; and God raises him, and with him Israel, from out of death."[3] There is now a new creation people of God, composed of both Jewish people and Gentiles, who have been delivered from sin and death—and from the old creation—through the new Moses, the Messiah.[4] This *new exodus* from spiritual death to new life is Paul's gospel: God "has delivered us from the power of darkness and brought us into the kingdom of the Son whom he loves, in whom we have redemption through his blood, the forgiveness of sins" (Colossians 1:13-14).

At first, as is well known, Paul was a vehement persecutor of the church, but then all his vast knowledge of Scripture, his robust theology, was jolted into place by a paradigm-shifting encounter with the risen Lord Jesus (Acts 9). He understood Jesus' resurrection from the dead, Jesus Christ himself, as God's utmost gift to humanity, the ultimate hope to which the hearts of God's people have always bent and the only possible—and profoundly logical—remedy for the great problem. Once the significance of Jesus' resurrection, and thus also of his sin-bearing crucifixion, had reached the full depths of his understanding, Paul realized that Jesus' resurrection was not only the redemption foretold in Scripture but the only real hope possible for the world. "If Christ is not risen," he would go on to declare, "then your faith is worthless, and you are still in your sins!" More than this, if our hope is restricted to this old creation life alone, then we—God's own people—are "of all people most to be pitied" (1 Corinthians 15:17, 19). The statement is comprehensive, encircling the Old Testament saints within its reach. Had Abraham died a fool, having set his hope squarely on this present life? Such a notion is, of course, ludicrous, for by God's own promises for his seed *after* him, Abraham understood that his own role was but one link in an ongoing chain, leading to the advent of the Messiah. No, the author of Hebrews pronounces, these all—Abraham and all God's people—died *in faith*, the substance of things hoped for; namely, they died in the hope of resurrection (Hebrews 11). Dying in hope, the psalmist had proclaimed: "You will cause me to live again, from

[3]Ramsey, *Resurrection of Christ*, 27.

[4]Such a reality, Paul makes clear, does not negate God's compassion and promises for Jewish people outside the church, but rather spurs on his own agonizing prayer for their obtaining of mercy and the fullness of redemption—of salvation, which is both from the Jews and, firstly, to the Jews (Romans 9-11; cf. John 4:22).

the depths of the earth you will raise me up again" (Psalm 71:20). Paul implies the same in explaining that there is no gospel—absolutely no good news, no hope—apart from the resurrection. But with the resurrection absolutely nothing could overturn or ruin the joy, the peace, and the glory. How confidently, as one who has himself been confronted by the risen Jesus, does Paul declare: "For me to live is Christ, and to die is gain," even that he has "a desire to depart and be with Christ, which is far better" (Philippians 1:21, 23; cf. 2 Corinthians 5:8)—he longs for a more complete departure, a more deeply experienced exodus.

No empty platitude, the reality of Jesus' resurrection entirely—and demonstrably—transformed Paul's life. He gladly endured beatings, whippings, stoning, shipwrecks, imprisonment, starvation, and insults for the sake of declaring the only hope to both Jewish people and Gentiles (see 2 Corinthians 11:23-28). When others, filled with foreboding, warned him that death awaited him in Jerusalem, Paul, unmoved and desiring only to fulfill his ministry with joy, continued onward to preach this gospel (Acts 20:22-24). Indeed, he had already considered himself dead, as having died to sin and to the old creation *in the death of Jesus*, to whom he was spiritually united—and now, in the resurrection of Jesus, already alive as a new creation, awaiting the new heavens and earth (cf. Romans 6:11). Language of exiting the old creation notwithstanding, Christianity is anything but escapism. Rather, the sure hope of resurrection from the grave leads to renewed engagement with the world, to selfless serving that shuns the fear of death with loving boldness. Paul's hope reached well beyond the grave and into the new creation of resurrection glory—assuredly so, for the Spirit had united him to the risen Lord Jesus.

Paul's entire theology was permeated and lit by the new exodus of Jesus' resurrection. He came to see that by his death Jesus sealed the end of the old creation; by his resurrection he brought the new creation into reality. He describes salvation as an exodus from the first Adam, along with the old creation, and an entry into the last Adam and the new creation: "For as in Adam all die, even so in Christ all shall be made alive" (1 Corinthians 15:22, 45). This teaching about Jesus, whom Paul calls "the last Adam," appears within the larger context of the new exodus, Jesus' resurrection: "For since death came by a man, the resurrection from the dead also came by man"

(1 Corinthians 15:21). The same Spirit who raised up Jesus from the dead also raises up God's people from spiritual death by uniting them to Jesus' exodus, his resurrection from the grave (Ephesians 1:19–2:6). God's people "are raised up together . . . in Christ Jesus" (Ephesians 2:6), they *participate* in his death and in his resurrection life and glory. At Jesus' second coming, the bodies of the redeemed will also be raised up in glory. The first and last Adams, then, form two sides of one theological coin: death and resurrection. For our purposes, those two sides may be understood as exile and exodus: the first Adam's disobedience led to humanity's exile away from God, which leads to death and everlasting judgment; the last Adam's obedience leads to humanity's exodus back to God, to life and everlasting glory.

Not only his theology but its application was also grounded in Jesus' resurrection. United with him in death and in resurrection by the Spirit, God's people already partake of the age to come, the new creation, spiritually—now. If anyone is in Christ, Paul proclaims, that person "is a new creation: old things have passed away—look! all things have become new!" (2 Corinthians 5:17). Although one never forsakes both tending and blessing the old creation, which will itself experience the same renovation as our bodies into a new creation (Romans 8:18-23), Christians have already experienced a departure from this age even while remaining within its bounds: through baptism, Paul writes, we have been united to Jesus' death and have been buried with him (Romans 6:1-11). You have died, he says, and your life is now hidden in Jesus as we await his return in glory (Colossians 3:3). But the apostle does not stop here; rather, it is for God's people now to follow Jesus through to the other side of the grave. He boasts in his spiritual union with Jesus and his crucifixion because it is the means of Paul's departure, of his own exodus—the cross, by which "the world is crucified to me, and I to the world" (Galatians 6:14). Well did Jesus say, "If anyone would come after me, let him deny himself, take up his cross daily, and follow me" (Luke 9:23). True growth in holiness is being conformed ever more closely to Jesus by the Spirit, a more deeply pressed application of our exodus by prayerfully putting to death *through the cross* all sinful dispositions and behavior, all sexual immorality, lying, violence, greed, and self-seeking, and by a renewed living for God in Christ *through his resurrection*, with all humility and gentleness, charity and kindness, pursuing godliness with perseverance and joy. One must, therefore, have a share in Jesus' own death and resurrection since new creation life, resurrection, is found only "in Christ," one of Paul's favorite phrases.

Such was Paul's driving passion—namely to be found in Christ, possessing his righteousness, which is from God by faith: "that I may know him, and the power of his resurrection, and the fellowship of his sufferings, being conformed to his death, if by any means I might attain to the resurrection of the dead!" (Philippians 3:9-11). Here on display is reasoning ablaze with heaven's light: *if by any means*! Who would disagree? Surely this attaining of the resurrection of the dead is the greatest of all human quests, one for which any person would willingly sacrifice all else—for what does all else amount to when one's carcass is lowered into the earth? Cures for our sicknesses, precious though they are, are again but temporary remedies, for the body ages, it breaks down, and we must die and then face our Maker. But give us the guarantee of resurrection from the grave and the assurance that we are reconciled with God and suddenly all despair is pulled up by its roots.

The resurrection from the dead: this is what is worth striving to attain if by any means. In the ancient story *The Epic of Gilgamesh*, Gilgamesh, confronted with his own transience by the death of his friend, begins a heroic quest for immortality, battling fierce predators, climbing high mountains, crossing treacherous seas, even the waters of death, and in short wasting himself physically throughout the pursuit so that even his sinews were filled with sorrow from the toil. And all this only to be told, at the end of his arduous journey, that he must turn around and go back home—for the gods would not convene any special assembly for the sake of granting him eternal life. "What then," Gilgamesh pleads, "and wither should I go? . . . Death lurks in my bedchamber, and wherever I turn, there is death!"[5] While, to be sure, there is biblical wisdom in embracing one's own mortality, *Gilgamesh* is nevertheless an anti-gospel:

> Gilgamesh, wherefore do you wander?
> The eternal life you are seeking you shall not find.

[5] *The Epic of Gilgamesh: A New Translation, Analogues, Criticism*, trans. Benjamin R. Foster (New York: Norton, 2001), 93 (XI 246, 248-49).

When the gods created mankind,
They established death for mankind,
And withheld eternal life for themselves.[6]

These words form a dark contrast against Paul's inspired preaching that God, out of his love for sinners, did not spare his own cherished Son but freely offered him as an atoning sacrifice to give the gift of eternal life to humanity (Romans 3:23-26; 5:8-11; 6:23; 8:32).

In the case of *Gilgamesh*, the quest was worthy even with the paltry understanding of immortality in ancient Mesopotamia, where it was basically relegated to ongoing old-creation life. That is the natural limit of our vision, to remain a part of this old creation, desperately shunning the grave. But, as Paul witnessed, the Bible reveals eternal life as new creation, as resurrection out of the grave—a physical reality that is spiritually transformed into a new and abundant life of glory, a life that has conquered death and emerged from the grave on the other side, absolutely and forever. Even so, who could fault Gilgamesh for having set out on such a pursuit? "If by any means," says Paul. Is this not why people so spend themselves, if only to keep one's chair at the banquet of life a few more passing moments?

To such weary souls, Paul's glad tidings of the new exodus resound: while resurrection life cannot be earned by the wretched strivings of humanity, it is—incredible joy surpassing wonder—a gracious gift of God, received simply by faith in the risen Lord, Jesus Christ. The Creator purposes to live on earth with his creatures, with his beloved people, now within a new creation. This Jesus, Paul says, is the "Son of God who loved me and gave himself for me" (Galatians 2:20). Including the idea of purchasing, redemption means that we are no longer our own for we have been bought with a price, even the precious blood of Christ, the Passover Lamb of God (1 Corinthians 6:19-20; see also 1 Peter 1:19). Ever after, Paul's life was a straining after Jesus, a living wholly unto God in him, serving him gladly. His life was an awaiting for the Savior, who will one day return and transform our lowly, old-creation bodies, so prone to sickness, disease, and waste, and conform them to his new-creation body of glory (Philippians 3:20-21).

---

[6]*Gilgamesh*, 75 (X 77-81).

Among the last words he would ever pen, the apostle Paul wrote: "Remember that Jesus Christ, of the seed of David, was raised from the dead according to my gospel" (2 Timothy 2:8).

CONCLUSION

The resurrection: this is the hope, the living hope, set forth in all the Scriptures and embraced by all of God's people throughout the history of the world. "Blessed be the God and Father of our Lord Jesus Christ," Peter exclaims, "who by his abundant mercy has given us new birth into a living hope by the resurrection of Jesus Christ from the dead!" (1 Peter 1:3). The sureness of this hope is grounded not only in the reality of the resurrection of Jesus but ultimately in the very being and character of God, who is the endless wellspring of life. Jesus, rebuking severely the religious elite who were denying the resurrection from the dead, confessed that God "is not the God of the dead, but the God of the living" (Mark 12:27). His own glorious resurrection was itself, then, a profession of the nature and goodness of God.

One blessed day God's people will find themselves at last blinking in the dawn's light of a new creation, together on the other side of history, on the other side of their own graves, experiencing the inexpressible joy of the redeemed, the nearly incomprehensible reality that, yes, the fear and the battle and death are done forever, and there will be no more tears or afflictions or tragedies or sadness—no more Satan, wickedness, sin, or decay. All evil, within and without, along with its bedfellows of gloom and sorrow, will be forever banished. God's people will be raised up in glory and brought into that life of cheer and peace in the land, for our Shepherd, who laid down his life for the sheep, says, "Behold, I make all things new!" (Revelation 21:5), and he is well able. "I am the Living One," he says, "I was dead, and, look! now I am alive for ever and ever and I hold the keys of Hades and Death!" (Revelation 1:18). He has in himself already brought our humanity to its destined beatific end before the face of God. Every soul who turns to Jesus Christ in sincerity will partake of the same glory, even the culmination of the Messiah's exodus: "Behold, the Dwelling of God is with humanity, and he will dwell with them, and they shall be his peoples—and God himself will be with them and be their God!" (Revelation 21:3).

Until that day breaks, Paul's question remains: Why should it be thought incredible by you that God raises the dead? He is, after all, the God of the exodus.

> O God, who by the glorious resurrection of your Son Jesus Christ destroyed death and brought life and immortality to light: Grant that we, who have been raised with him, may abide in his presence and rejoice in the hope of eternal glory; through Jesus Christ our Lord, to whom, with You and the Holy Spirit, be dominion and praise for ever and ever. Amen.[7]

[7]*Book of Common Prayer* (New York: Church Publishing, Inc., 1979), 223.

FURTHER READING

Alexander, T. Desmond. *From Eden to the New Jerusalem: An Introduction to Biblical Theology*. Grand Rapids, MI: Kregel, 2008.

Bruce, F. F. *The New Testament Development of Old Testament Themes*. Milton Keynes: Paternoster, 1968.

Estelle, Bryan D. *Echoes of Exodus: Tracing a Biblical Motif*. Downers Grove, IL: IVP Academic, 2018.

Fox, R. Michael, ed. *Reverberations of the Exodus in Scripture*. Eugene, OR: Pickwick, 2014.

Fishbane, Michael. "The 'Exodus' Motif/The Paradigm of Historical Renewal." In *Biblical Text and Texture: A Literary Reading of Selected Texts*, 121-40. Oxford, UK: OneWorld, 1998.

Morales, L. Michael. *Who Shall Ascend the Mountain of the Lord? A Biblical Theology of Leviticus*. Downers Grove, IL: IVP Academic, 2015.

Perrin, Nicholas. *Finding Jesus in the Exodus*. New York: FaithWords, 2014.

Roberts, Alastair and Andrew Wilson. *Echoes of Exodus: Tracing Themes of Redemption Through Scripture*. Wheaton, IL: Crossway, 2019.

Zakovitch, Yair. *"And You Shall Tell Your Son . . ." The Concept of the Exodus in the Bible*. Jerusalem: Magnes Press, 1991.

AUTHOR INDEX

SCRIPTURE INDEX

ALSO AVAILABLE

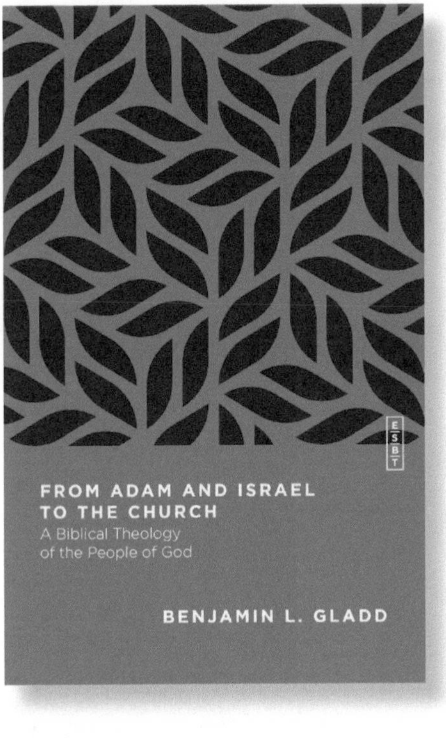

Finding the Textbook You Need

The IVP Academic Textbook Selector
is an online tool for instantly finding the IVP books
suitable for over 250 courses across 24 disciplines.